D0500151

THE WAY TO
TIN PAN ALLEY

THE WAY TO TIN PAN ALLEY

AMERICAN POPULAR SONG, 1866-1910

NICHOLAS E. TAWA

SCHIRMER BOOKS
A Division of Macmillan, Inc.
New York

Collier Macmillan Publishers
London

Schirmer Books
A Division of Macmillan, Inc.
866 Third Avenue, New York, N.Y. 10022

Collier Macmillan Canada, Inc.

Library of Congress Catalog Card Number: 89–38174

Printed in the United States of America

printing number
1 2 3 4 5 6 7 8 9 10

Library of Congress Cataloging in Publication Data

Tawa, Nicholas E.
    The way to Tin Pan Alley : American popular song, 1866–
1910 / by
    Nicholas E. Tawa.
        p. cm.
    Includes bibliographical references.
    ISBN 0-02-872541-7
    1. Popular music—United States—To 1901—History and
criticism.
    2. Popular music—United States—1901–1910—History and
criticism.
    I. Title.
    ML3477.T42   1990
    782.42164'0973'09034—dc20   89-38174
                                                          CIP
                                                          MN

CONTENTS

Preface   ix

1. THE PUBLIC FOR POPULAR SONG   1

Public Attitudes   5
Identifying the Public for Popular Songs   8
Popular Songs in the Home   12
A Shared Ambience   14

2. THE COMPOSER OF POPULAR SONGS   21

The Songwriter's Origins and Training
Ground   23
Songwriting Techniques   29
The Songwriter and Public Opinion   31

3. THE PUBLISHERS OF POPULAR SONGS   37

Analyzing the Public's Tastes   39
Publisher and Composer   41
Modern Business Practices   44

4. THE PUBLIC PERFORMANCE OF POPULAR SONGS   **55**

Careers on the Stage   57
Performer and Audience   61
Singing in Places of Entertainment   66
Variety, Vaudeville, and Musical Drama   72
The Singing Game   77

5. UNDERSTANDING AMERICAN POPULAR SONGS   **83**

The Utility of Popular Songs   86
Lyrics and Themes   91
Musical Style   95

6. CONSERVATIVE SONGS   **99**

Holdover Songs of Sentiment   101
Buoyant Songs of Remembrance   111

7. SONGS FOR A CHANGING SOCIETY   **119**

The Modifications in Serious Songs   123
Portents of Change in the Livelier Songs   131

8. ACKNOWLEDGING THE INCONSTANT HUMAN CREATURE   **137**

Acceptance of Reality   144
Themes of Isolation   153
The New Woman in Song   155
A Miscellany of Fresh Themes   157

9. TEXT AND MUSIC IN THE NEW SONGS   **161**

Sentimental Songs   166
Artistic and Semiartistic Songs   172

Waltz Songs   175
Coon and Rag Songs   181
March Songs and Other Rhythmic Songs   193
In Summation: The Roots of Tin Pan Alley   198

ANTHOLOGY OF SONGS   207

Absence Makes the Heart Grow Fonder   209
All Coons Look Alike to Me   212
Amber Tresses Tied in Blue   216
Angels Meet Me at the Cross Roads   219
Hello! Ma Baby   222
I Had $15 in my Inside Pocket   226
I'm Going to do what I Please   229
Let Me Call you Sweetheart   233
Love Me, and the World is Mine   236
Over the Hill to the Poor House   239
Winter   242

Notes   247
Bibliography   265
Selective Bibliography of Songs   273
Index   285

PREFACE

This book is about the American songs that had broad appeal in the four decades or so after the American Civil War. The songs published from 1866 to 1890 predate Tin Pan Alley. Many of the later ones, but by no means all, were associated with the music publishing world that came to be known by that term. In addition, a small but significant group of successful songs had little to do with the popular-music industry. No matter where the songs originated, if they received extensive public sponsorship, they form a part of this study.

This book is about those men and women who enjoyed, wrote, and published these compositions; about the singers who performed them and where they did so; and also about subjects, textual structures, and musical styles of these songs. This book does not give a strictly chronological history of popular song in post–Civil war America but rather is concerned with the industrial society of the last third of the nineteenth century and the Americans for whom popular musical entertainment was provided.

The earlier chapters inquire into the attitudes and needs of the musical public and the response to these attitudes and needs by the songwriters, singers, and entrepreneurs who supplied the music. Other chapters investigate the verbal and musical qualities of the songs written at the close of the Civil War and the alterations that gradually took place in some songs even as others continued to maintain antebellum values and show a continuity with antebellum tastes.

ix

The last two chapters examine the songs that were the typical products of the musical world from around the turn of the century. Although we freely use the term *Tin Pan Alley* to apply to all of the popular-music activities that began in the 1890s, in truth the term came into common currency only after 1903, when a majority of popular-song publishers had finally moved their premises to the Twenty-eighth Street area of New York City and when Monroe Rosenfeld employed the term to describe these publishers in an article for the *New York Herald.* This is why the book is entitled *The Way to Tin Pan Alley.* As prominent as Tin Pan Alley became in the first half of the twentieth century, it was still aborning in the very late nineteenth century and beginning of the twentieth century.

Many past writers on the cultural history of the United States have dismissed American popular songs from the last third of the nineteenth century as trifles to be brushed aside, apologized for, or criticized. Only a handful of songs, mostly by African-American composers, have received some praise.

Critics have often applied tests of musical uniqueness, the embodiment of an artistic personality, and the sensitive exploration of a poetic text to this music, and of course have found it wanting. However, these criteria derive from standards set by the classical music world and, if relevant at all, are applicable to art songs.

Art songs were usually created by highly trained composers who intended them for vocalists and accompanying pianists of some technical ability. Their expected audience was small and composed of Americans with a large degree of musical sophistication. Because a few of these songs managed nevertheless to attract a much larger public—their melodies proving agreeable, their texts easily comprehensible, and their performance not too demanding—they deserve consideration as a special category of popular song.

American popular songs composed between 1866 and the end of 1910 were based, for the most part, on different premises than those of art songs. They had different functions and were meant to please a huge audience. A large majority of this audience paid little attention to uniqueness, the composer's personality, or sensitive explorations of a poem's meanings. Indeed, to a member of this audience the first might betoken an unacceptable quirkiness, the second an exclusionary eccentricity, and the third an excuse for not writing a memorable tune. This audience would elevate into popularity only those works whose subjects were relevant to their human condition, whose language was that of the common man, and whose music proved delightful and stirred feeling.

Convinced that popular music after the American Civil War constituted a genre of considerable importance in America's cultural development, the author has tried to understand this music's premises and functions, and has asked what it meant to be a musician in the postbellum years. Hundreds of the songs have been analyzed to determine their subject matter, textual format, and muscial style. For each of the eight categories of popular song delineated in the later chapters, fifty or more works indicative of their type were critically examined. Their selection was based on the comments of contemporary writers and on the titles mentioned in Sigmund Spaeth's *A History of Popular Music in America*, Julius Mattfield's *Variety Music Cavalcade, 1620–1969*, and David Ewen's *All the Years of American Popular Music*. Those songs that appeared most often in the three books just mentioned and were also most frequently mentioned in the autobiographies and commentaries of performers, publishers, and observers of the post–Civil War entertainment world were the compositions chosen for analysis. An aid to selection was the substantial agreement among all the author's sources about which songs were the most significant.

In all, around 500 songs were thoroughly dissected. (The Selective Bibliography of Songs in the back of this book lists 230 of them, with composer, librettist, and complete copyright information. Song titles in the text that are followed by an asterisk can be found in the Selective Bibliography of Songs.) The statistics presented are based on these compositions. At least an equal number of randomly selected songs were examined in order to check the author's findings. The actual sheet music for most of these compositions came to the author around ten years ago, when he was presented with almost ten thousand songs that once belonged to Norman J. Wentworth, an old-time professional vocalist. (The songs are now housed at the University of Massachusetts at Boston.) Those titles the Wentworth collection lacked were easily obtained at Harvard University's Houghton Library.

Although considerable information is given about the songs themselves, little can be done to re-create the ambience of an actual performance, that magical moment when a talented entertainer stepped onto the stage, skillfully sized up the audience, and launched himself or herself into a creative routine during which exact timing, sharp-witted patter, personal magnetism, and gifted vocalization brought a song home to the viewers. This every reader must imagine for himself.

More than a few of these songs have melodies that are still attractive and set to texts that continue to have meaning. Moreover, they reveal craftsmanship of a high order. They express an extraordinary

American society that once existed in all its singularity. They tell us and enable us to feel what it meant to live, laugh, and grieve during decades of hectic activity, rapid social change, and economic uncertainty. Given half a chance, they can still speak to us over the years, if we will but listen.

THE WAY TO
TIN PAN ALLEY

1 THE PUBLIC FOR POPULAR SONG

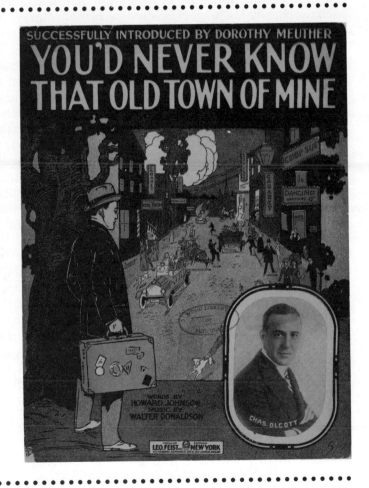

The American popular song discussed here is solo vocal music set to verse and accompanied by one or more musical instruments. Its well-defined tune is brief and recurs strophically to successive stanzas of the verse. A songwriter designed such a composition to be readily performed and understood, and hoped it would have a wide appeal. He was normally an American but was sometimes a European active in American life who had learned to conform to American vernacular patterns of culture, which he embraced as his own.

The period covered is marked off at one end by the conclusion of the Civil War and at the other end by the approach of World War I. These were years when the distinction between art and popular music gradually became apparent, with the latter more and more understood to comprehend a language characteristic of the ordinary American and to promise some expectation of monetary profit. Most of this music was suited to the requirements of and emanated from the new variety theater. In turn, the variety theater was always sensitive to the changing tastes of the American industrial society that took on a distinctive shape in the final three decades of the nineteenth century.

The years from the 1790s through the 1860s represent the formative stages of American popular song. During this period the definition of the American democracy as one rooted in the demos rather than in an aristocracy manqué took hold, and the growth of a culture typical of the demos began to be discerned.[1] The last decade of the nineteenth century and the first decade of the twentieth century found American vernacular culture, including popular song, with well-established and generally accepted ways of doing things, which, though oftentimes unwritten, were observed by its adherents.

One articulate adherent, intent on delineating the criteria proper to the vernacular rather than to the artistic expression of the time, was Mark Twain. Criticism of his writing as deficient because it was not sufficiently artistic in nature and aim had stung him. In a letter to Andrew Lang in 1889, Twain rebutted his critics by saying that art and popular compositions should be judged by standards proper to each. It was nonsense to assume that if a work "doesn't meet the cultivated-class standard, it isn't valuable. . . . It condemns all the rounds of art which lie between" the most prosaic and the most exalted. "It requires Whitcomb Riley to sing no more till he can sing like Shakespeare, and it forbids all amateur music and will grant its sanction to nothing below the 'classic.' " This assumption imposes the "superstition" that the "august opera" is more valuable "than the hurdy-gurdy and the villagers' singing society. . . . The superstition, in a word, that the vast and awful comet that trails its cold lustre through the remote abysses of space once a century and interests and instructs a cultivated handful of astronomers is worth more to the world than the sun which warms and cheers all the nations every day and makes the crops grow." Not the "little minority who are already saved . . . are best worth trying to uplift," but rather the "mighty mass of the uncultivated who are underneath." This mass "cannot have the opera, but the hurdy-gurdy and the singing class lift them [sic] a little way toward that far light. . . . Indeed I have been misjudged from the very first," Twain concludes. "I have never tried . . . to help cultivate the cultivated classes. . . . but always hunted for bigger game—the masses. I have seldom deliberately tried to instruct them, but have done my best to entertain them."[2]

Thus, during any examination of late-nineteenth-century popular song, one should heed Twain's admonition that it is a reflection of a broad humanity. Lawrence K. Frank has stated: "All men, everywhere, face the same life tasks, share the same anxieties and perplexities, bereavements and tragedies, seek the same goals in their cultures: to make life meaningful and significant, to find some security, to achieve some social order and to regulate their conduct toward values that make life more than organic existence." Frank's "all men" find the facing, sharing, and seeking made more manageable through personal involvement with a variety of cultural artifacts, not least among them being popular song. Song, therefore, cannot be truly understood without a regard for the consensus that called it forth and for the standards applied to it by the vast public that sponsored and valued it. Further insights result after inquiring into the "socio-economic, political, scientific, religious, and aesthetic matters" that affect it.[3] For example, popular song's development owes a great deal to the rise of public transportation—urban trolley lines connecting suburbs to a city's core and railroads connecting cities to the hinterland's towns—which aided in the formation of an immense and homogeneous market for musical recreation, and to an advancing technology that made possible high-speed printing presses, cheaper paper, and efficient methods of production and distribution.[4]

Lastly, the reader should not fall victim to the kind of thinking that historically goes back to the ancient Greeks and Romans, in which a distinction was made, ipso facto, between patrician and plebeian tastes, denominating the former as superior and the latter as contemptible. This attitude still persists among many twentieth-century American art composers and performers.[5] George Boas writes that evaluators of cultural works still feel "what is plentiful, and perhaps therefore cheap, is worse than that which is rare." Even the word "common" in "common people" continues to be suggestive of the ordinary, the undesirable, and the worthlessly vulgar.[6]

By the end of the nineteenth century, popular songs were plentiful, cheap to buy in sheet-music format, heard frequently in inexpensive performance by professionals, and increasingly suggestive of common people's concerns and values. In no way should they thus be deemed worthless. Furthermore, for most Americans of the time they were more desirable and worthwhile to experience than the relatively complex and lengthier artistic compositions, since they lacked the musical education, sophistication, and exposure to appreciate them.

Nevertheless, popular song felt the influence of the unrestrained materialism and preoccupation with status that increasingly affected individual Americans. This influence is detectable in the self-centered, rather than other-centered, tendencies in the song lyrics, the commercialized cookie-cutter sameness in much of the music, and the attempt of cynical publishers to manipulate the public into accepting whatever musical products were offered to it. To voice these criticisms alone, however, is to see things in overly simplified black and white. The post–Civil War audience for popular song was really an aggregate of several overlapping publics, each large in number, and was characterized by heterogeneity. From the countless offerings of composers and publishers, the songs that became the most popular were those that were highly entertaining and communicative to one or more of these audiences. Moreover, their lyrics and music reflected some commonly held set of principles of taste and worth.

In short, the American people of this period were not mindless acceptors of everything presented to them, however clever and persistent the efforts of the mass-culture producers. Late-nineteenth-century publishers continuously faced the problem of issuing songs inexpensive enough for ordinary people to purchase and inclusive of enough common values to attract as many people as possible. A constant task for music publishers was the synthesis of diverse tastes into intelligible and wieldy musical units. The underlying problem in all these discussions of late-nineteenth-century American civilization and beyond is how to single out principles of taste and achievement in vernacular creative products whose producers kept marketability, monetary gain, and broad public appeal in mind.

The problem is compounded by the realization that each subdivision of the musical public was made up of individuals no two of whom had identical tastes, backgrounds, and educations. However much a musician or publisher might hope to influence public taste, neither could ever fix its character. However much a song seemed fabricated according to some preconceived plan, its excellence depended on the meaning an audience discovered in it, which was not necessarily that envisioned by its creators or concoctors. Thus, a commodity offered for sale and marketed to make a profit became transmuted into a composition prized by the general public.

PUBLIC ATTITUDES

Witnesses of the period have attested to what has been said above. One such witness, Brander Matthews, insisted that attitudes were not all of a piece, nor were demands for entertainment homogeneous. Writing about the theater at the turn of the century, he stated: "There is no such entity as 'the public'wanting a definite thing." Both Irving-Terry company and the Weber-Fields company played to crowded houses in the same city at the same time. "There are as many separate publics as there are separate attractions; these several publics intersect, and every individual belongs to more than one." For example, a huge public existed for Buffalo Bill's Wild West, and a far smaller public for the symphony concerts; yet, many persons "with a catholicity of taste" enjoyed both these entertainments.[7]

When nineteenth-century Americans listened to their songs, they did not demand to experience subtle probings of the psyche, nor ultraserious profundities, nor a quasiritualistic involvement in some aesthetic mystery—which German writers claimed were the be-all and end-all of art song. They demanded enchantment, or at least a measure of delight, from the music. They also longed for some surcease from the oppressive realities of their day. Witness William Dean Howells's recollection of a blackface singer and monologist who was part of a variety-show billing:

> What did he say, what did he sing? I don't know; I only know that it rested the soul and brain, that it soothed the conscience, and appeased the hungerings of ambition. Just to sit there and listen to that unalloyed nonsense was better than to "sport with Amaryllis in the shade, or with the tangles of Naera's hair," or to be the object of a votive dinner, to be forgiven one's sins; there is no such complete purgation of care as one gets from the real Afro-American when he is unreal, and lures one completely away from life, while professing to give his impressions of it.[8]

Even the most hard-bitten listeners could find enchantment in a popular song's tune and be moved by its sentiments, so long as no great pondering over meaning was involved. Eugene Field, in his poem, "Prof. De Blaw," refers to miners in America's West, around 1890, and the music they craved to hear:

> The toons wich the professor would perform with sech eclaw
>   Would melt the toughest mountain gentlemen I ever
>   saw
> . . . .
> But the toons that fetched the likker from the critics in the
>   crowd
>   Wuz *not* the high-toned ones, Professor Vere de Blaw
>   allowed.
> 'Twas "Silver Threads among the Gold," an' "The Gal that
>   Winked at Me."
>   An' "Gentle Annie," "Nancy Till," an' "The Cot beside
>   the Sea."
> Your opry airs is good enough for them ez likes to pay
>   Their money for the truck ez can't be got no other way;
> But opry to a miner is a thin an' holler thing,—
>   The music that he pines for is the songs he used to sing.[9]

Surely a large number of nineteenth-century Americans resembled the father of Tony Hart in their expectation of song and dance when they went to the theater for entertainment, even if the evening featured a Shakespearean tragedy and an outstanding actor like Edwin Booth. "Well, father," said Tony Hart, "how did you like Mr. Booth's Hamlet?" His father replied that $1.50 was too much to pay and thousands of better actors could be seen for less money: "I waited for tree hours to hear him sing, but not a chirp outa him—and he couldn't do a damn step."[10]

In those moments when he tried with the best will in the world to comprehend something considered of high aesthetic worth, the average American might find himself more puzzled than otherwise. Like Henry James's Mr. Newman at the Louvre, he might end up "with an aesthetic headache,"[11] or experience pain, as did one of Finley Peter Dunne's characters when he listened to Wagner:

> She wint at it as though she had a gredge at it. First 'twas wan hand an' thin th' other, thin both hands, knuckles down, an' it looked, says Slavin, as if she was goin to leap into th' middle iv it with both feet, whin Donahue jumps up. "Hol! on!" he says. "Why,

pap-pah," says Molly, "what d'ye mean?" she says. "That's Wagner," she says. "Tis th' music iv the future," she says. "Yes," says Donahue, "but I don't want me hell on earth. I can wait f'r it.'."[12]

Awareness of American attitudes like those just mentioned was one significant reason why many European visitors to and writers on the United States declared American civilization to be uninteresting and culturally inconsequential. To Matthew Arnold even a tragic figure like Abraham Lincoln lacked distinction and had nothing elevated about him, although he did give a romantic dash to American history by being assassinated. Arnold then approvingly mentions one Frenchman as saying the emphasis on popular instruction and standards had produced mediocrity of intellect, vulgarity of manner, and superficiality of spirit; and another Frenchman as taking umbrage at the vernacular humor of Mark Twain, "so attractive to the Philistine." Indeed, American vernacular culture appealed to "childish and half-savage minds . . . not moved except by very elementary narratives composed without art, in which burlesque and melodrama, vulgarity and eccentricity, are combined in strong doses."[13]

Cultivated Americans like Henry Finck echoed Arnold's sentiments and those of the Frenchmen he quoted. Finck wrote that while at Harvard he and his friends "spent much time playing the Schubert songs, and how we *did* enjoy them! They were at that time (1870s) entirely neglected by the stupid and incompetent public singers," who were addicted to cheap ditties.[14]

Americans like Finck felt annoyance because the public did not elevate the musical artists they valued to heroic status. Finck failed to see the vitality and strength of a New World music unbeholden to European refinements of taste or to a contemporary American elitist art. He could not reconcile himself to the fact that the public accepted neither his criticism nor the artistry he cherished.

In September 1867 an argument in support of the average American's taste appeared in *The Nation* in a letter entitled "A Plea for the Uncultivated" and signed "A Philistine." The writer included himself among the "great mass of workers, who are the mud, the common clay, upon whom conventional society may set its feet, but who cannot partake in the culture which is the chief good to be attained in life." He attacked as unjust the way certain rich and educated people were declared to be "cultivated," while the middle and lower classes were left out or described as engaging in useless activity: "We know that except for our work, the culture of the scholar who despises our pursuits would be impracticable." The public must reject the label "Philistine" but should not ward it off by gaining a "smattering" of culture. Instead, they should carve out for themselves a

> position as high as that of others who now look down upon them by virtue of a clear perception of the fact that by their work the abundance of things is increased, the comfort of humanity promoted, the leisure of the scholar made possible, and true culture . . . diffused among all, and not monopolized by a few.

The writer captured a fresh social consciousness in postwar America, one that made its first appearance during the Jacksonian years. He protested that men and women like him, who drudge all their lives in exhausting and lowly jobs, have too often experienced disregard and scorn. Implicit in his letter was the position that social equality and those things that are valued by the majority should hold authority alongside claims advanced by any powerful minority group. This view, according to James Bryce in *The American Commonwealth*, was widely accepted in the United States, although Bryce feared it might lead to the dogma that the majority is always right and that "it is vain to oppose or censure the majority."[15]

. . . .

IDENTIFYING THE PUBLIC FOR POPULAR SONGS

. . . .

Despite what may be said about the change in religious and moral values in the postwar United States, the fundamental core of rural society remained obdurately traditional in its view of secular entertainment. Theater in general and the variety stage that introduced popular song continued to be suspect if they betokened loose living and corrupt morality, particularly to the millions of Americans untouched by life in the large metropolises or by the rough-and-tumble atmosphere of the raw settlements in the Far West. Most of their cultural activities had grown out of church activities, as Herbert Quick tells us in his description of Mason City, Iowa, in the early 1880s. A town of three or four thousand people, Mason City had an "opera house" where stage performances were mounted, sometimes by a traveling company like the Andrews Opera Company, a "family organization with headquarters somewhere in southern Minnesota." This company occasionally provided musical entertainment in the town's opera house. Musical people of the town also organized their own stage shows to the vociferous objections of strict churchgoers. In Mason City the amateur acting, dancing, and singing on the stage once called forth a "terrible sermon" from the Methodist minister, which infuriated the women participants who were Methodists. They felt especially insulted and angrily left the church premises when he preached against the "great whore which did corrupt the earth with her fornications."[16]

In contrast, many inhabitants of cities and large towns, who found themselves torn from their traditional moorings, derived no comfort from an urban environment both impersonal and profane. To them, theater and popular song provided consolation and refreshment. Some of these inhabitants had left their rural American homes out of economic necessity and perhaps a sense of adventure in order to live and work in cities. Others were immigrants or the offspring of recent immigrants to the United States—the Irish, Central and East Europeans (including many Jews), and those born around the Mediterranean basin. Many of them were footloose and determined to make their way in strange and inhospitable surroundings. They were but slightly affected by handed-down beliefs inapplicable to the New World setting. Eager to acclimate themselves to conditions unknown to their parents, they turned to the theater and popular songs for relaxation and for making themselves au courant with present American thinking. In addition, many of them pursued careers in the field of entertainment, many Irishmen becoming song-and-dance performers and an extraordinary number of East European Jews becoming the music publishers of Tin Pan Alley.[17]

The postwar years also found African-Americans afflicted by the virulent racial prejudices and discriminatory treatment of white Americans. Indeed, some popular songs promoted by white Americans had an obviously nasty side to them. As always, popular culture indulged less in the sophistication that causes hate to be subtly inflected, prejudice to be veiled, and amorality to be described as visionary. These offenses are found in a few art songs. A more naked hostility and lack of moral sensibility is evident in the belittlement of African-Americans in several "coon songs," and of Chinese, Jews, and Italians in some songs about recent immigrants. Yet, it is also true that for the first time African-Americans were allowed certain circumscribed liberties. They were permitted to join the theater audience provided they occupied seats in the gallery ["nigger heaven" was a pejorative term that came into use in these years]. The postbellum years saw an increase in all-black performing companies, all-black theaters, and highly regarded popular songs by black composers.

As one might expect some educated African-Americans shared the bias of their white counterparts against American popular music in favor of European art music. W. C. Handy remarked about the taste shown by black educators at Teacher's Agricultural and Mechanical College, in Huntsville, Alabama: "In this school, like many others, there seemed to be an unwritten law against American music and any inferior song of foreign origin was considered 'classical.' " On the other hand, he said, when working in a steel mill during the early 1890s, he and the son of his white boss had a common love for popular music: "We liked the same books and enjoyed singing the same popular songs of the day, *That Is Love, Down Went McGinty* and *White Wings*."[18]

Aware of the bedrock of opposition from many Americans and anxious to attract as many people as possible, entrepreneurs like P. T. Barnum described the buildings where they promised stage entertainment free from moral taint as "museums." They hoped the euphemism would allay the suspicions of morally upright critics. The frequently encountered term *opera house*, used to indicate a building that featured mainly light musicals and variety shows, was perhaps an attempt at high-toned phrasing that would appeal to those who favored art music. In the last decade of the century the term *vaudeville* would be used to denominate those variety theaters that promised to present, or at least to go through the pretense of presenting, diversions free of obscenities and sexual innuendoes. The aim here was to encourage families and those conforming to more stringent concepts of correct behavior to attend.[19]

A majority of those Americans once adamantly against impropriety slightly modified their views in the postbellum years because of the altered social conditions and the persistent need for recreation. Women, especially urban and middle-class, found that the increase in the variety of foods brought to their doors from all over the world, advent of canned goods, improved refrigeration, purchase of washing machines, and employment of aluminum cookware freed them as never before from household routines, increased their leisure time, and encouraged greater "participation in the world that lay beyond the domestic walls." Note the steps that theater managers like Tony Pastor and B. F. Keith took to win women over to their entertainments after they realized their growing importance in public life. When F. F. Proctor instituted "clean" vaudeville shows, with emphasis on music, around 1890, a judge from New York City told him: "I've been going to your show every week for the past two months with my wife and little girl and little niece, because you've got the kind of show that keeps a family together. . . . Men don't go sneaking off alone to corrupt places of entertainment now that you have provided in your 23rd Street Theatre a source of real inspiration and joy."[20]

Rural inhabitants, because of swifter and more efficient means of transportation and communication, became more readily acquainted with the developments taking place in the cities, yet felt as much as ever the desire to relieve the tedium brought on by lack of mobility, inflexible routine, and rare contact with people other than the handful they always encountered.[21]

Writing about the farm people of the Midwest during the 1880s, Hamlin Garland described the young men and women as sad, beaten down by the toil exacted by the land, yet "hungry for the world, for life." At a social gathering near Milwaukee, music was produced: "The magic of the music sobered every face: the women looked older and more careworn, the men slouched sullenly in their chairs, or leaned back against the wall. It seemed . . . as if the spirit of tragedy had entered this house. Music had always been . . . [an] unconscious expression of . . . unsatisfied desires." They "seemed to find in these melodies, love songs, and especially in a wild, sweet, low-keyed negro song, some expression for" their "indefinable inner melancholy."[22]

Garland wrote that farm people of every sort flocked to the closest village or town when entertainment was available. In a northern town of Iowa

> They climbed the narrow, precarious stairway which led to the door of the hall. Every seat of the room was filled. . . . The hall seated about three hundred persons, and the stage added considerably to the fun of the evening by the squeaks it gave out as the heavy man walked across, as well as by the falling down of the calico wings at inopportune moments. At the back of the room the benches rose one above the other until those who occupied the rear seats almost touched the grimy ceiling. These benches were occupied by the toughs of the town, who treated each other to peanuts and slapped each other over the head with their soft, shapeless hats.[23]

Small-town audiences from Indiana to California desired a "human quality" in performers and "simple fun" in the entertainment. They were enthusiastic when given a "delightful illusion of being transported to a "part of that glistening paradise" that belonged to the stage and the singers. Reality was transmuted "into paradisiacal fancy," however makeshift the scenery and sound effects; the commonplace world was left at the door to the hall.[24]

By 1900 the spectrum of available public musical entertainment was wide indeed, from the raunchy songs heard in disreputable saloons to the decorous ballads sung in circumspect vaudeville houses.

Every taste, whether licentious or moralistic, was catered to. The fact that the taste for American songs was international is stressed by E. J. Kahn, Jr., who writes that tunes sung in the Harrigan and Hart shows were also heard in London, Paris, and Vienna.[25]

On the whole, if any large identifiable group could be pointed to as the principal audience for popular song, it would be the American working class, the occupiers of the seats in the gallery.[26] Winston Churchill stated that it was the gallery, rather than the orchestra, "where are the human passions which make this world of ours; the gallery played upon by anger, vengeance, derision, triumph, hate, and love; the gallery, which lingers and applauds long after the fifth curtain, and then goes reluctantly home—to dream. And he who scorns the gallery is no artist, for there lives the soul of art."[27] Edward Harrigan stated how he hated to perform in a theater without a gallery, since he took most seriously the verdict of his "twenty-five cent critics." In fact, he habitually sat incognito among them in order to gauge the effect of his presentations.[28]

POPULAR SONGS IN THE HOME

In an age without radio, television, and recordings, if people desired musical diversion, they had to actively engage in playing an instrument and singing songs when not at the theater. Publishers knew this and therefore issued thousands of songs with piano accompaniment, expecting that millions of Americans had pianos in their homes and that they enjoyed gathering around the piano to sing. In 1870, one out of every 1,540 Americans bought a new piano; in 1890, one out of every 874 did so; and in 1910, one out of every 252. These were years when piano prices had gradually decreased while other prices had risen, owing to more efficient and specialized manufacture of the case, action, soundboard, and plate, and to the adoption of assembly-line methods. Efficient factories produced a smaller, affordable upright piano that soon supplanted the square piano in the home. Moreover, disposable income had increased, and more and more workers were able to direct a portion of their wages into areas other than food, clothing, and shelter. A surprising number of working-class Americans sought instruction in singing and playing a musical instrument, especially the piano. For those unable to afford private instruction, musical instruction was now a regular part of the public-school curriculum and provided at least minimum competency in singing.[29]

Interestingly, Isidore Witmark, one of the most astute song publishers of Tin Pan Alley, stated that although his firm thrived on the recognition that songs were a part of one's home activities, it was not so much in large cities but in the smaller communities that he did the most business. City people had all sorts of professional performances they could attend and were never at a loss for an inexpensive evening's entertainment outside of the home. On the other hand, beyond the large cities, a greater dependence on home life existed. This resulted in a more constant use of the piano and an insatiable demand for popular songs with piano accompaniment, issued as sheet music.[30]

Women had fueled the demand for popular songs during the antebellum years, and they continued to do so.[31] Theodore Dreiser once described his mother's moist eyes and twitching lips, indicative "of her deepest feelings," when experiencing her son Paul's "I Believe It for My Mother Told Me So."[32] Dreiser wrote of a lonely Sister Carrie seated at her window, rocking to and fro:

> She was too wrought up to care to go down to eat, too pensive to do ought but rock and sing. Some old tunes crept to her lips and, as she sang, her heart sank. She longed and longed and longed. . . . She was sad beyond measure, and yet uncertain, wishing, fancying. Finally, it seemed as if all her state was one of loneliness and forsakenness, and she could scarce refrain from trembling at the lip. She hummed and hummed as the moments went by, sitting in the shadow by the window, and was therein as happy, though she did not perceive it, as she ever would be.[33]

George Cable described a small town in northwestern Louisiana where there was a hotel of sorts, built of pine boards and exhibiting "pale wall-paper and a transferable whitewash." Yet it had a piano and a disconsolate landlady's daughter "who seven times a day played and sang 'I want to be somebody's darling,' and had no want beyond."[34] This bore out the claim of E. M. Wickes that once people, and particularly women, are attracted to a song, they are not satisfied until they can sing it "day in and day out for a certain length of time," reproducing a favorite song "a hundred times, yes, a thousand." He added that if a young woman has taken a fancy to a song, she wakes up with it on her lips, sings it at work, and goes to bed humming the chorus.[35]

What has been stated notwithstanding, men and boys also enjoyed and sang popular songs. For example, Thomas Edison wanted "I'll Take You Home Again, Kathleen"—a song he so valued that he sent its author, Thomas Westendorf, $250 in gratitude for composing it—to be sung at his funeral. Dreiser described hearing newsboys late at night going down the street and singing in mellifluous harmony his brother Paul's "On the Banks of the Wabash." Mark Twain, in a letter to his wife, described how he and twenty journalists passed the time very pleasantly one night in Chicago playing billiards, talking, and then singing songs until six in the morning.[36]

James Muirhead, who visited the United States in 1888 and 1890–93, wrote of entering Yosemite Valley with a band of Americans, including a San Francisco youth who had a "delightful baritone voice" and "entertained the guests in the hotel parlour at Wanona by a good-natured series of songs. No one in the room except myself seemed to find it in the least incongruous or funny that he sandwiched 'Nearer, my God, to Thee' between 'The man who broke the bank at Monte Carlo' and 'Her golden hair was hanging down her back,' or that he jumped at once from the pathetic solemnity of 'I know that my Redeemer liveth ' to the jingle of 'Little Annie Rooney.' "[37]

· ·

A SHARED AMBIENCE

· ·

Isaac Goldberg said of this period that "Tin Pan Alley at once follows the taste of the crowd and creates that taste. The influence between public and Alley is strangely reciprocal; it is a living circuit in which the interchange is constant. Each has re-made the other in its image, until something like complete fusion has been effected."[38] A song was very much a product of its milieu. It conformed to the public's view of reality. Whether "passionate" or "neurotic," it was a "recognizable representation of that reality," and the "materials" employed "for its construction" were "by and large, public property."[39] It conveyed a unified fantasy life pertinent to American society, so that what the composer said had unconscious significance for his contemporaries. The "I" was inseparable from the "we," and it was the collective experience, possibly not otherwise "articulated or brought into the open, but which nonetheless" exerted "its influence," that defined what was appropriate to the piece.[40]

As a case in point, in *Sister Carrie* a Mr. Ames, while giving a young woman advice on her career, states:

Well, the expression in your face is one that comes out in different things. You get the same thing in a pathetic song, or any picture which moves you deeply. It's a thing the world likes to see because it's a natural expression of its longing. . . . The world is always struggling to express itself. Most people are not capable of voicing their feelings. They depend on others. That is what genius is for. One man expresses their desires for them in music; another one in poetry.[41]

To put it another way, Howells states that vaudeville, with its large quotient of popular song,

must grab something that is more than its own. It must venture into regions yet unexplored. It must seize not only the fleeting moments, but the enduring moments of experience; it should be wise not only to the whims and moods, but the passions, the feelings, the natures of men; for it appeals to a public not sophisticated by mistaken ideals of art, but instantly responsive to representations of life. Nothing is lost upon the vaudeville audience, not the lightest touch, not the airiest shadow of meaning; [to try] to elevate the vaudeville [means] to kill it.[42]

The public treasured popular song because it represented ordinary people like themselves. They had struggled to survive in this world and had come to know the frustration of ambition and the small joys and larger griefs of living. Soon they would "vanish from a world where they were of no consequence; where they achieved nothing; where they were a mistake and a failure and a foolishness; where they have left no sign that they have existed—a world which will lament them for a day and forget them forever." Accordingly, a popular song helped give meaning to their lives, however transitory, and transposed this meaning "into a simpler key for the untrained voices that sing our popular songs. For song . . . even in Tin Pan Alley phrases, however blunderingly, however stereotypically," captured the "fundamental hopes and disillusionments of this, our common living." The music was capable of relieving monotony or depression at the same time that it aroused "deep and significant emotions," from aesthetic delight in structure, through feelings of great joy and grief.[43]

To describe in what manner a singer touched the audience and fused the mood of a song with that of the listener eluded even the most verbal of Americans. One can, of course, discover a voyeuristic aspect to the song-singer-audience relationship. The public could seem to be a presumptuous onlooker, seeking an easy and questionable emotionalism, but this was not the sum of the public's experience. Once

Howells saw a half-grown girl portraying a forlorn nobody from a poorhouse, carrying a rag doll and singing "Oh Dear, What Can the Matter Be." Then she put the doll to sleep by crooning "By Low, Baby." Finally, an old man offered the poor young thing a home, which scene, if the offer had not been made, Howells claimed he could not have borne, for his heart was in his throat with pity, and tears were in his eyes.[44]

In "To a Soubrette," Eugene Field stressed the fact that the intimacy between singer and listener was on a one-to-one basis:

'Tis years, soubrette, since last we met;
    And yet—ah, yet, how swift and tender
My thoughts go back in time's dull track
    To you, sweet pink of female gender!
I shall not say—though others may—
    That time all human joys enhances;
But the same old thrill comes to me still
    With memories of your songs and dances.
· ·
I used to sit down in the pit
    And see you flit like elf or fairy
Across the stage, and I'll engage
    No moonbeam sprite was half so airy;
Lo, everywhere about me there
    Were rivals reeking with pomatum
And if, perchance, they caught your glance
    In song or dance, how did I hate 'em![45]

A fine vocalist established a strong empathy with each individual seated beyond the apron, with one responding in perfect sympathy to the other. The individual experienced a variety of emotional resonances from the song itself and from the singer's movement of hands and body, facial expression, and tone of voice. Imaginative identification became complete.[46]

Ernestine Schumann-Heink once said she loved to sing "The Rosary" to American audiences because she knew that every bit of it went straight to the heart of each listener. The listener initially reacted with a spontaneous burst of applause as he recognized the first familiar phrase. Then she could see on every face before her "that what is in my heart is in theirs, and we are both swept along." Assuredly, a "song like that" made "all hearts beat together."[47] Composed by Ethelbert Nevin, "The Rosary" won an immense American following at the turn of the century.

Her statement that her audience was transported "to that anguished cry for a happiness that has escaped us" is not merely a purple flourish. A fundamental change was taking place in American thinking during the postwar years. A tilt toward equating happiness with things of this world took place, with a corresponding willingness to forgo the promises of heaven. Every member of the audience was a part of an America where little by little an unchecked materialism burgeoned and where preoccupation with economic position and social status could produce calamity in the individual psyche and in the civil framework. A rush to profits was trampling the public interest. Here was a situation that certainly affected every member of the audience and willy-nilly had to affect popular song.

The songs favored by the American public before the Civil War insisted that happiness came from God. Humans found happiness through a state of blessedness. The ultimate pleasure was virtuousness represented by an abatement of drive, ambition, and craving for things of this world. Whatever the actual practices of antebellum American society, its songs set forth the ideal of mental and spiritual tranquillity. Mankind could only strive to attain this ideal; which was arrived at solely through death. Most pre–Civil War comic songs did not mock this societal consensus, although they often satirized those areas of behavior, thought, and activity that transgressed it. They also freely ridiculed people who sought happiness in materialism—the accumulation of wealth, ostentatious living, exclusive self-concern.[48]

Beginning with the 1870s, the perspective of the songs slowly changed. Happiness associated with the pleasure-pain principle gained increasing ascendancy in popular song, not in all songs but enough to show the weakening of the older themes and growing preoccupation with one's personal relationship to the world as found. The greatest happiness for many an American who was thus portrayed was derived from the greatest possible increase of pleasure for the individual as set against the maximum avoidance of pain. Here was a new shared ambience of public, performer, and publisher.

The directing of value considerations toward oneself was a popular, albeit somewhat distorted, manifestation of the doctrine of utilitarianism associated with John Stuart Mill, Jeremy Bentham, and William James. Happiness was defined by worldly achievement measured in wealth, power, and fame, a concept fanned by a new scientific focus, rising economic expectations, and faith in progress. The struggle for spiritual self-completeness, knowledge of self, and the willingness to commit the self to others were superseded in the thoughts of many by an egoistic hedonism and the test "What can you do for me? What is in it for me?" This change, an outcome of the growing industrial society, was the Achilles heel of the culture, including popular song.

Greed and self-interest, to be sure, have manifested themselves in human societies of every age and place. Yet, they have rarely had such persuasive argumentation in their favor as took place in the late nineteenth century. The practice of illiberality was countenanced in unconcealed ways that the settled American society of the antebellum years would have frowned upon. The public for popular song was the victim and, when given the chance, often the inflictor of this illiberality. Survival of the fittest in a social jungle took hold to the detriment of giving charity and God their due. If we discover the greater incidence of these themes in the texts of the songs, it is as one should expect.

De Tocqueville had warned that the American democracy could not survive without an outer-directed religion and philosophy of life. Max Lerner, reacting to the competitive capitalism, market economy, and cold business spirit that took over in the post–Civil War decades, wrote a century after De Tocqueville: "To a great extent the old codes and the old consensus based on them dissolved. Americans were confronted with the most difficult task that a society ever has to face—that of finding organic continuities to keep its life from being pulverized."[49]

Once the "I" of popular song had been an innocent child of arcadia who had to enter into the treacherous world of experience, a place located emphatically outside of him that operated like a furnace burning away whatever imperfections he may have had in order to prepare him to enter the greater Arcadia—heaven; now the modern "I" of song, a surrogate for the public's "I," recognized that evil was not a separate entity, that a person was a mixture of many things that somehow had to be brought into balance—like cruelty and kindness, bad and good, self-love and other-love. Only by bringing his conflicting impulses into equilibrium could he hope to arrive at a state he could describe as happy. From song after song we get the impression that the contemporary "I" was urban, though with recent rural antecedents—whether native country boy or transatlantic emigrant. He stood without the support once given by religion, family, and community. He existed in an unstable, unfamiliar world that was proving destructive. He worked in industrial settings that consumed the spirit of workers.[50]

As shall be discovered in the songs that are later examined, a conscious yearning for love as an antidote to loneliness was a hunger brought on by severe emotional deprivation. Relationships with others often proved either difficult to establish or unsatisfying. The songs revealed the public mind preoccupied with the problem of how to commit oneself to another and still maintain one's freedom of action. Again and again the "I" was perceived as an independent entity wary of submission to another, fearful of suppressing one's own personality.

The postbellum age was characterized by a new and rapidly accepted term, *neurasthenia*, use to describe the common mental and emotional state of men and women suffering from nervous exhaustion. George Beard, who coined the word, defined two of its symptoms as fear of responsibility and loneliness, both concomitants of the new urban industrial civilization. Even humor, including the humor of American comic songs, was subject to this neurasthenia. Beard claimed:

> American humor, both in its peculiarities and in its abundance, takes its origin, in part, in American nervousness. It is an inevitable reaction from excessive strain of mental and physical life; people who toil and worry less have less need than we for abandonment— of nonsense, exaggeration, and fun. Both the supply and demand for humor of a grotesque and exaggerated form are maintained by this increasing requirement for recreation; not the vulgar, the unrestrained alone, but the disciplined, the intellectual, the finely organized man and woman of position, dignity, responsibility and genius, of strong and solid acquisitions, enjoy and follow up and sustain those amusements which are in our land so very common, and which are looked upon, and slightly so, as American.[51]

Thus did Beard sum up the condition of Americans who sponsored the songs made most popular because they pictured the American condition and gave it an aesthetic embodiment that they found meaningful and pleasing.

2 THE COMPOSER OF POPULAR SONGS

Around 1800, nearly all the songs popular in America were written by British composers. The changeover from British domination of the genre began in the twenties and thirties and was quite advanced by the late forties and the fifties. American composers of the postwar years (or, in several instances, European-born composers acclimated to the United States) would become the suppliers of popular works in accord with the public's demand for musical entertainment.[1]

On the whole, the songwriters of the postwar years displayed enormous knowledgeability of their special idiom, guided by the precept that the music public might think through words but wanted to feel through music. In this regard, Russell Nye wrote: "Satisfying a large audience involves no less skill than pleasing a smaller or more sophisticated one; popular artists can and do develop tremendous expertise and real talent." Furthermore, a "song is not necessarily worthless because people hum it. . . . Sometimes, with skill and talent alone, a popular artist may transmute [even] mediocre material into something . . . good."[2]

Unfortunately for American composers, however pleasing people might find a song, they rarely kept the author in mind for any period, if at all. Theodore Dreiser stated that the authors of songs pleasing to the millions (without a doubt he had his own brother, Paul Dresser, in mind) are quickly forgotten, as are yesterday's great singers. Everybody in the song world might know about and discuss the composers of currently successful compositions, but after a few failures that same composer would be forgotten by people in the trade.[3]

In his book of instruction on writing the popular song (1916), E. M. Wickes gives a rather ominous prefatory warning to beginning composers:

> The public seldom becomes interested in any particular song writer, as it does in a fiction writer, a dramatist, or an inventor, and the best that a successful song writer may hope for is a financial reward, and a modicum of admiration in a circumscribed set. The popular-song writer quickly follows his own creations into oblivion. Once in a great while a man writes a classic that is taken up by the masses, and he and his work live in the memory of mankind long after he is dead. Ethelbert Nevin accomplished this with his high-class song, "The Rosary."[4]

(Several decades later, we question to what extent Nevin and "The Rosary" continue to live in mankind's memory.)

If certain songwriters were known to their public (an awareness normally coincident with the time of the greatest popularity for their songs), the familiarity was not attributable only to their talent as composers. One such composer, David Braham, was undoubtedly one of the best-known songwriters of the 1870s and 1880s. Born in England in 1834, he came to New York in 1856 and worked as an orchestra conductor, composer, and arranger. In the 1870s he teamed with Edward Harrigan (the lyricist) to write the songs for the tremendously popular Harrigan and Hart farcical playlets on American urban life. Interviews and journalistic articles connected Braham with this series of burlesques and brought him into the public eye.[5] Nevertheless, what fame he had diminished during the 1890s and did not outlast his death in 1905.

Most composers of winning songs failed to receive even this ephemeral distinction. Far from being "commercial hacks," as they were disparagingly called, many composers sold their songs to publishers for a pittance, or, as in the case of Sam Lucas and James Bland, gave songs away or allowed others to publish them under their own names, not necessarily for remuneration.[6] Given the lack of personal recognition and financial success, one ventures to suggest that artistic inspiration must have accounted for their drive to compose songs. They had an overriding affection for music in the popular vein, however much they might declare themselves to be practical men tailoring a product for maximum acceptance.

· ·

THE SONGWRITER'S ORIGINS AND TRAINING GROUND

· ·

Popular-song composers active in the last third of the nineteenth century usually came from lower-middle-class families: they were children of shopkeepers, barbers, printers, farmers, artisans, and the like. Usually no other family member had a strong inclination toward music making, nor was there evidence of musical talent in their ancestry. They did not normally display prodigious musical gifts during childhood. Of none of them could one say "Hats off, a genius!" For some, entry into a songwriter's life seemed accidental rather than deliberate. For a majority, the hunger to perform music and to create songs did not produce a desire to undergo extensive musical training. Their backgrounds and early attitudes did not predict what they would become.

If we drew a composite picture of the typical songwriter, we might find that his parents were unsympathetic to a musical career and urged the child to take up a trade. What musical knowledge the songwriter had was self-taught (as with Charles Harris) or picked up fortuitously (as Gussie Davis did while a custodian at a music conservatory). Because of a yearning to make music, the fledgling songwriter left home and accepted any available job as an entertainer, a job that often involved singing, and thus learned how to carry out their vocation and almost by happenstance commenced songwriting. Quite a few songwriters then lead disorderly personal lives, entered unstable marriages, sometimes drinking heavily, spending money freely when they had it, and learning to go without when they didn't—not an unusual state of things. Impermanence accompanied them on the road, whether as salesmen (the employment of several fledgling songwriters) or as performers with a traveling entertainment troupe.

For some, professional musical employment was not of great significance in gaining a reputation in the popular-song world. Numerous composers had meager musical backgrounds when they produced their first hit. One of them, Joseph P. Skelly, who wrote about four hundred songs, including the hit "Why Did They Dig Ma's Grave So Deep?" (1880), was originally a plumber and was known to be indolent, a spendthrift, and constantly intoxicated. So great was his need for alcohol that he would sell his songs outright to publishers for a few dollars. Edward B. Marks and Joseph W. Stern were traveling button salesmen when they wrote the lyrics and music for "The Little Lost Child" (1894). Gussie Davis, one of the first African-Americans to win international fame as a composer of songs, was first a janitor. It was while employed as a porter that he wrote lyrics and music for "In the Baggage Car Ahead," one of the most popular songs issued in 1896.

Some composers, to be sure, did have musical educations and strong musical backgrounds. Kerry Mills, noted for two big hits—"At a Georgia Campmeeting" (1897) and "Meet Me In St. Louis, Louis" (1904)—was a violinist and taught at the University of Michigan before he established a sheet-music publishing house in New York. Ernest Ball, composer of "Will You Love Me in December as You Do in May?," was an alumnus of the Cleveland Conservatory. Hart Pease Danks, who achieved success with "Don't Be Angry With Me, Darling" in 1870 and even greater success with "Silver Threads Among the Gold" in 1873, had studied under choral conductor L. E. Whiting and was himself a singer, leader of a music society, and writer of hymns when he turned to popular song. Carrie Jacobs-Bond had studied piano and musicianship with two competent musicians before she published "Just A-wearyin' for You" and "I Love You Truly" in 1901. J. Rosamond

Johnson, a black musician educated at the New England Conservatory, went on to compose "Under the Bamboo Tree" (1902). Finally, composers of complete artistic orientation who nevertheless wrote songs pleasing to the millions, like Edward MacDowell and Mrs. H. H. A. Beach, had thorough musical training.

Early experiences in the popular-music world might seem inauspicious, although they invariably provided songwriters with indispensable training in understanding the demands of their vocation. Around the turn of the century, Irving Berlin was a boy working the streets and cafés of the Bowery with the street singer Blind Sol. He then became a singing waiter at Pelham's Café, and later a song plugger for the Von Tilzer publishing house. Like Berlin, other composers got their sea legs working for publishers. Gus Edwards began as a song plugger, singing and publicizing new song publications from theater balconies, on ferryboats, and in saloons and lodge halls before he entered the vaudeville circuit and composed "By the Light of the Silvery Moon" in 1909.[7] Jean Schwartz earned his living as a Coney Island pianist, a sheet-music demonstrator in a department store, and a song plugger for Shapiro-Bernstein before he issued his hit "Bedilia" in 1903.[8] Ernest Ball was first Witmark's sheet-music demonstrator, then the firm's staff composer, after he wrote his hit "Will You Love Me in December as You Do in May?" Theodore Morse, born in Washington, D.C, later ran away to New York, where he worked in a music shop before turning sheet-music salesman; later, in 1903, he would author "Dear Old Girl."[9]

Paul Dresser, an outstanding composer of sentimental ballads, shows how varied the composer's practical training might be. He started humbly as a

> singer and entertainer with a perambulating cure-all oil troupe or wagon ("Hamlin's Wizard Oil") . . . both end- and middle-man with one, two or three different minstrel companies of repute . . . a black monologue artist; a white-face ditto, at Tony Pastor's, Miner's and Niblo's of the old days, a comic lead; co-star and star in such melodramas and farces as "The Danger Signal". . . .[10]

Like Dresser, most musicians active as songwriters in the years before the 1890s had initially worked in minstrel shows, especially if they were African-Americans. James Bland, the outstanding composer of "Carry Me Back to Old Virginny" (1878), was a member of the all-black Billy Kersand minstrel troupe. The outstanding variety entertainer Bert Williams (famous for the comic musical satire "Nobody" of 1905) traveled with minstrel shows before teaming up with George Walker and entering the variety circuit.

When the variety theater began to supplant minstrelsy, composers like Joseph Sullivan (of "Where Did You Get That Hat?" fame) appeared on the entertainment bill as blackface comedians or song-and-dance men. Joseph Howard (writer of "Hello! Ma Baby" in 1899), after running away from home, sang in saloons and billiard parlors, then appeared as a minstrel and finally as a variety performer. Benjamin Harney, composer of rag songs, performed in saloons before appearing in minstrel shows and later in variety.

The give-and-take of the variety theater (denominated as vaudeville in its politer versions) was the principal training ground for many if not most popular-song writers. Charles K. Harris played banjo and first participated in amateur, later in professional, variety productions prior to writing his immense hit "After the Ball" in 1892. George M. Cohan was a song-and-dance variety performer, first appearing with his parents and sister. Harry Von Tilzer appeared in variety after he had worked as an acrobat in a circus, a pitchman for a medicine show, and an actor in a repertory troupe. He published his first song in 1892 and had his first hit in 1898 with "My Old New Hampshire Home."[11]

Among the musically educated composers of popular songs were several whose activities centered on the more sophisticated musical-dramatic stage, such as Reginald DeKoven, writer of "Oh! Promise Me." Other educated composers, to whom writing for the musical stage was secondary at best, thought of themselves as serious artistic creators. The wide popularity of a few of their songs was not primarily the result of a conscious effort to please the masses. For example, Ethelbert Nevin studied music with Franz Böhme in Dresden, Karl Klindworth in Berlin, and Stephen Emery in Boston. His "Mighty Lak' a Rose" and "The Rosary," which were conceived for an art-loving clientele, became widespread hits because of the satisfying sentiment of the verse and attractiveness of the lucid melody.[12] Nevertheless, the majority of these composers at one time or another had a connection with the variety theater, usually as performers. Fewer were affiliated with the light operas of the musical stage, and only a handful wrote for the recital hall.

The connection with variety was a vital one, since so much of what was crucial to the health of the popular-music organism depended on the constant analysis of the audience's reactions to the presentations on the variety stage and the flexibility that stage offered for swiftly changing what was sung and the way it was sung—from the less to the more acceptable—a flexibility not as readily achievable in the more fixed format of the musical-dramatic theater and formal recital hall.

A number of the most successful compositions were written by performers for their own acts. At first, they might not think out the implications of publishing their song successes, a deficiency that publishers were quick to turn to their advantage. As Hazel Meyer stated, "Many of the songs so written were exploited by publishers, who neglected to share the profits from them with their writers."[13]

What spurred performers to write for themselves? Chauncey Olcott, to cite one, began composing out of necessity. When he started his career, any promising material would do so long as he could employ it to produce a favorable impression. Soon he had used up compositions by others that suited his manner of presentation. To continue to grow as a performer he had to write his own songs, which he did during the summer, composing music to his own lyrics while strumming on a guitar. Since he portrayed an Irish character onstage, his pieces took on strong Irish hues—as in "My Wild Irish Rose" (1899).[14]

In the earlier decades of the sixties through the early eighties, when popular music had not yet become big business, performing experience was less necessary for continuous success. Two of the most esteemed popular composers from these earlier decades were William Shakespeare Hays and Hart P. Danks. Hays, who greatly enjoyed music as a youth, began writing songs at nineteen years of age for his own amusement. Because his melodies had considerable charm, his accompaniments were easy to execute, and his finished compositions projected authentic feelings, his works (like "We Parted by the River-Side" and "Driven from Home") won great favor with the masses.[15] Likewise, Hart P. Danks began writing for the pleasure it gave him, having nothing else in mind. When he was sixteen years old, his family moved to Chicago, where he did some choir singing. F. O. Jones wrote in 1886: "Soon after removing to Chicago he began to try his hand at composing, but his father, who had no idea of his following music as a profession, looked upon all this as foolishness and put the young man to work at his own trade, that of a builder." Church musician William Bradbury encouraged the young Danks to continue with his attempts at musical composition, which resulted in several song hits. Jones adds: "Mr. Danks does not aspire to be ranked as a classical musician, but his music is of fair order, flowingly written, and well appreciated by the masses."[16]

As mentioned earlier, deficiencies in musical education were not usually detrimental to achievement in the popular world. Admired songs grew out of the experiences of ordinary life and dealt in common truths. To a certain extent, education hindered arrival at such truths. The composer worked out a melody, stumbled over the harmonies, and somehow—aided by an arranger (the professional arranger became a fixture in the popular-music world from the nineties on)—cobbled the melody and harmonies to an accompaniment.

Charles Harris provides an example of a Tin Pan Alley practitioner from the last years of the nineteenth century who never acquired much theoretical musical knowledge. He explained:

> The reader will naturally wonder how it was possible for me to write music to a song when even to this day [1926] I cannot distinguish one note from another. The answer is simple. As soon as a melody occurred to me, I hummed it. Then I would procure the services of a trained musician for the purpose, hum or whistle the melody for him and have him take it down on paper with notes. He would then arrange it for the piano.[17]

Like Paul Dresser and Irving Berlin, Harris, though lacking musical education, refused to be deterred by his deficiencies and plunged into a composer's career in spite of the frustrations of writing the music in his head and indifferent to the potential criticisms of knowledgeable musicians ready to ferret out every flaw, real or imagined, in the musical fabric. As James Whitcomb Riley wrote, in his poem "A Wrongdillion":

> Nay, nothing—Nay nothing affects him the least!
> They may say he sings less like a bird than a beast—
> They may say that his song is both patchy and pieced—
> That its worst may be his, but the best he has fleeced
> From old dinky masters not only deceased
> But damn'd ere their dying,—Yet nothing the least—
> Nothing affects him the least![18]

The educated composer, on the other hand, had to realize that theoretical skill alone got him nowhere and could hinder the launching of a career in songwriting. Ernest Ball had to temper his learning with the give-and-take of the stage before he could make headway in the entertainment field. After serving an apprenticeship in variety and achieving expertise as an entertainer and singer, he grew adept at satisfying the American public's taste for ballads, ballads that appealed "to the culture musician as well as to the boy in the gallery. His melodies were of the kind that reach the heart, having the intangible something which impresses itself indelibly upon the listener."[19] This "intangible something" owed more to native talent and its shaping by the requirements for successful stage performance than to the conservatory education he received in Cleveland.

Even after thorough study and experience with the ins and outs of popular song, African-Americans and women, both black and white, found it more difficult than white males did to establish themselves as songwriters. Already mentioned were one or two African-Americans who managed to exist in two worlds, one black and the other white. After many difficulties they succeeded as songwriters catering to a white public. Nevertheless, only a few black Americans made the breakthrough. The struggle for recognition in the face of indifference and insult ultimately defeated most of them. The firmly locked office doors of publishers and theater managers proved unopenable. The deterrents of racial prejudice and minority-group isolation continued to affect them well into the twentieth century.

Few women succeeded in becoming composers, although they were required for roles in musical drama. Physical attractiveness and sexual allure helped give some of them access to the theater, and stage presence and persuasive vocalizing produced a loyal following. In these ways a good number of women won fame as actors, entertainers, and singers, yet comparatively few created songs. Marion Dix Sullivan and Augusta Browne were two early exceptions, having gained fine reputations as popular-song writers during the 1840s and 1850s.

It was not until the end of the century that several other women began writing songs, having proved that they had learned enough about the popular music world to compose. The gathering strength of the feminist movement, led by militants like Elizabeth C. Stanton and Susan B. Anthony, which sought equality with men, undoubtedly made women more aware of their capabilities and emboldened one or two to compose music. Isaac Goldberg writes that from the days of Maude Nugent's "Sweet Rosie O'Grady" (1896), "there have been hits by the ladies. Clare Kummer began her career with 'Dearie.' Carrie Jacobs-Bond has sold 5,000,000 copies of the imperfect song entitled 'The End of a Perfect Day.' Hattie Starr was widely known, thirty years ago, for her 'Little Alabama Coon' [1893] 'Somebody Loves Me' [1893], and other ballads. Miss Starr, indeed, who wrote her own words and music, found the field of composition so profitable that she abandoned the stage for it."[20] Nevertheless, women composers remained the exception until well into the twentieth century.

SONGWRITING TECHNIQUES

As the nineteenth century drew to a close, the study of the ins and outs of popular song grew more and more essential not only for the composer but also for the lyricist, whether male or female, black or white. At times the composer found the lyrics already written and fashioned a melody to fit them; at other times the composer might write the melody on a lead sheet (a manuscript containing the melody and perhaps a sketch of basic harmonies and an indication of the sort of expression desired), which was then presented to a lyricist for word-fitting. Isidore Witmark called it an economic device "meant chiefly for the lyricist, as a guide or 'lead' in fitting his words to the contours of the tune." When the lead sheet also contained the fitted text, it went to a publisher for approval and arranging, or it might go first to an arranger for the completed musical product before presentation to a publisher.[21]

Hattie Starr was fortunate in her ability to write both words and music, thereby exercising more complete control over the final outcome. Paul Dresser had a similar ability. An idea for a song could come from anywhere."On the Banks of the Wabash" (1897) was created during a meeting of Dresser and his brothers, Edward and Theodore Dreiser. Edward, as quoted by his daughter Vera, states that out of the blue

> Theodore said casually, "Say Paul, why don't you write a song about a river? How about the Wabash?" Paul was delighted and said, "Theo, you draft out some words!" He wrote out words for the first verse and gave it to Paul. Paul changed some of it, polished it, wrote the second verse, the chorus, and music. . . . Theo . . . never wanted and even resented being given any credit for it.[22]

In contrast to Dresser, a composer like David Braham specialized in fitting melody to a text already invented by a lyricist (usually Edward Harrigan). He said he could write music while riding on a train to and from New York, since the clatter of the wheels masked all other distracting sounds and concentrated his senses. He started by scrutinizing the verse. He painstakingly invented one line of melody at a time to conform to the word accents and to the subject's moods; then he devised an appropriate accompaniment. He was also sensitive to the strengths and failings of the performer introducing the song. If the singer was to be Tony Hart, for example, whose voice had little weight or sustaining power, he was to be handled cautiously so as to conserve his strength; for Hart, Braham produced uncomplicated melody confined to a few notes that of necessity were restricted in compass.[23]

The blanket accusation that all popular songwriters are facile hacks, which has been levied by critics from the art world, is simply not true. High professionalism characterized the activities of a Dresser or a Braham. They were well aware and critical of what they were doing. The necessity for finding a combination of text and music that struck the listener as inevitable was uppermost in their thoughts. George Gershwin spoke for all of his colleagues before and after his time when he said that composing a popular song was not an easy affair. "Personally, I can think of no more nerve-racking, no more mentally arduous task than making music. There are times when a phrase of music will cost many hours of internal sweating. Rhythms romp through one's brain, but they're not easy to capture and keep; the chief difficulty is to avoid reminiscence." Gershwin then stresses that the popular-song composer needs talent and knowledge of the idiom, "abetted by emotion."[24]

Theodore Dreiser never regarded his brother Paul Dresser's songwriting efforts as hack work. Rather, Dreiser wrote, his brother Paul

> was always full of music of a tender, sometimes sad, sometimes gay, kind—that of the ballad-maker of a nation. He was constantly attempting to work them out of himself, not quickly but slowly, brooding as it were over the piano wherever he might find one and could have a little solitude, at times on the organ (his favorite instrument), improving various sad or wistful strains, some of which he jotted down, others which, having mastered, he strove to fit words to. At such times he preferred to be alone or with someone whose temperament in no way clashed but rather harmonized with his own. Living with one of my sisters for a period of years, he had a room specially fitted up for his composing work . . . within which he would shut himself and thrum a melody by the hour, especially toward evening or at night . . . until over some particular one, a new song usually, he would be in tears![25]

Ultimately, the successful popular composer had to have a special talent, claimed the songwriter Harry Von Tilzer, creator of "The Bird in the Gilded Cage" (1900) and "Wait 'Till the Sun Shines, Nellie" (1905). It was a "gift endowed by Nature. You cannot woo it, pilfer it, or manufacture it." Without this ability, the practical knowledge of how to write a song, however proficient the outcome, was useless.[26]

THE SONGWRITER AND PUBLIC OPINION

Given the ability and the practical knowledge of how to construct a popular song, perseverance was the other essential. Mark Twain's comment concerning the "unwritten law about human successes," in a letter sent in 1887, applies more to popular-song writing than to any other vernacular activity. First, an apprenticeship without appreciation or pay had to be endured, during which the aspirant had to prove himself.[27] Regrettably, the road to success was littered with failures and one-hit composers. The failures included those people without ability or without the drive to peddle their songs from publisher to publisher and performer to performer.[28] Composers who had achieved only one hit or who had run dry after a period of success were tragic figures, according to Theodore Dreiser. They were quickly displaced in the mind of the public and publisher by other writers: "Soon it is the old grind again, and then, if thoughtless spending has been his failing, shabby clothing and want. You may see the doubles of these in any publishers's sanctum at any time, the sarcastically referred-to *has beens.*"[29]

The evaluation of the composer's songs was a matter of the marketplace. Even the more successful writers, like Bert Williams, tried out many songs that had to be thrown away because they did not succeed. He did not waste his time insisting that he had composed excellent music that the public was too ignorant to appreciate. Instead, he kept on trying out new songs until something received genuine approval as measured by audience response and monetary return. This was his measure of quality.[30]

Harry Von Tilzer explained that at one time the composition of songs was more play and relaxation, but in his day (after 1890) it was more and more like a business, demanding business methods: "A song writer may still sing to suit his own tastes, provided they harmonize with those of his fellow men. His work has become a commodity with a cash value, and in order to augment the value he must subordinate his own personal tastes to those of the music-buying public."[31]

Most infuriating to the composer of popular songs was the criticism levied at him by writers who judged what he did on elevated aesthetic grounds of no pertinence to the reality he had to live with. In 1906, George M. Cohan grew angry about the criticism coming at him from high-toned writers, especially James Metcalfe, who wrote that Cohan's "combinations of music are curious things, consisting mainly of several bars of well-known patriotic or sentimental songs strung together with connecting links of lively and more or less original musical trash. The words fitted to those curious contraptions are of the kind of unmetrical stuff that children compose and call poetry." To this, George M. Cohan replied:

For the benefit of some damned fools I've met, let me say that my success comes from the fact that I know and have studied the business in which I manage to knock out a very good livelihood. I write my own songs because I write better songs than anyone else that I know of. I publish these songs because they bring greater royalties than any other class of music sold in this country.[32]

Care had to be taken less somebody else get hold of material still in manuscript and pirate it. James Weldon Johnson said that when he and his brother Rosamond arrived in New York from Jacksonville in 1899, they went to see Isidore Witmark in order to get him to publish their songs:

He appeared to be favorably impressed by the songs and choruses. Just as we finished, Harry B. Smith and Reginald DeKoven, then the two greatest American writers of light opera, entered. Mr. Witmark introduced us as two young men who had written an opera. "Well," said Mr. Smith, "let's hear it; we might be able to steal something from it." Mr. DeKoven and Mr. Witmark laughed. We didn't quite see the joke—if it was a joke—and, remembering Mr. Kerrison's warning, gathered up our precious manuscript and made a quick exit.[33]

Later, the two Johnsons would collaborate with Smith and DeKoven, but over the years their apprehensions about piracy increased rather than decreased as they saw all around them individuals ready to gain possession of anything that was not closely guarded.

There was a basis for their fears. Composers borrowing from other composers without permission can frequently be detected. For example, Monroe Rosenfeld, alias F. Heiser and F. Belasco, was a prolific composer who produced over one thousand songs, in some of which he used other people's tunes and ideas for lyrics. One hit of his, "And Her Golden Hair Was Hanging Down Her Back" (1894), had a melody composed by Felix McGlennon. Another, "With All Her Faults I Love Her Still" (1888), had a tune that closely resembled one by Theodore Metz.

After waiting and trying and worrying, when a songwriter found that one of his songs had gone over and was on everybody's lips, it seemed, as James Weldon Johnson remarked, like living under the influence of a "heady beverage," success. It "magically blotted out the memory of all our disappointment and defeats and carried us up into a region above doubts and fears. . . . There is a line in the blues which runs: I got de world in a bottle an' de stopper-in-a ma hand. No single line of poetry that I know of contains a more graphic figure to suggest the reaction to success."[34]

Although the demand in the marketplace seems to have determined the type of songs written, most successful popular composers of ability found no conflict between their own taste and that of the public. Brooks Atkinson quotes Oscar Hammerstein II as saying in 1955, about George M. Cohan's immense popularity: "A song writer's genius, or rather Cohan's genius, was to say simply what everybody was subconsciously feeling." Atkinson adds that the words and music in Cohan's songs were sublimations of the mood of their day.[35]

William Dean Howells stated that the songs of the variety stage reveal "touches of truth so exquisite, so ideally fine, that I might have believed I was getting them at first hand and pure from the street-corner." He recognized that these truths often seem to be imprisoned in "false terms," or to be labored "out of shape." Nevertheless, they survive and gladden the soul. Indeed, he would not insist on whole rather than touches of truth. He requests no more than the authentic "moments of life," and explains: "We can stand only a very little radium. . . . A touch of truth is perhaps not only all we need, but all we can endure in any one example of art."[36]

Because the touches of truth were ones of intimate feeling, not intellect (a focus on which songwriters and public were agreed), no aesthetic distance remained between the songwriter and his creations. When both Charles Harris and Paul Dresser wept over their sentimental ballads, they were reacting like members of their American and European audiences in this age of sentiment.[37] Paul Dresser had a childlike and sincere perspective on life. The emotionalism that saturated his lyrics won over the like-minded masses.[38]

To sum up what has already been written about this relationship between composer, song, and public, the author can do no better than again to quote Theodore Dreiser about his brother Paul. Paul Dresser specialized in highly charged ballads like "Just Tell Them That You Saw Me" and "On the Banks of the Wabash." His creative mood was almost one of "deep depression, which ended a little later in marked elation or satisfaction, once he had succeeded in evoking something which really pleased him." Dreiser confirmed that late nineteenth-century popular-song writers like his brother accurately delineated the moods, hopes, and responses to life of plain men and women and thus illuminated the common man's democracy that was the United States.[39] Stripped of all pretense, the popular songs ran the gamut of feeling from extreme sadness to extreme happiness and entertained the listener. Many compositions gave out the "kind of gaiety, poetry and romance which . . . had as much charm as anything in this world can well have."[40]

What the composers and the performers who entertained with their songs did, they did perfectly well. As David Belasco said of Bert Williams, they "performed an important work, rendering a valuable service to society," for they "made this world a happier, brighter place to live in than it would have been" without them.[41]

Songwriters did indeed work to fashion a saleable product, but in their finest products is also evidence of creative imagination. The usual definition of a composer is one who writes music. A popular-song writer, however, fits a more expanded definition of the composer, one who orders and resolves conflicts within and between people (even as he hopes to resolve them in himself), one who eases tension in the senses and nervous system. None of these composers is or aspires to be a Bach or Beethoven. In an unassuming way the composer reaches out to the millions left untouched by the mighty ones in music.

3 THE PUBLISHERS OF POPULAR SONGS

Old-line music publishing firms, like Charles H. Ditson of Boston and William Pond and G. Schirmer of New York, conducted generalized operations. They published songs they hoped would win popularity, but they also published hymns, music books, vocal and instrumental studies, performance pieces for students, and piano music—marches, dances, variations, and arrangements of orchestral overtures. Their catalogs offered for sale music from the most complex to the simple, works imported and domestically composed. They expected some compositions to command a long-lasting interest and have a small but consistent sale year after year; others would attract short-lived but, they hoped, widespread interest. The latter category included "popular" types of compositions aimed at the general public. A single house might offer as many as thirty thousand different titles for sale.[1]

Music publishing firms did not, in normal circumstances, aggressively and incessantly publicize their music. When a song caught the public's fancy, they still required most public performers to purchase copies, for they were not geared to give them "professional copies" free of charge. Five-and-ten-cent stores found a majority of their songs too expensively priced and insufficiently in demand by the masses to consider handling them. Several publishers of this type wished their lyricists to be poets, their composers to have proper academic credentials and their songs to appear "high-class." They felt certain that the quality of the verse and music would impress enough of their steady customers to recoup expenses. Several of them maintained music stores for retailing their offerings and jealously guarded their selective lists of subscribers who might show interest in recent issues.[2]

The division between the old-line and the popularly oriented sort of publisher became quite distinct when bold and energetic firms concentrating only on popular music made their appearance—Thomas B. Harms in 1881, Willis Woodward in 1883, and M. Witmark & Sons in 1885. The trend toward making a distinction between firms devoted to what they saw as estimable and significant works and those devoted to entertaining and popular works grew apparent throughout the publishing world. Gertrude Atherton stated that when she came to New York City in the late eighties and saw an old-line publisher about taking on her new novel, she got the reply "The traditions of my firm do not permit me to publish your little book, much as I should like to for your sake. But you may have better fortune with one of these newer firm that are unhampered by traditions." The author then added with satisfaction that later "this dignified old firm" went under,[3] an ending that was also visited on several dignified old music publishers.

During the nineties a number of the newfangled firms moved to buildings around New York City's Twenty-eighth Street. Unlike the older publishers, centered in various cities throughout the country, those devoted to the sheet-music publication of popular music—its cultivation, dissemination, and publicizing—were inclined to concentrate in one area of New York City. These firms were directed by men such as Isidore Witmark, Edward Marks, Charles Harris, Leo Feist, Maurice Shapiro, Louis Bernstein, Joseph Stern, Harry Von Tilzer, Jerome Remick, Thomas Harms, and Kerry Mills. Few of these men boasted long American ancestry; many originated in the ranks of recent Jewish immigrants to the United States.

Isaac Goldberg declared the change to be a historic and racial revolution. As firm after firm was founded on a shoestring ("A chance hit and a couple of hundred dollars was [sic] sufficient to open an office"), what was once an "almost exclusively Gentile" profession now "took on a Jewish complexion." After naming several of the people cited above, he states that they were the true pioneers of popular-music making and popular-music publishing in the United States, a phenomenon without parallel in the rest of the world.[4] Isidore Witmark pointed out, however, that the eighties introduced some pioneering but hazardous ventures into publishing. Nonetheless, these men paved the way for the next decade of young people entering publishing, providing them with the certainty that popular-song publication could promise substantial gains.[5]

· ·

ANALYZING THE PUBLIC'S TASTES

· ·

Economically speaking, the music publisher operated a private business for profit. From a societal point of view, the new-style publisher might resemble an overseer, with power to intervene anywhere in the popular-song chain (from creation through production to consumption). In the interests of the public (interests that fused with self-interest), he investigated and acted upon its needs, desires, and complaints. He attended the theater, observed audience response, and solicited the advice of theater managers and performers.[6]

From 1867 to 1910, the popular-music publishing industry still addressed a wide spectrum of tastes, from more or less sophisticated to rather coarse. Within broadly conceived permissible parameters, publishers offered songs in a variety of styles on a variety of subjects.

There were slow and sweet sentimental ballads, cakewalking coon songs, gracious waltzes, fast and syncopated rag songs, cheery topical ditties, fervent hymns, ethnic takeoffs, and fervid love serenades. Although the aim was substantial sales, thinking was not yet dominated by an iron conformity of entrepreneurs concentrating on the main chance to the exclusion of preferences of one or more substantial subgroups. A million-dollar blockbuster might be the dream, but a sale of tens of thousands was not despised.

A music publisher kept a varied selection of new songs in reserve so as not to be found in an unguarded state. If he sensed an alteration, however minute, in public preference, he was prepared to saturate the theaters and the retail music outlets with compositions accommodating the altered preference. If a song issued by a competitor won a widespread following, he immediately charged the songwriters in his employ to come up at least with its equal. Where styles were heading and the direction of coming trends were uppermost in his mind.[7]

On January 28, 1908, Charles Denier Warren, a branch manager in the Witmark firm, reported that taste was changing in New York. The public wanted songs better designed than the current coon and rag songs. He sensed a more "artistic" leaning of the public, evidenced in the sudden popularity of Ernest Ball's "Love Me and the World Is Mine." Sentimental but not effusively gushing compositions were setting a new fashion. Publishers and their songwriters, he claimed, were taking their lead from works like that of Ball.[8] Although the rag-derived song did not die, Warren had alerted Witmark to a current trend that required investigation.

Once launched, the usual hit could sell well for three to six years. Yet, nobody could predict an event that could wipe out sales. Harry Kennedy's "Cradle's Empty, Baby's Gone" (1880) was very popular in New York City, especially among the shop girls; however, a sudden outbreak of infant deaths extinguished interest in the song.[9] Again, an event could take place that would put a song over. Charles K. Harris's "Break the News to Mother" (1897), whose subject was a dying Confederate soldier, was not expected to be a success because the Civil War was long past. But when the Spanish-American War broke out, both soldiers and civilians found the song suited to the temper of the changed times.[10]

From what has been said above, it should be clear that publishers were fearful of loss, swift to drop everything in favor of the current rage in music, and reluctant to take chances. They also were fusionists, assimilating different cultural tendencies, responding to any cultural drift of the moment. To remain in business, they could ill afford to identify themselves with any one song style, or to dictate a specific taste in subject or music to their customers. Even in the late twentieth century, with a more profound knowledge of mass psychology and a greater expertise in marketing, music publishers cannot work conspiratorially or "operate authoritatively."[11]

Nevertheless, by the end of the nineteenth century music publishers had begun to believe that a song that showed promise, in terms of contemporary public tastes and the composition's individual attractiveness, could benefit from judicious assistance. Directors of publishing firms were fascinated by the question of how tastes and opinions might be predicted and controlled. Joseph Wood Krutch wrote that, beginning in this nineteenth-century period, "Even in the realm of the popular arts, commercial exploiters" spoke "frankly of 'making' a star or a song hit rather than 'discovering' him or it. They have their methods and the methods very frequently work. When the beginnings of popularity are detected, its full flowering can be directed and controlled."[12]

In short, a song that was already well received could be helped along to "hit" status through management and the observance of fixed procedures. A conceivable exception was a topical song rushed out to seize an opportunity, such as the discovery of electricity, or the invention of the telephone or motorcar, the marriage of President Grover Cleveland, the kidnapping of Charley Ross, or the surprising number of women who suddenly took up the Grecian Bend. There was no time to nurse it along. All too soon the subject was yesterday's history; so also was demand for this kind of song.[13]

PUBLISHER AND COMPOSER

Composers capable of consistently writing profitable songs were the bedrock of the music publishing industry. The publishing house of J. L. Peters certainly valued its relationship with Will S. Hays. In the two decades before 1880, he composed around 300 successful songs, exploiting subjects centered on lovers, home, and mother. A single song, if well received, sold around 350,000 copies. Peters eventually sold 20 million copies of Hays's compositions.[14]

During the eighties and nineties, the population of the United States burgeoned and the larger firms among the new music publishers specializing in popular song grew even bigger and swallowed up smaller or more infirm houses. Witmark and Sons, founded in 1886, took over ten other firms within a few years and soon boasted a vast song catalog. Fortunes were being made through the sale of popular music. By the beginning of the twentieth century, some 2 billion sheet-music copies of songs were being sold in a single year. From 1902 to 1907, around 100 songs had sold 100,000 copies each; 50 had sold more than 200,000 each; 30 had reached 250,000; and 4 had been truly big sellers, with a piece like "In the Shade of the Old Apple Tree" (1905) quickly selling over 700,000 copies.[15]

In contrast to the few successful firms were the many that failed to publish enough profitable songs to enable them to continue. They were forced to sell what assets they had to pay off debts and permanently close their doors.[16] Given that publishers must compete successfully to survive, let along thrive, issuing music admired by and afforded by a multitude of persons undoubtedly colored and even dominated all other considerations, such as cultural enhancement and the nurturing of deserving composers.

The ability to spot promising pieces when first encountered was of considerable importance. One reason the Witmarks thrived as publishers was Julie Witmark's experience as a professional singer, which gave him the ability to recognize what would please people in all parts of the United States. Isidore Witmark also developed this sense. When he perceived that Ernest Ball, who wrote the enthusiastically endorsed "Love Me and the World Is Mine" (1906), could produce consistently agreeable songs for the public, he gave him a twenty-four year contract as staff composer, with an annual guaranteed wage—an action that helped the firm to market Ball's future song successes more efficiently, quickly, and cheaply.[17]

On the other hand, these same publishers rejected more than a few songs that eventually developed enormous followings. Banks Winters found no publisher for his "White Wings." No one sensed the song's possibilities or wished to develop an audience for it. Finally, a performance at a Boston theater catapulted the song into fame. Willis Woodward, who was prevailed upon to publish it in 1884, added an outstanding profit maker to his catalog. "In the Good Old Summer Time," words by Ren Shields, music by George Evans, met with a similar rejection. Publishers claimed that variety performers and audiences would endorse it at best for the three summer months, and even then its success was too chancy. Finally, in 1902, Howley, Haviland, and Dresser issued it and sold over 1 million copies.[18]

It is logical to conclude that an objectified, systemized, and certain knowledge to guide publishers' dealings with composer and public was by no means reliably established. Moreover, hundreds of people from every part of America were trying their hands at writing popular songs and sending their manuscripts to publishers. Sometimes over a thousand manuscripts a month arrived at a publisher's door. For all the know-how of the Witmarks, they got so buried under manuscripts that they often resorted to accepting songs on a hit-or-miss, trial-and-error basis.[19]

Although royalty payments to popular-song composers were not unknown—Stephen Foster and George Root had been so reimbursed during the fifties—publishers more often bought songs outright. Normally composers were delighted to get $25 for a song, especially before 1890. Publishers would then charge up to 75 cents a copy. By the nineties, due to competition, more efficient production methods, and improved technology, the sales price per copy dropped to 40 cents; ten years later, to 25 cents. Performers paid much less, and beginning in the 1900s they almost always received copies free of charge. Jobbers who took over wholesale lots of songs for distribution to retail outlets got them with a 50-percent reduction.[20]

The young Witmark house, still financially shaky, bought "The Picture That Is Turned Toward the Wall" from Charles Graham, sold thousands of copies of it beginning in 1891, and thus established the firm on a solid footing. Graham received only $15 for his composition. Thomas Westendorf received a token payment from the John Church publishing house for "I'll Take You Home Again, Kathleen," published in 1876. Americans went wild over it. Fortunately for Westerndorf, the publisher was willing to show his gratitude for the fortune he made, albeit in a small way, by sending the composer $50 a month over several years. Such twinges of conscience did not bother many other publishers. Luckily for Harry Von Tilzer, it bothered Shapiro and Bernstein after they purchased "My Old New Hampshire Home" from him for $25 and issued it in 1898. The song immediately entered the vaudeville repertoire and was taken up by numerous singers. The firm then handed $4,000 to Von Tilzer and offered him a partnership.[21]

Few songwriters were as astute as Hart P. Danks in profiting from songs. Charles Hamm said that, unlike Westendorf, Danks was a great pragmatist who managed to support himself through his songs. He moved to New York, where he supplied his songs to different houses, demanding as much money as the market would bear and selling to the highest bidder. Danks even made arrangements to sell his songs in England through a London firm. In both America and England, "Don't be Angry with Me, Darling" (1870) and "Silver Threads Among the Gold" (1872) were big sellers.[22]

Some songwriters, provoked at what they thought was the publishers' insensitivity and greed, founded their own firms. Charles K. Harris, angered at the 85-cent royalty check that Witmark gave him for

"When the Sun Has Set," proceeded to open his own office, where he issued his "After the Ball" in 1892. When it sold over 2 million copies, he was the one who made a fortune. One publisher after another turned down Kerry Mills's "At a Georgia Camp Meeting." An exasperated Mills started his own firm and published the composition in 1899. After Mills hawked his publication wherever he could, getting music retailers to carry it and performers to feature it, the song met with great demand on the vaudeville circuit and he earned more money than he could have dreamed of getting from a publisher. "Meet Me Tonight in Dreamland," words by Beth Slater Whitson and music by Leo Friedman, provides a final example. It was sold outright to William Rossiter, who denied the authors a share of his respectable profits. Therefore, when Rossiter's brother Harold opened his own office, the authors decided to give him, not William, the song "Let Me Call You Sweetheart" to publish for royalties. Published in 1910, the song went on to accumulate even larger profits than the previous composition, making the authors and Harold Rossiter happy.[23]

Clearly, if composers failed to become their own publishers, they stood to lose by their songs. Since most composers submitted their work to already established publishing firms, they almost invariably suffered by their business deals. Some composers made out very well financially from their songwriting activities, whether through the operation of their own publishing firms or the receipt of royalties or fees. More received middling incomes from their compositions. Most earned little or nothing. If money was the object, for the great majority of musicians it was undoubtedly easier to attain through performance rather than songwriting. In rebuttal, publishers claimed that they had to bear the expense of numerous song failures and their seemingly large profits were necessary to offset these. They insisted that few songs were published as the composers wrote them; each one had to be gone over by the publisher and altered if it proved troublesome for a singer's voice or difficult for an audience to understand. Nevertheless, when an unconscionably shocking profit was made from a song and offsetting losses were nil, the publisher was still not apt to show magnanimity toward the poor songwriter who had made the profit possible.

MODERN BUSINESS PRACTICES

William Rossiter provides an excellent example of the new, pugnaciously enterprising, and profit-oriented publisher. Born in England in 1867, Rossiter came to Chicago in 1881 and started off as a drafts-man before entering popular entertainment. He has already been mentioned as denying Beth Whitson and Leo Friedman a share in the immense earnings his firm derived from their "Meet Me Tonight in Dreamland," which sold over 2 million copies. Like so many of the younger breed of publishers, he had started as a songwriter and variety entertainer, promoting his own compositions on the stage, in retail stores, and anywhere he could command an audience. After establish-ing his music business, he pioneered assertive advertising campaigns for his most recent publications in newspapers and journals, including theatrical trade journals like *The New York Clipper*. As further insur-ance against failure, he had a financial interest in several variety acts which, of course, showcased the newest songs issued by his firm. Another activity that won him fame was the printing of bargain-priced songbooks for the general public, a strategy that he first adopted for the World's Columbian Exposition in Chicago in 1893. Whatever his ul-timate financial intentions were with regard to songwriters, he paid court to those who showed the most promise, thereby assuring himself one or two sensational winners like Shelton Brooks's "Some of These Days" (1910) and "The Darktown Strutters' Ball" (1917). However, he did let Charles K. Harris's "After the Ball" get away from him.[24]

So important were successes to publishers that they immediately took action when they came upon any copyright infringement. (By 1891 an international copyright law offered protection from piracy in other countries.) Moreover, if publishers found a vital source for in-come unprotected by the copyright law, they lobbied to correct the omission. In the case of the player piano and phonograph recordings, we see evidence of the extreme measures used by publishers to protect their interests. The courts decided in 1906 that reproduction of songs by means of piano rolls and recordings did not come under the copy-right law as then written. Music publishers lobbied Congress for a correction but to no avail because, as the publishers learned, without a constituency from various congressional districts to back them noth-ing would happen. Isidore Witmark stated that he then conceived the plan of combing publishers' files for the thousands of names of men and women who had submitted songs for publications. Each of them re-ceived a letter saying their song might have been published if it had not been for losses incurred by free reproduction of songs by mechanical means. This forced publishers to cut down on the number of compo-sitions they could issue. The situation corrected, they would reconsider the submitters' manuscripts. Therefore, they urged all submitters to write their congressmen demanding copyright revision.

A flood of letters from amateur songwriters and their friends inundated Washington. When Representative Frank D. Currier of New Hampshire, chair of the Patents Committee, proved obdurate in his defense of the status quo (Witmark claims he was "controlled" by the "other side"), the assistance of other politicians was solicited to put pressure on the committee. A lobbyist was hired to talk to the fence sitters and disseminate "educational" material among them. Free tickets to shows were dispensed to any congressman who wanted them. At last a compromise copyright bill emerged that provided a 2-cent royalty for each side of a phonograph disk containing copyrighted material and a 2-cent royalty for each publication however mechanically reproduced.[25]

Innovative tactics were also employed when, in 1907, it was found that large department stores—among them Siegel, Cooper and Company, and R. H. Macy's in New York—were discounting sheet music down to 6 cents a copy, thus undermining the price structure that publishers felt essential to maintain. Again, the courts decided against the publishers. According to Isidore Witmark, the publishers banded together and fought back by advertising and staging 1-cent sales of the same music. They also hired people to go to the department stores with the 1-cent advertisement in hand and complain vociferously, so that all customers could hear them, about establishments like Macy's, which lied when they claimed that they would not be undersold. The department stores were forced to come to terms with the publishers.[26]

Any audience-pleasing material that was not copyrighted experienced quick appropriation by others. E. J. Kahn, Jr., said that songs and entire theater acts might be stolen if left unprotected. He gave an instance of a Harrigan and Hart show opening in Pittsburgh to a local critic's complaint that he had already heard all of the music and most of the lines in other shows. Kahn describes one occasion where a Harrigan and Braham song was filched before its first public performance: an Italian bandleader who heard it in rehearsal then used it at a beer garden not far from the theater.[27] A militant watchfulness over copyrighted music and a readiness to give battle in the courts when infringement was detected might be difficult and time-consuming activities for songwriters, who usually lacked the resources to guard their productions, but they were necessary activities for music publishers who wished to survive.

The term *Tin Pan Alley*, used to describe the popular-song industry that emerged during the nineties (with publishers' offices extending from Fourteenth to Twenty-eighth streets, in New York City is supposed to have originated with Monroe H. Rosenfeld around 1903.[28] The larger role of these publishers is clear in Theodore Dreiser's comment, made in 1900, that the publishers along Broadway from Madison to

Greeley squares coordinated the world of popular music. He saw them operating in a regulated manner in order to achieve a common purpose. A vivid portrayal of the inside of a music-publishing house then follows:

> There is an office and a reception-room; a music chamber, where songs are tried, and a stock room. Perhaps, in the case of the larger publishers, the music-rooms are two or three, but the air of each is much the same. Rugs, divans, imitation palms make this publishing house more bower than office. Three or four pianos give to each chamber a parlor-like appearance. The walls are hung with the photos of celebrities. . . . In the private music-rooms [are] rocking-chairs. A boy or two wait to bring *professional copies* at a word. A salaried pianist or two wait to run over pieces which the singers may desire to hear. Arrangers wait to make orchestrations or take down newly schemed out melodies which the popular composer himself cannot play.[29]

Dreiser's words underline the fact that New York City had become the publication and distribution center for popular songs. Variety artists, band and orchestra directors, and singers—both those with theater engagements and those down on their luck—visited publishers looking for new material and an exchange of theatrical gossip and information, or if idle and without money, looking for handouts and job openings. The publisher concentrated his attention on these professional visitors, knowing he had to create a demand for a song within a reasonable time or put it aside, knowing they would welcome anything that struck them as fresh, adaptable to their acts, and flattering to their singing styles. If there was a bothersome spot in a song for a singer, an arranger was present to effect a modification. If the orchestra leader required a special orchestration for his ensemble, the arranger would immediately write one for him. To encourage future performance, the publisher had copies of the newest songs already printed on cheaper-grade paper. Any professional who might possibly sing one of them received a free copy.[30]

Reactions were carefully observed. If the professionals seemed to like a song on first hearing in the publisher's music chamber, then small retail stores and large department stores all over the country were sent discounted copies for resale. After the song's progress was monitored nationwide for a few months, perhaps some public interest became evident, some reordering of the song had taken place, or some reports had come back from singers on favorable audience reaction. That was the moment to commence advertising the song in newspapers and journals and on the jackets of other songs that were already selling well. Professionals distant from the publishing house were asked to write for free copies of the music. Songsheets containing the words were offered the public. Orders for the songsheets were taken from theaters, circuses, and other places that catered to audiences with music of some sort.[31]

From the nineties on, publishers studied their market with a care unknown in earlier decades. They noted, for example, that there was little sale of songs from May to September. For this reason they held back on those new songs that showed the greatest promise of becoming hits and introduced them in the fall and winter. This is because in those months all of the theaters were open, people were home from vacations at the seashore or in the countryside and readily attended musical performances, and fresh songs were required for singing around the piano at home.[32]

All new musical compositions had to experience acts of initiation whereby they were commended to the public and introduced into the performance circuit. During the post–Civil War period, knowing publishers practiced multifarious promotions for newly introduced musical compositions, promotions that had been hitherto unknown to the trade or observed in a more desultory manner.

Advertising was one essential recourse. Daniel Boorstin wrote that in the postbellum decades the calling of products to the attention of the public emerged as a major American art and a manifestation of the assertive, pugnacious democracy that came into being at the time. Sometimes ruthlessly and certainly relentlessly, publishers shared in the endeavor of business-centered democracy "to widen the audience and to broaden its appeal. There is no better example of the power of new American circumstances to break up old rigidities, to allow the world to flow."[33]

As early as 1862, Henry Clay Work's song "Kingdom Coming" underwent a boostering campaign that foreshadowed the way promoters would tease the public into taking notice of a composition. For several days before arriving in a town, Christy's Minstrels enigmatically set forth the mysterious message of "Kingdom Coming!" in newspaper items and on publicly displayed placards. The troupe then appeared in a stage show of the same name and offered the song for sale. From April to November more than twenty thousand copies of the work were sold in this manner. That no scheme bore repetition was proven when the similarly promoted "Babylon Falling" failed to intrigue the public. In 1864 the publishing house of Root & Cady, through its house publication *The Song Messenger*, offered a free copy of Work's "Come Home, Father!" to people who could read the lyrics and hold back their tears. Thousands read it; ten claimed copies.[34]

In later years, publishers would acknowledge that advertising in journals and newspapers alone, however novel, would not suffice to put a song across because the public also had to hear and become familiar with the music. Nevertheless, they did note a success here and there that was achieved primarily through this means. Raymond Moore, member of a minstrel show, entertained audiences with performance of "Sweet Marie" (1893), his musical setting of lyrics by Cy Warman. Nevertheless, it was the publicity given the song by the *New York Sun* that was material in building enthusiasm for the composition. Charles B. Ward's "The Band Played On" (1895), lyrics by John F. Palmer [Palmer is said to have been largely responsible for the music as well], achieved an equally enthusiastic response when sponsored by the *New York World*, which printed both its words and music. After the mid-nineties, sheet-music songs would be commonly encountered as newspaper supplements.[35]

Favorable publicity achieved through diverse means was certainly a goal of music publishers from the earlier years,[36] but it was not until the post–Civil War period that it became a dominant factor in publishers' thinking.

Plugging, one of the primary promotional tools, is defined by Edward B. Marks as

> any public performance which is calculated to boost a song. . . . Forty years ago [ca. 1893] . . . with its initial break in the beer hall, a song might work up to the smaller variety houses, and finally to Tony Pastor's, on Fourteenth Street, or Koster and Bial's, whence some British singer might carry it home to London. If it scored there, it might come back here as a society sensation. And the whole process, from bottom to top, might take several weeks, during which gross sales mounted steadily.[37]

A plug might mean loudly singing a song on a major urban intersection or in front of a music store displaying the title in its window. A plug might be the sending of a singer-pianist to perform on a raised platform in a department store, in the midst of sheet-music counters. The hope was to familiarize shoppers with its tune and entice them to buy. A plug might be negotiating with an Italian *padrone* to have his organ grinders push the song on the streets. Around the turn of the century, publishers might plug a song by recording it on a player-piano roll or on a phonograph cylinder or flat disk, then offering it free to influential performers or at a competitive price to ordinary customers.

Marks states that at the beginning of his publishing career, he would put in a full day in the office, then get his campaign for a new song going at night by weekly visiting some sixty saloons, beer halls, and other "joints" that offered musical entertainment. (His partner Jo Stern visited about forty a week.) Accompanying him was a plugger called Louis the Whistler, who would give the patrons slips of paper containing the words of the chorus, then encourage everyone to try to sing along with the orchestra. Louis himself would whistle the melody and, when he discovered a table occupant with a decent voice, have him sing a solo chorus. Gradually, if all went as planned, the entire crowd would be singing along and would, therefore, remember it in the future.[38]

When Charles K. Harris gave orchestra leader Frank Palma a box of cigars to arrange "After the Ball" and gave J. Aldrich Libbey $500 to sing it in the show *A Trip to Chinatown*, he was making preparations to have the piece plugged. Libbey says a proper plugging campaign for an unknown song, utilizing a professional singer of some repute, required around $1,300, some of which went for a lithographed picture of the singer on the song's title page, copies for free distribution, a year's advertising in a theatrical journal, and a cash advance plus an arrangement for ongoing payments to the performer who was hired to introduce it on the stage.[39]

Placing songs with highly regarded entertainers and important music dealers was a treasured skill. Julie Witmark sang and plugged the Witmark firm's songs wherever he traveled in the United States. His personal charm helped to win over men like Patrick Healy of Lyon & Healy, Chicago, and Leander Sherman of Sherman, Clay & Co., San Francisco, as well as their clerks and buyers. They agreed to carry the Witmark music line. He befriended and placed songs with the most popular performers at Tony Pastor's, among them Joe Hart, Katie Hart, Tony Hart, Bessie Bonehill, Vesta Victoria, Marie Lloyd, Lottie Gilson, Arthur West, Danny Collyer, and Monroe and Rice. Pluggers of this sort were indispensable to publishers. Meyer Cohen placed songs for the Joseph W. Stern Company; Mose Gumble, for Shapiro-Bernstein, then Remick. Pluggers bought singers their meals and drinks, paid their hotel bills, had new outfits tailored for them, and subsidized their acts; they flattered them, sang to them, and persuaded them in the streets, restaurants, their rooms, and backstage. This was "outside" plugging. Firms also retained "inside" pluggers—that is to say, skilled musicians (the "salaried pianist" that Dreiser mentioned earlier) with agreeable voices who played and sang the firm's offerings for visiting entertainers, taught them how to sing the music, and made changes to suit individual needs and mask individual deficiencies.[40]

Publishers were most reluctant to accept songs by an unknown unless they were introduced by leading artists first. Gambling on an inexperienced songwriter might prove profitless. Publishers wanted to save themselves the expense of having the pieces "sung, played, hummed, and drummed into the ears of the public, not in one city alone, but in every city, town, and village" to make them popular. If the novice's song was thus tested and emerged triumphant, then they would consider its publication.[41]

The more popular performers expected reimbursement for introducing unfamiliar pieces. Stars like Belle Baker, Fanny Brice, and Sophie Tucker received large undercover payments for their commercial favors. *Variety,* April 7, 1906, described the practice as a "menace to vaudeville," since it led to a monopoly by a handful of publishers and to showcasing songs that were monotonously similar in sound and subject. Three months earlier, the Gus Edwards Publishing Company had denounced "payola," insisting that it was one firm that refused to give in to greedy singers' demands and that Lillian Russell, Louise Dresser, and Nettie Vesta were singing its new issues without exacting secret fees.[42]

Successful singers "are out for themselves," wrote Theodore Dreiser in 1900. They expect "some arrangement by which" they will "receive a stated sum per week for singing a song." It is the publisher's decision whether a singer "is worth subsidizing or not." An ordinary "gentleman of the road" may come to a publisher and ask for $25 or so, because he is short of money. The publisher must then decide whether the singer can "do the songs of the house twenty-five dollars' worth of good next season." A famous "lord of the stage" may come in, and the publisher knows he must get the "glad hand and the ready check, and he is to be petted, flattered, taken to lunch, dinner, a box theater party—anything—everything, really." Finally, there "is the sub-strata applicant in tawdry make-believe clothes whose want peeps out of every seam and pocket." Because he is down-and-out and without audience appeal, he is not worth anything to a publisher and gets short shrift.[43]

The variety-stage headliners took a song on a circuit that embraced the major cities of the United States as well as many smaller cities. They were a great influence on people's acceptance, which was easily measured by the local burst of sales in a song wherever it was being performed by one of these stars. Moreover, if a headliner made a song an integral part of his act, he could keep the public's attention engaged for a period of years, adding to the song's profitability.[44]

Other plugging methods developed by the more aggressive publishers helped the performer make a success of an unfamiliar song. One such method involved planting a "stooge" in the audience. When Harry Von Tilzer wrote music and his publishing house issued "Please

Go 'Way and Let Me Sleep" (1902), he thought up the gimmick of seating himself in the audience and pretending to be asleep while snoring loudly. Finding his performance disturbed, the minstrel entertainer Arthur Deming would begin to scold the sleeping man. Harry Von Tilzer would then rise listlessly and sing the chorus from his seat—an inspiration that was widely reported in the newspapers and admired by the audience whenever it was repeated. In the same year, when Nora Bayes introduced "Down Where the Wurzburger Flows" at the Orpheum Theater in Brooklyn, she broke down and Harry Von Tilzer continued to sing until she recovered. Again, the audience enjoyed the exchange, and he continued to be her stooge for the rest of the week.[45]

The stooge sometimes was a boy selected for his pleasing voice. Seated in the balcony, he was supposed to be so "spontaneously" carried away by the song that he could not help but get up to sing along with the performer onstage. Or he could disguise himself as a water boy or a refreshment seller, someone who ostensibly was there to serve members of the audience.[46]

Other ideas were tried, such as using song-slides to illustrate the text. This was said to have started around 1892, when George H. Thomas, an electrician at the Amphion Theater in Brooklyn, accompanied "Where Is My Wandering Boy Tonight?" (1877) with the projection of a single slide depicting a young man at a saloon bar. This gave Edward Marks and Joseph Stern, writers and publishers of "The Little Lost Child" (1894), the idea of preparing a series of slide-photographs taken at a Brooklyn police station to be shown along with this song's performance. Before long, other publishers were investing in colored slides to help win the affection of audiences.[47]

Another way to ensure a song's success was to hire a claque to promote acceptance through clamorous applause and uninhibited shouts of approval. The claque alone might be relied on, or it might be used in conjunction with a stooge or slide show or both to create an overwhelming impression of enthusiastic approval.[48]

Toward the end of the century, a portion of the public attending a song's initial performance was sampled for its reaction and the opinions expressed were used to forecast the eventual acceptance of the work. Audience response was also measured by the number of song copies sold in the theater lobby during the run of the act featuring a composition. However, these measures of public opinion had to be interpreted with considerable caution, since future events frequently proved the poll wrong, and a song might come into its own only after several failures to win an audience.

Yet, no matter how clever and persistent the publicity given a song, at the end it had to succeed on its own merits—as a composition whose words and music merited attention for their own sake. A "lord of the stage," widespread advertisement, and the use of stooges and other pluggers might inflate a song's importance, but they could not turn a bad song into a good one. On the other hand, it was also true that a song with much to recommend it to the public might easily go nowhere without carefully-thought-out promotion and sponsorship. This was the task of the publisher.

4 THE PUBLIC PERFORMANCE OF POPULAR SONGS

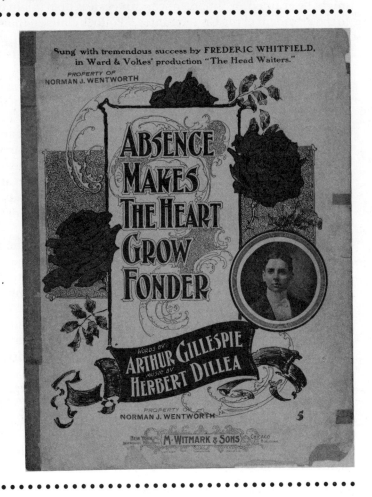

The performers (many of whom, of course, were also songwriters) came mostly from the ranks of the lower middle class and from families that included scarcely any and usually no other stage entertainers. Most sought stage careers because they yearned for excitement or because they felt that they possessed an undeniable talent for the stage.

Many entertainers yearned for the "intoxicating music of applause," the "consciousness of the strained attention of the thousands who have paid to see" them, praise by newspaper critics, and respectful interviews quoting their every word, according to Channing Pollock, a noted Broadway entertainer, in 1911. A top performer might be granted an "importance scarcely less than might be accorded to the President of the United States." Pollock claimed that the women who took up life on the stage were often "daughters of poverty and squalor," who appreciated luxury and wished to extricate themselves from their oppressive surroundings, even if it meant escape only for a moment in the chorus line. Oliver Logan, who was strongly opposed to the exploitation of women, wrote in 1869 that women were now being hired for the theater as never before and made to go unclad and sing songs of "indecent constructions," "accompanied by the wink, the wriggle, the grimace, which are not peculiar to virtuous women, whatever else they are." In particular, Logan denounced women's appearance in the variety theater, claiming that it was not a theater: "Until the reign of the nude women set in, variety-halls were the resort of only the lowest and vilest, and women were not seen in the audience.[1]

Whatever Logan's objections, the stage seemed to offer young men and women deliverance from mundane evils and appeared to be an intriguing venture calling for little capital to achieve distinction. What was more, the door was open to anyone, whatever his education, background, ethnic origin, or economic class.

De Wolf Hopper, a stage entertainer active around the turn of the century, confirmed Pollock's words when he stated that the performers he knew did not, "with rare exceptions, drift on to the stage. They [made] a dead set for it." It was not just for the sake "of meal tickets" that they did so. They crossed the "footlights out of an egotistic desire to strut before an admiring world." They hoped "romantically to win a fortune along with their pictures in the papers, but always they have been willing to starve cheerfully if accompanied by adequate publicity." Applause to performers is like drugs to addicts, he concluded.[2]

56

CAREERS ON THE STAGE

All performers learned that they had to start from the bottom, ready to do anything to gain a place on the stage. In 1871 Henry Clay Barnabee was a relatively unknown singer who could not afford to turn down any offer. The day after he arrived in Boston with a soprano, they were asked to sing at a funeral. "Our fee was ten dollars, and we grabbed it convulsively." When the unknown Bert Williams was making the rounds of San Francisco's saloons playing the banjo and singing, he was offered a job as a "Hawaiian," playing guitar and singing with a Hawaiian group. He immediately accepted it. Chauncey Olcott said he developed a special determination to make it on the stage, no matter what the discouragement. After several failures to find employment, he learned that he had to take anything that came along. Pride and choosiness were luxuries he could not allow himself. Olcott therefore developed a song repertoire that enabled him to accept whatever offer was made, from singing for change on the street to appearing on the operatic stage.[3]

The need for money and the hunger for prestige spurred most beginning performers. Barnabee said with some tongue in cheek that, when a starting singer in Portsmouth, New Hampshire, he understood that to become well known he would have to widen his sphere of action and "allow the mellowing effulgence of [his] talents to beam upon other communities." His efforts, he was certain, would bring him a "new pot of money, besides sundry laurels." Therefore, "with my accustomed readiness to gather in all that was coming to me, I immediately began preparing to leave my familiar New England haunts." This meant putting together a traveling company, which eventually included another singer, a cornet player, and a pianist, to visit other parts of the United States.[4]

Given the special talent and initial performance experience, the popular singer then hoped to find someone with influence to further one's career. Felix Isman said both David Warfield and Fay Templeton were fortunate in this regard. Of the former, Isman wrote: "It remained for Weber and Fields to give Warfield his big chance [ca. 1898], and it was not until he had proved himself on their stage that Belasco turned his glance toward the boy he once had heard singing on a San Francisco street corner, and made of him a star."[5]

Realistic singers knew that to achieve, or maintain themselves in, the big time they had to search forever for special songs that would distinguish them from the horde of other entertainers. A common acknowledgment among entertainers was that the performer was only as good as his or her material. Around 1890, Maggie Cline said she was looking for a boost to her career and hoped to discover a novel piece suited to her powerful voice and boisterous personality. She met John W. Kelly, the songwriter. "I asked him if he had any loose songs about him and he said he had one that no one wanted on the opera stage and I could have it, but not for a cent less than two dollars. I took the song and paid cash, and for twenty-three years I've used it in my business." The song that suited her style of delivery and made her famous was "Throw Him Down, McCloskey."[6]

The most popular singers had compositions written to order for them. Frequently, publishers willingly paid the cost, hoping that variety headliners and other singers with public followings would create a demand for these songs. Publishers would even pay the singers to sing them![7] Sophie Tucker stated that around 1906, when she was singing in the German Village, a New York restaurant, publishers noted her popularity with the clientele. Soon they were bringing her new songs suited to her voice and singing style. These compositions were most welcome, since her motto had always been "Get something new. Keep fresh. Don't get stale singing the same songs."[8]

Singers were likely to introduce a song anywhere in their act, whether appropriate or not, if they thought the audience would approve of the result. If they inserted the composition into a variety presentation, the problem of coordinating song and act was minimal. However, if a musical play was involved, the plot might be less amenable to adaptations. Nevertheless, if a show was doing poorly and the introduction of a new song might save it, most producers did not worry about assimilation. When, at the beginning of the nineties, *A Trip to Chinatown* was introduced on the stage, ticket sales were slow. Then Harry Conor came upon "The Bowery" (lyrics by Charles H. Hoyt and music by Percy Gaunt). He introduced it into the show, although it had no connection with what was taking place on the stage. The song became a hit and filled the theater, enabling the show to run for 650 performances.[9]

DeWolf Hopper stated that although the staged story and the music were often "unfriendly," promising songs always took precedence over the plot's logic. To accommodate the music, the story might leap from a Louisiana cane field to the ice of Greenland to exotic India, then to a "Montana ranch by way of the Bowery." It was not unusual to see central European peasants and soldiers sing a rollicking drinking song then suddenly reappear "as cotton pickers cakewalking to the strains of 'Georgia Camp Meeting.' " Connecting the songs to the story was a constant strain: "In order to do this it was necessary now and then for the tenor to be reminded by a catchup bottle in a Vienna rathskeller of Apple Blossom Time in Delaware." Or, for example, if a story was left stranded on the island of Sulu and the authors wanted to incorporate a song about Doctor Crook, gumdrops and Eskimos, the dialogue would run something like this:

"She: Isn't it warm here in Sulu?"

"He: It is indeed. I wish I were back again in dear old Franz Joseph Land [a part of Russia, on the Arctic Ocean].

"The conductor, who had been waiting with poised baton, would give it a flourish and the pack would be off in full cry on the gumdrop song."[10]

The greatest sin a performer could commit was not to entertain, not to delight the audience. Tremendous tension built up in singers who were called on again and again to give good accounts of themselves while they performed. Even the stars, in constant fear of toppling from their high positions, felt this tension. Lotta Crabtree, after appearing young, relaxed, and in good humor in the theater, was known to sometimes drive insanely around the countryside to work off her tension. On the stage, she made the crowds feel she was one of them; off the stage, she was lonely and alone, without friends. At one time, in a small western town, "she drove about for hours in a hack through a storm with water and mud up to the heels." At another time, "someone remembered seeing her curled up at the end of a railway coach alone and forlorn, smoking surreptitiously during a long journey. She sometimes smoked as furiously as she drove, smoking black cigars." None of this strain was ever evident when she performed.[11]

Singers were convinced that a very thin line divided today's successful performer from tomorrow's seedy has-been. Before them was Theodore Dreiser's vivid portrayal of the ballad singer down on his luck, desperately trying to keep up appearances:

> Once a day he makes the rounds of the theatrical agencies; once, or if fortune favors, twice a day he visits some cheap eating-house. At night, after a long stroll through the fairyland of theaters and gaudy palaces to which, as he sees it he properly belongs—Broadway, he returns to his bed, the carpeted floor of a room in some tolerant publisher's office, where he sleeps by permission, perhaps, and not even there, too often. . . . Outside, as he stretches himself, may even now be heard the murmur of that shiny, joyous rout of which he was so recently a part. The lights, the laughter; the songs, the mirth—all are for others. Only he, he must linger in shadows, alone.[12]

Insecurity haunted the performer at all times. As often as not, when on top of the heap, the singer dressed extravagantly, spoke with maddening self-adulation, dealt condescendingly with others, and tolerated no competition from able but lesser singers. Allen Churchill described Eva Tanguay as one of the most fiercely competitive performers in a world where self-centered ambition was a must for survival. Onstage, she tried to give everything she had to each performance; offstage, she was on guard against any entertainer likely to usurp her position.[13]

Nora Bayes, although a preeminent performer and famous for her rendition of "Down Where the Wurzburger Flows" (1902) and "Take Me Out to the Ball Game" (1908), was instantly on the alert when the still-unestablished Sophie Tucker made a hit in the *Follies* opening in 1909. Bayes felt that her star status in the production was about to be threatened by an upstart. Furious at Tucker's success, Bayes had her cut back to one number only. Sophie Tucker said that she was thankful she was not fired. Tucker was learning that "tough breaks" were plentiful in show business, and one had to learn to take them. The entertainer, she said, had to be "hard-boiled," had to protect herself; there was no room for "self-pity" or "hurt feelings."[14]

Most performers had no life beyond the theater. They usually socialized with other theater people, few others. Everybody talked shop, wrote Channing Pollock, but in the theater it was the only thing they talked about, never art, science, literature, or politics. Essential reading was the theatrical news, nothing else. Once, when Pollock mentioned the San Francisco earthquake and the calamity it turned out to be, a performer replied: "By George, yes! Cost me twenty weeks I had booked over the Orpheum circuit."[15] Summing up her life, the singer Helen Bertram was quoted as saying: "When we quit the stage we have only the memory of the songs we have sung and the parts we have played," nothing else.[16]

What was the performer's monetary reward for the ceaseless worry, striving to achieve professional excellence, and uncertainty about future prospects, which were just delineated? During the eighties and nineties and into the 1900s, the average song-and-dance man in variety or minstrelsy might get from $10 to $30 a week, and a singer demonstrating some ability to please an audience with his or her singing might get from $15 to $35. If the singer got top billing, then $150 to $250 a week could be the reward. Normally, the management paid traveling expenses.[17]

Yet, these were performers' wages only when they were working. Regrettably, many a week offered no work, and the entertainer had to survive on whatever savings he or she had accumulated. The bookings for a variety circuit might have ended; a minstrel troupe might have gone bankrupt; a show might have closed with no new opening in sight; an entertainer might have gotten sick or temporarily or permanently lost his touch with audiences. When one considers that, in order merely to subsist during these years, a yearly income of around $600 was necessary,[18] it becomes clear that a hand-to-mouth standard of living was the norm.

Chauncey Olcott stated that in the eighties he sang in a minstrel troupe for $40 a month. As his popularity increased, so did his salary—reaching $50 a week. Then fortune smiled and he was hired to sing opposite Lillian Russell, in *Pepita*, at $75 a week. Sophie Tucker, who started her career around the turn of the century stated that she earned no money at first. Later, she won a singing job at New York's German Village restaurant that paid her $15 weekly. She had to sing from fifty to one hundred songs a night to earn that money. A customer's request for a song came with a tip of 50 cents to $1, but all tips went into a pool shared by her, seven other singers, and two pianists. Eventually, both Olcott and Tucker went on to command top wages.[19]

PERFORMER AND AUDIENCE

The popular-entertainment stage is an "ancient and honest" institution, stated Ludwig Lewisohn in 1907. The singer does not ask that you believe something natural and real is being presented—all one has to do is see the vocalist's makeup and fantastic costume to realize reality is not intended, nor an imitation of nature. The singer, instead, "possesses the appealing beauty of things utterly artificial, utterly unreal, utterly useless and fragile."[20]

The sum total of the popular singer's artifice was a magnetic personality that captivated an audience. This was more true of the years after the Civil War than before. In the earlier part of the century, a pleasing voice quality, however untrained, and a simple, unforced style of singing were more important criteria of excellence. Mannerisms that deflected attention from the song's melody and meaning were little countenanced.

After the war, the song became an integral part of an entire image that the brightly illuminated performer transmitted from a raised platform. As a musical illusionist, the singer freely interpreted a song to suit the act, altering key, dynamics, words, melody, and pitch of individual tones. Yet, words were always clearly articulated and rarely distorted for the sake of a beautiful musical sound. (This was especially true in minstrelsy and variety, less true in musical plays that approximated European operettas and called for vocal production approximating that of European singers.) Fidelity to one's own performance style and stage personality took precedence over the accurate replication of the composer's and arranger's intentions.

James L. Ford wrote:

> The profession was nearer and dearer to the popular heart . . . partly because the illusion of the footlights was more carefully retained, but chiefly because the personality . . . entered so largely into the matter. . . . Lotta [Crabtree], aptly characterized by John Brougham as "the dramatic cocktail," could appear in almost anything provided she sang "The Sweet Bye and Bye," a simple ballad that never failed to reach the hearts of her audience.[21]

Lotta Crabtree, according to Constance Rourke, first attracted attention with her swaggering and romping on the stage, always ready to sing, dance, play the banjo or hand organ with all the force of her youth and vivacity. She learned to change with the theater situation, to be tough or fragile, unrestrained or whimsical, oddly ingratiating or standoffish. She would sing with a smoldering ardor that did not always correspond to the trifling subject matter of some of her songs. Every word she vocalized was heard clearly in the farthermost corners of the gallery and was given a strength and significance not always intended by the lyricist.[22]

The magic between singer and audience was not so easily defined. Caroline Caffin, who attended the performances of many of the singers in variety, found it difficult to explain the audience's response to certain singers. To be sure, the public was expert in interpreting and anticipating every nuance of a performance, yet, at the same time, why one artist and not another received special favor remained a mystery. One woman's voice might be thin, her face plain and dancing primitive, yet she won salvos of applause. Another sang sweetly, danced gracefully, and boasted a pretty face and pleasing figure, yet won only a tepid reception. Force of personality made the difference, Caffin concluded.[23] Possibly, descriptions of four prominent women of the stage—Nora Bayes, Eva Tanguay, Lillian Russell, and Fay Templeton—and two men—George M. Cohan and Bert Williams—will indicate what is meant by force of personality.

Caffin remarked on how strongly the audience responded to Nora Bayes's "sparkling languor." She greeted the audience "with a slow, sideway glance" that seemed "to sweep, curving out from her eyes over her face." Teeth and dimples flashed for an instant, "and again the face is almost serious, with a little wistfulness, as though she would hate to think that you might not like her." She next sang so simply "that it is hard to catch the artifice of it." A special "throaty sob" was present even when the song was jolly. At other times she could appear roguish, or arch, or delicate and gentle, "which makes you want to meet her halfway."[24]

Caffin was quite amazed by the audience's reception of Eva Tanguay, a song-and-dance entertainer who could not sing or dance, was not beautiful, witty, or graceful, but who knew the secret of dominating her public "more entirely than anyone on the Vaudeville stage."

Caffin wondered: "How shall we account for the almost breathless intensity with which the audience awaits her entrance? . . . Here she comes, with quick, fluttering steps and restless outstretched hands, a dynamic personality of all nerves and excitement," full of "intense vitality." There is a whirlwind of sound, the restless and aimless patter of her feet, and singing with a "voice that has no music in it." She chants and shrieks over the loudness of the orchestra.

> Naively, childishly self-conscious are her songs—if one can call them songs. [The audience hears a] recitation of her own eccentricities, her extravagance, her defiance of all conventions, with a refrain of "I don't care" [the song, by Jean Lenox and Harry O. Sutton, came out in 1905]. . . . There is no appeal in her attitude toward her public, just a saucy grin. "I don't care" she seems to say; "this is my stunt—like it or not, it's fun to do it, so I don't care." And the audience likes it. Why?[25]

In contrast to Eva Tanguay was the young Lillian Russell, with her own kind of splendor that embraced the audience at Tony Pastor's when she first appeared there in the eighties. She was quite pretty, had an exciting figure, and sang sweetly. Her lyric soprano voice, although not rich, was transparent, of fine quality, and accurately on pitch. Her songs "hinted gently at the delights of trysting 'down by the babbling brook,' or 'where the old millwheel splashes,' " which "struck a responsive chord in the heart of every man in the audience. Here, each of them felt, was the quintessence of sweetness and purity. She was just the kind of girl any fellow would like to marry and teach the facts of life to." This was the innocent image she presented to audiences at a time when she was already married, had borne and lost a child, then divorced her husband in order to singlemindedly dedicate herself to furthering her career.[26]

Popular performers had a strong sense of timing that added immensely to their musical renditions. Fay Templeton's feel for rhythm, for exact timing, phrasing, and accentuation, guaranteed there would be no dead delivery of a song. All of her movements, made at precisely the right moments, heightened the effectiveness of her singing. "Even the most ordinary flutter of her handkerchief and you can get from it all the joy of syncopated accent, the accent which goes not with the best but in a recognized relation to it." Her rhythmic movements and gestures formed an embroidery to her performance. The smallest detail was "adjusted in its time and emphasis in relation to the whole."[27]

In the musical *Little Johnny Jones*, George M. Cohan would look forlornly after the homeward-bound ship that had abandoned him in England and begin to sing softly and with infinite sadness "Give My Regards to Broadway" to murmurs from the orchestra. Then the ship reappeared in the distance as a rocket flared up. Cohan timed it so that the orchestra would now start up without holding back, getting faster and happier as his voice grew increasingly excited, reaching a climax just as the curtain came down. Viewers could not help but applaud madly. In another part of the musical, the noisy crowded stage suddenly became quiet and empty of people. Cohan, left all alone, sorrowed over his inability to find his fiancée, then sang-chanted "Life's a Funny Proposition," which discourses about birth, life, and death. When he arrived at the song's chorus about "life's" being a "funny proposition," he knew it would be wrong to deliver it gloomily or in a moralizing tone. Therefore, he changed his pacing and rendered the "lines in pleasant bemusement, as if unaccountably intrigued. The audience was bemused as well."[28]

Bert Williams had an infallible sense of timing and an ability to effect subtle shifts of emphasis that more than made up for his easily strained and rough voice. By stressing important phrases, by introducing long pauses to suggest ironic subtlety, and through wryly uttered "asides," he encouraged the audience to laugh so hard it forgot about his voice quality. He created a pathetic stage figure, hesitant in its delivery of lines, executing a song like "Nobody" to the "plaintive sound" of a slide trombone, which he made "apparently desperate efforts to catch up with."[29] Bert Williams would make his debut in the Ziegfeld Follies in 1910, becoming one of the first African-American performers to be featured alongside white performances in an important Broadway production.

By this date, African-Americans, helped by the cakewalk and coon-song craze of the nineties, had begun to break out of the all-black shows. In variety-vaudeville alone, there were now about 1,400 black entertainers, of whom 270 were principals.[30] In the late nineties and early part of the twentieth century, some women singers, among them Carry Scott and Louise Dresser, were using African-American children (called "pickaninnies") to sing and dance in their acts. Louise Dresser said that in 1899 she sang Paul Dresser's songs at New York's Masonic Roof Garden, then later on the Orpheum vaudeville circuit: "At the end of the act I introduced two pickaninnies who sang in German, as well as their own darky melodies, accompanying themselves with guitar and mandolin. We finished the act with a rollicking song, one boy playing a cornet, the other a tuba horn, the orchestra, of course, playing with us."[31]

There were also white performers affecting what were ostensibly black-American idioms. In the sixties, seventies, and eighties there were song-and-dance entertainers in blackface who appeared with minstrel troupes and variety acts. In the nineties, with the rise in popularity of the coon songs, came the "coon shouters," among whom five women were prominent—May Irwin, Imogene Comer, Lottie Collins, Sophie Tucker, and Marie Cahill. Bullyragging—that is to say, a somewhat overbearing swaggering delivery—characterized the appearances of most of them. They vociferated more than they sang, took great freedoms with their melodic rhythms, and imposed microtonal variations in pitch (intervals smaller than a halftone) on certain of their notes. Lottie Collins singing "Ta-ra-ra-bom-der-e" (1891), May Irwin "The Bully Song" (1896), and Marie Cahill "Under the Bamboo Tree" (1902) provide important examples. When Collins first began singing her number, her rendition was circumspect, in dramatic contrast to the raucous, shrieking, and high-kicking chorus line that came in on the refrain. The last song came at a time when the coon type of song was being transformed into the rag song, and, in this instance, the words and music were by the African-Americans Bob Cole and J. Rosamond Johnson.[32]

In one regard, the minstrel and variety singers of the postwar period had an approach similar to those of the first half of the century. When afforded the opportunity, they sang "in character"—that is to say, they acted out their songs.[33] If the action suited the song and was rendered by a singer with a dynamic personality, the effect could be telling. One can understand why, in an era when personality had become a significant key to success, entertainers were constantly on the lookout for songs whose subject suited their stage identities and music their singing approach.

Henry Clay Barnabee writes that he always acted out his songs with some stage business, even a dramatic sketch, that would lead into what he was about to sing. In one sketch, "The Unprotected Female," he stepped onto the stage dressed as a young woman, in the character of a person who had turned down many a marriage offer and now realized she was turning into an old maid. This realization led into a song bewailing her fate. Barnabee states that so effective was the characterization, he was once severely attacked by New Hampshire suffragettes for the act.[34]

The Preeminent popular singers could convey the character of a song with even the most sparing of facial or bodily signs. The *Dramatic Mirror*, reviewing Fay Templeton's singing in Cohan's *Forty-Five Minutes from Broadway* (1905), including the title song, commented on her "artistic economy of gesture, her ability to get large effects with little motions, her strange power to make a modest droop of the eyelids, so to speak, re-echo through the whole house, and her magnificent control of comic repose."[35]

···

SINGING IN PLACES OF ENTERTAINMENT

···

Singing was heard in restaurants, free and easies (drinking halls), saloons, beer halls, and wine bars, normally located in cellars, on ground levels, or on the next story above, and, less often, on upper stories or roofs. The least pretentious of these places had a piano to accompany the singing, whether by a paid soloist, by somebody singing for tips, or by the clientele. The plushier places retained one or more professional singers with some reputation and backed them with ensembles ranging from a small band to a large orchestra. Writing about New York City in the eighties and nineties, David Ewen described Minnie Schulte as a voluptuous blonde who attracted patrons to her husband George Huber's Prospect Gardens. Maude Nugent, famous for her song "Sweet Rosie O'Grady" (1896), was featured at the Abbey, on Eighth Avenue. Jessie Lindsay gained renown for her singing of "Daisy Bell" (1892) at the Winter Garden in Union Square. The still-little-known James Thornton was a singing waiter at Bal Mobile in Greenwich Village.[36]

Sophie Tucker said she started off singing in restaurants only for meals and whatever gratuities the customers cared to offer her. A big popular hit of 1897 was "Break the News to Mother." Although thirteen years of age, Tucker had in that year already found work in a restaurant. She would stand by the entry and sing this song and others like it, with all the drama and sentimentality at her command, until, she says, the patrons wept into their food-filled plates. When she finished singing, she waited on tables and unfailingly received tips for her entertainment. If the weather was warm and the door stood open, people on the street stopped to listen.[37]

Except for the minstrel theater, musical entertainment in the United States during the antebellum period resembled that of England and, as often as not, featured European, especially British, singers. Then in the postwar years young Americans in large numbers aggressively sought reputations as popular entertainers. Many started their careers in free and easies, others in restaurants. Eventually they hoped to appear in variety, vaudeville, or musical drama. They brought with them a zest, vigor, and pungency typical of the spirit that permeated America during the last third of the century.[38] Yet, it was these ungenteel drinking places and these restaurants reeking with the smell of food that were the cradles of the new American talent. In them the novice entertainers learned how to please all kinds of audiences, perform up to fifteen shows a day without dropping of fatigue, experiment with unique presentations and dance steps, and write or adapt material, including songs, to suit themselves and their audience.[39] Although the performers were sorely tested by the boisterous and perhaps vulgar demands of their uninhibited patrons, the pressures helped them develop the versatility to adapt swiftly to the changing requirements of impatient audiences.[40]

In many American towns there were meeting halls and public houses where convivial people could gather informally to enjoy themselves drinking, smoking, and singing. These free and easies, which multiplied into the hundreds after the Civil War, included both circumspect music halls and disreputable saloons. In these places amateurs and lower-tier professionals offered songs, dances, comic readings, and anything else that might amuse the table occupants.

Jonathan Baxter Harrison, in *Certain Dangerous Tendencies in American Life*, published in 1880, described a postwar free and easy in a New England factory town. He stated that he entered a second-floor hall, 50 feet long by 25 feet wide, with a bar at one end and a small platform on which was a piano at the other end. Fifty people, most of them mill workers and one-quarter of them young women, sat at eight to ten tables, waited on by a woman who dispensed mostly beer. He saw a young man get up from a table, ascend to the platform, and sing, "in tolerable accord with the weary, protesting piano, a melancholy song about a sailor lover who sailed away from his mistress and never returned." Finished, the vocalist received applause. At this point, a tipsy young woman asked Harrison if he was going to get up next and "shout" something, but before she could pursue her question further, somebody made her leave the hall.[41]

A young black man was invited to abandon his table for a moment and sing. After mounting the stage, he sang various songs, ranging from the comic and silly to the sentimental and pathetic, which brought tears to the guests' eyes. These last "he sang and acted with a kind of suppressed intensity of manner and expression." Next, Harrison visited a couple of the other music halls in town. All the attendants at these halls had come from the mills. In each a youthful pianist received $4 or $5 a week in addition to his board. Those who sang received $1 per night. The real business of these halls, Harrison concluded, was the sale of liquor—the piano music, singing, and recitations were meant to attract patrons.[42]

Harrison, who met the black singer several times at these halls, found out he was a composer whose songs had been published in Boston. "His business was negro minstrelsy and theatricals . . . with the principal companies in this country." His mother had died a year ago, and in order to honor her memory he had decided not to appear in public for a year. The singer said of his performances in free and easies: "I sing a little in this private way to accommodate my friends here, and because it is not good to be doing nothing."[43]

While staying at the principal hotel in town, Harrison met some people who were not mill workers. He told them that he had noticed a variety troupe was in town and intended to entertain at the local academy of music with acts "all of the highest character." He asked if the mill workers would attend. No, came the reply, since they could not appreciate first-class performances and preferred "their own low amusements," among which the execution of popular songs ranked high.[44]

Cities had their own free and easies that catered to an assortment of customers. For example, on New York's Bowery, "Owney Geoghegan's notorious 'Free and Easy' was filled every night with roistering youths, gamblers, and prize fighters," along with "slumming swells," writes James T. Powers. In addition, on Broadway's east side could be seen parallel rows of round colored lanterns that led down to gaily lighted cellars. These were also free and easies, where the principal drink served was beer, no cover charge was exacted, and the main entertainment was furnished by the waiters singing "Mother songs" (sentimental ballads about a loved elderly mother living in a humble, rural home).[45]

Across the continent, in San Francisco, Bert Williams was trying to make a start in show business by appearing in dimly lighted, smoke-filled, and crowded free and easies, most of them catering to sailors in the unruly waterfront district. The sound of scampering waiters, clinking beer and whiskey glasses, and loud conversation compelled Williams to shout his songs in order to catch customers' attention. From the winter of 1893 to the fall of 1895, in a free and easy called Jack Halahan's Cramorne Theater (later renamed the Midway Plaisance), he worked as a team with George Walker. Here entertainment was continuous from 1:30 P.M. to 4 A.M. Williams and Walker presented songs and short comic acts, while other entertainers did variety routines and off-color sketches.[46]

It was the cheapest variety house, where entertainment was secondary in importance to the selling of drinks, that usually came under the rubric of free and easy. In most instances, when the formal relationship of a theater stage to an auditorium with row seats for an audience was observed and stage performance took precedence over the dispensing of liquor, the term *free and easy* was a misnomer. Thus, when Chauncey Olcott's mother, around the late seventies, financed his entry into the entertainment world by opening a "song and dance bar," where he was the drink waiter and singer, the place was indeed a free and easy.[47] When Gustav Walter, in the San Francisco of the mid-seventies, opened The Fountain, a cellar cabaret serving drinks and amusing its patrons with a few variety acts and a small orchestra, Walter's place was also a free and easy. However, when he opened the larger Vienna Gardens in 1881, then The Wigwam in 1884, and finally the Orpheum in 1887, he was progressing from the variety saloon–type of free and easy to variety theater. The Orpheum, which was built as a genuine theater, charged admission and separated the drinks bar from the place where entertainment took place. Its remaining link, and a fairly common one for the time, was the shelf placed on the back of each row seat, where beer and whiskey glasses purchased from aisle vendors could be placed.[48]

Other terms were used to describe establishments, neither saloons nor theaters, that suggested the free and easy. Some that were not theaters, although designated as such, were really "box houses," according to Eugene Clinton Elliott. He writes that in Seattle in 1876, when the Theatre Comique—a saloon plus theater—opened, it was properly called a box house. The designation meant that the balcony was partitioned into curtained alcoves or boxes (here twenty-four) where patrons could remain unseen while viewing the stage and having "girls" attend to their needs. Such houses had poor, amoral reputations, although they did provide lively shows of the minstrel or variety sort. Seattle was then an untamed town, full of lumberjacks, woodsmen, and thieves. Walking along the unpaved gas-lit streets at night was dangerous. In 1882 the Bijou Theater, another box house, began life, and two years later a new Bijou that more closely resembled a true theater. At last, in 1888, the Standard Theater opened under John Cort's management. It had a proper stage, row seats for the audience, and drinks served in the same manner as in San Francisco's Orpheum.[49]

Another kind of establishment was the "dime museum," which charged admission for viewing an exhibit, then allowed the guests to attend a variety show of about an hour's duration without extra charge. Since mixed audiences, including married couples and possibly children, attended, the blue sketches of the rougher variety saloons were banished. One such, in the seventies, was the successful Bunnell's Museum at Broadway and Ninth Street, in New York City. M. B. Leavitt claimed that Bunnell's initiated the continuous variety show—that is to say, when the last act was completed, the show began again with the first act.[50] In the eighties, dime museums grew quite popular and were usually buildings divided in two: one for the exhibits, the other for the variety show, which repeated itself five or more times daily. Douglas Gilbert cites several of them, in New York, Chicago, Boston, Philadelphia, Minneapolis, Saint Paul, Cincinnati, Pittsburgh, and Allegheny, Pennsylvania.

Whether a restaurant, free and easy, variety saloon, box house or dime museum, all were establishments where the beginner could learn how to handle himself or herself in front of an audience. To these establishments should be added the summer resort hotel, which invariably provided musical entertainment. Since many of the hotel managers, like the operators of most of the other establishments described, were leery of paying high wages, they also might hire people with little or no experience. On the other hand, the more fashionable or snobbish hotels maintained practiced singers and musicians commanding an expertise commensurate with the expectations of their affluent and possibly more sophisticated guests. The latter type of resort hotel was likely to feature the less-raucous popular songs and dances plus an admixture of European-oriented salon music.

William Dean Howells described visiting a resort hotel at the end of August, where he listened to music performed by professional musicians on the hotel's long veranda during the afternoon and in the ballroom during the evening. Before his stay was completed, the management dismissed the musicians, just before the season's end, which made him and other people unhappy. Gone was the gaiety, the pleasure he had watching young people dance to the band's playing, and the anticipation of enjoyment each afternoon and evening. He described the change as "cataclysmical" and admitted: "I missed it [the music] poignantly, if one can miss a thing poignantly."[52]

Another avenue leading to professionalism and open to all newcomers was the amateur-night show put on in a variety theater. One writer defined it as "tryout" during which the "baiting of the performer is as much a part of the show as the slaughter of horses at a bull fight."[53] Some of the famous singers could point to appearances on the amateur stage during the period when they were getting their first foothold in show business. There were even professional amateur performers—those who scraped a living out of the tiny sums paid them for amateur performances. Whether neophyte or veteran amateur, the singer had to face an audience ready both to jeer at ineptness and to relish any flair for entertainment.

Although he gave no date, John DiMeglio stated that Miner's Bowery Theater initiated amateur nights on Fridays in imitation of the English music halls. He described Eddie Cantor's first frightened appearance there, when Cantor watched those who preceded him onstage being ridiculed and eventually getting the hook. Cantor's entry was saluted with overripe fruit and noisy wisecracks until he came out with a quip that caught the audience's fancy: "They roared. They let me go on. There were even cheers from the gallery, Stick to it, kid, you're lousy!" Coins pelted the stage, and Cantor won first prize plus the privileges of pocketing the several dollars thrown at him. DiMeglio also wrote of Fanny Brice's breaking away from singing in her family's saloon, at thirteen or fourteen years of age, to appear at amateur night at Brooklyn's Keeney's Theater. She so delighted the audience that an abundance of coins was thrown at her. So successful was she that she continued appearing at amateur nights, bringing along her brother Lew to pick up the coins, and thereby earned around $60 to $70 a week. Another entertainer, Jimmy Savo, began at New York's Olympic Theater when he was still a newsboy. He came onstage with his unsold papers under his arm, needing a haircut, and wearing his patched coat and pants with holes in the knees. His dog Nelly scampered onto the stage after him and would not leave. Undismayed, Savo sang "Wait 'Till the Sun Shines, Nellie" (1905), winning such strong approval that he, like Fanny Brice, found himself a consistent winner as he made the rounds of the amateur nights about town. Both performers said that appearances at amateur nights provided the sought-after entry into the professional theater.[54]

Nora Bayes, born Leonora Goldberg, made her start at Chicago amateur nights, where she quickly discovered her strengths and weaknesses. For example, through such appearances she learned that when she sang an Irish song under her real name, her personality and throaty contralto voice made her sound "like a bouncy refugee from Tipperary." Voice and name did not seem to go together, so the name was changed.

Sophie Tucker stated that she broke away from her restaurant job by appearing at Chris Brown's amateur nights, where, in addition to the tough audience, the auditorium contained producers and booking agents scouting for talent. She was such a hit that Joe Woods, a booking agent, hired her to sing in blackface and put her on a small-time circuit, billing her as "Sophie Tucker, Manipulator of Coon Melodies."[55]

VARIETY, VAUDEVILLE, AND MUSICAL DRAMA

M. B. Leavitt considered the variety show to be an offshoot of minstrelsy. He thought that the first variety show in the United States was probably presented at Boston's Adelphi Theater, and that Frank Rivers organized the first touring variety company, which opened at Boston's Howard Athenaeum in 1861 and played there for eight weeks. He further claimed that Robert Fox ran a variety theater in New York's Mozart Hall around 1857, anticipating by eight years the ventures of Tony Pastor and Sam Sharpley. He said the reason that variety and, later, vaudeville were so enthusiastically endorsed by the public was that there seemed to be "more humanity, more of homely, every-day life" in them "than in almost any other form of entertainment." The average play cannot contain "a little of everything," but there is in variety and vaudeville "singing, dancing, conversations, laughter, tears, animals, acrobats, contortionists and usually one or two good plays well written and acted." And to see all of this, it costs "half or one-quarter of the price of a Broadway theatre ticket."[56]

The influence of minstrelsy is indicated in Charles K. Harris's statement about Smith's Variety Theater, in Saginaw, Michigan, during the seventies. He wrote that 25-cents admission was charged to view a show that opened with a circle of men and women, similar to the positions taken by minstrel performers. Songs, dances, and sketches followed one another; then at the close came "either Oliver Twist or a musical act entitled Black-Eyed Susan, given by the entire cast." The town also had an academy of music where legitimate drama and musical plays were mounted.[57]

During the years immediately after the war, theaters featured all-male blackface minstrel performance, a form of entertainment

begun in the thirties and still drawing good-sized crowds. Nevertheless, variety, which included men and women performers, slowly
supplanted minstrelsy. During the seventies and into the eighties, a
theater might present either one or the other type, depending on what
was available for booking. Eugene Clinton Elliott observed that in
these years both minstrel troupes and traveling variety companies
played in the more respectable theaters, leaving to the box houses and
saloons a more disreputable brand of variety entertainment.[58]

Yet, many of the early variety theaters were not far removed from
the box houses and saloons in the entertainment offered and the nature
of the audience. Otis Skinner described the theater in Leadville, Colorado, in 1882 as consisting of a bare hall with makeshift stage and an
auditorium containing rows of benches rather than seats. Leadville

> was a wide-open town, saloons, gambling houses, dance-halls and
> variety shows, all ablaze after night-fall. . . . The chief variety
> theatre was a tawdry affair, afflicted with much cheap gilt and
> bright paint, where sorry-looking 'serio-comics' in lurid dresses
> sang to an audience that threw silver dollars at their feet. These
> daughters of Danaë would ogle and nod as they sang and worked
> very hard to start the silver shower, which, when begun, resembled
> a hail-storm. The ability of these nymphs to sing, dance, and pick
> up coin in simultaneous action was much admired. I saw one poor
> black-face banjo player bob and pantomime at the occupants of the
> bench rows without result until, either in pity or disgust, a drunken
> miner threw him a dime.[59]

Whatever the program shown in, and the status of, the variety
theater of the seventies and eighties, diverse song and dance acts
overshadowed all other kinds of entertainment—Dutch or Irish caricatures, blackface or whiteface song-slapstick-and knockabout, ur-
bane or rough and ready repartee cum song, down-South or out-West
vernacular, and song-acrobatic exchange were a few of the
possibilities.[60] Placards on the side of the stage identified the several
acts billed for the night. Small-town theaters held under 1,000 people;
towns and cities had theaters seating from 1,000 to 3,000 people.[61]

Advancing technology was applied to the building of theaters.
T. S. C. Lowe invented low-cost gas illumination in 1875, Thomas
Edison the incandescent lamp in 1880. Cities rapidly installed gas
streetlights and electric power lines. Theaters used the improved lighting to illumine the stage. Arthur Meier Schlesinger claimed: "Improved lighting not only dispelled much of the darkness of urban night
life but also many of its dangers." It "gave an enormous stimulus to
after-dark amusements and the theater."[62]

Certainly the best-known variety theater was the one Tony Pastor opened in Paterson, New Jersey, in 1865 and moved to New York City in the same year. Risqué acts were frowned upon. The aim was to give wholesome entertainment that would provide enjoyment to respectable men and women. Pastor's Opera House introduced Lillian Russell, Weber and Fields, Kelly and Ryan, George M. Cohan, Lottie Gilson, May Irwin, Sophie Tucker, Gus Williams, Vesta Victoria, Maggie Cline, and Eddie Foy.[63]

Instrumental support for the acts, especially the singing and dancing, was needed. A pianist was mandatory; if two musicians could be afforded, a drummer was usually added; if three, a violinist or cornetist. If several instruments could be afforded, a clarinet, trombone, and string bass were added to the four already named. The instrumentalists often knew by heart an enormous amount of music; they could easily sight-read whatever was placed before them, or fake an accompaniment to almost any song a vocalist proposed to sing and in whatever key required. Obviously, the orchestra could make or break any vocalist, and it was habitual for singers to curry favor with the orchestra director and his players, at times paying them to be supportive.[64]

Theodore Dreiser's description of the Opera House in Warsaw, Indiana, provides us with a view of the workaday theater ensemble outside of the large cities. This town, with a population of seven thousand, was host to all sorts of traveling companies. A seven- or eight-piece orchestra, conducted by a local carpenter who also led the town band, was provided for these visitors. The instruments in the orchestra, played by carefully groomed men in dress suits, were two violins, a cornet, a bass viol, cello, flute, and percussion. The musicians could perform on other instruments if needed. When not in the theater, these men worked as barbers, clerks, and grocers.[65]

Vaudeville developed from variety in the 1890s. Tony Pastor, whose pre-1890 Opera House format was a prototype of the vaudeville theater to come, hated the word, saying it was a disparaging term for variety meant to indicate that the entertainment met with the approved standards of the time. Benjamin Franklin Keith was blamed for the new and overly fussy designation. Keith had opened up a dime museum in Boston in 1883, then the B. F. Keith Theater in 1894, which offered "vaudeville." Shortly thereafter, he opened Keith's Union Square Theatre, in New York City, offering "Refined Vaudeville" whose acts, according to Dayton Stoddart, were "fumigated to appeal to women and children, and with the revolutionary development of continuous performance." The term had been used in the United States as early as 1840, when an advertisement of a "Vaudeville Saloon," where a variety program could be enjoyed, appeared on a handbill distributed in Boston.[66]

Vaudeville was a response to the new middle class's desire for entertainment that did not subvert its sense of decorum. From 1870 to 1910, this group grew from 756,000 to 5,609,000 persons. The vaudeville audience aimed at was more precisely the lower middle class—white-color workers, tradesmen, and prosperous skilled workers, according to Shirley Staples. She cites a 1907 study of Greenwich Village that showed that those Americans making below $500 a year (laborers, kitchen helpers, cigar-makers, pressers, street cleaners) spent next to nothing on entertainment, finding the 15-cents to 50-cents admission charge better spent elsewhere. Those averaging $1,050 annually (police, longshoremen, masons, grocers and the like) spent $17.72 a year, on average, for entertainment. Those earning more devoted a much larger sum to entertainment and attended vaudeville performances with greater frequency.[67]

Catering to the tastes of this last group (which included the author William Dean Howells, the poet Eugene Field, and President Woodrow Wilson) were enterprising and ruthlessly competitive promoters like Benjamin Franklin Keith, Edward F. Albee, F. F. Proctor, and Marcus Loew. By 1900–05 they and others like them had established around 2,000 to 3,000 vaudeville theaters in the United States and Canada, with 1,000 of them having large enough facilities to accommodate first-class productions. The biggest promoters not only controlled chains of theaters but also the theatrical companies that traveled from one theater to another. They selected the acts to be included in a variety show and prescribed the circuit the show would make from one town to another. Attractions were offered every day except Sunday. New York City alone originated over 310 shows a season. In 1880 about 5,000 entertainers were traveling the variety-vaudeville circuits; by 1905, more than 21,000 were thus engaged.[68]

In October 1899, *Scribner's Magazine* printed an article by Edwin Milton Royle on the new vaudeville theater. Royle wrote that it differed from anything in Europe because no seats were reserved and some theaters had continuous shows sometimes lasting from 9:30 A.M. to 10:30 P.M. (intended to catch both the early risers with time on their hands and the afternoon shopping crowd), while others were two-a-days. Even if a theater offered continuous entertainment, headliners did only two turns a day; the lesser fry were denied this privilege. Stars appeared in the last or next-to-last act. The song-and-dance men had to clean up their acts, and between them vaudeville was denominated the "Sunday-school circuit." Women who attended had to appear respectable. Clean, wholesome family entertainment was the aim.

Some eight to sixteen separate acts, most about twelve minutes and none over thirty minutes long, composed a complete show. An open-door policy for new talent was generally observed, with one day a week set aside for giving newcomers a trial. If they seemed promising, they were placed on the bill for a performance before an audience. If they survived this test, they became regulars.[69]

Yet, vaudeville never remained completely free of purient allusions. Witness the article "The Decay of Vaudeville," author unidentified, that appeared in the *American Magazine* of April 1910. It mentioned "The Cubanola Glide," a harmless enough cakewalk sort of song, more silly than objectionable, that was frequently performed in vaudeville. Then it went on to state: "But there is one team, recently seen in one of the Broadway vaudeville theatres, a 'first-class house,' mind you, one of whose members sings this song and accompanies it with a dance so suggestive and so reeking with implied indecency that it is an insult to any respectable woman who happens to hear it." One longs "to leap upon the stage and punch the fellow who sings it and the stage manager who allows him to do it."[70]

After 1910, variety-vaudeville began to lose its ascendancy in America's entertainment world. Motion pictures, phonograph recordings, radio, the loss of intimacy in the larger theaters, and the rising charge for admission, necessitated by the demand of stars for extravagant prerogatives and salaries, helped decrease the public's attendance.[71]

Theaters featuring full-length musical dramas containing popular songs had an American history going back to colonial times. For the most part, however, these plays were comic operas or operettas imported from Europe or written in America by émigrés from Europe. The Gilbert and Sullivan and the Victor Herbert operettas immediately come to mind. By the nineties, Americans had begun to compete successfully with their European counterparts. Reginald DeKoven's comic operas, starting with *Robin Hood* (1890), at last achieved considerable acclaim both in the United States and Europe. "Oh Promise Me," from this musical, was his outstanding contribution to song. More genuinely American in atmosphere, language, and musical idiom were the Broadway musicals by George M. Cohan, beginning with *Little Johnny Jones* (1904) and *Forty-five Minutes from Broadway* (1905). Moreover, numerous song hits that seemed peculiarly American emerged from them. The prominent and continuing relationship of popular song to musical drama, nevertheless, did not come about until the end of World War I. Without question, up to 1910 the great majority of popular songs by Americans were introduced in variety and vaudeville.

. . . .

THE SINGING GAME

. . . .

On the lowest rung of the singing trade were the musicians who performed on street corners, in barrooms, on ferry boats, and at fairs, who afterward passed the hat for a collection. They were known as buskers, or guttersnipers. Tom Fletcher, an African-American vaude-villian born in 1862, explained:

> This type of entertaining was called *"buskin"* or *"tinkering."* It was also very popular in New York where different combinations [soloist to quartet] would pick out a paying route which oftimes would keep them in food and shelter. . . . Sometimes, while entertaining in a barroom, the performers would get an offer from one of the patrons to appear at a stag party or smoker, the patron guaranteeing an evening's take out of his own pocket. Such an offer for an evening during the week was usually grabbed without hesitation, but for a Saturday night the guarantee had to be no less than three dollars a man.[72]

Guttersniping, according to Robert Edmund Sherwood, an entertainer born in 1858, meant playing music in the street and passing a hat for expense money. At some period in the career of many minstrel and variety performers, it has been a necessary activity. He told of once, when he was traveling with Bruce's Modern Minstrels, how the manager absconded with all of the profits, leaving the company stranded in a small town. To pay for room and board, the men took to the streets, performing for any passersby willing to listen to them. Finally, in a copy of the *New York Clipper*, a trade newspaper, Sherwood saw an advertisement asking for "ten mouthpieces and two drums" to join a circus in Chicago. Boldly he sent off a telegram reading "Minstrel band want to quit road. Can join at once, subject to approval. Here for two days. Wire [train] tickets for twelve men." It was a relief to all of the company when the tickets arrived.[73]

Many performers remained street musicians because their limited talents allowed them to progress no further. A vivid depiction of the habitual urban street musician from the viewpoint of a passerby comes from William Dean Howells:

> Ought one to give money to a hand-organist, who is manifestly making himself a nuisance before the door of some one else? I have

asked myself this when I have been tempted, and I am not yet quite clear about it. At present, therefore, I give only to the inaudible street minstrels, who earn an honest living, and make no noise about it. I cannot think that a ballad-singer on Sixth Avenue, who pours forth his artless lay amid the roar and rattle of the elevated trains, the jangle and clatter of horse-cars, the bang of the grocers' carts, and the thunder of the express-wagons, is practically molesting anybody. . . . It is always amusing to have him stop in his most effective phrase to say, "Thank you, thank you, sir," and then go on again. The other day, as I dropped my contribution into the extended hat, I asked, "How is business?" and the singer interrupted himself to answer, "Nothing-to-brag-of-sir-thank-you," and resumed with continuous tenderness the "ditty of no tone" that he was piping to the inattentive uproar of the street.[74]

These same street musicians were accustomed to sleeping in "charity hotels," alongside beggars and ne'er-do-wells of one kind and another. In these hotels, all lighting was extinguished at 10 P.M. Between 9 A.M. and 5 P.M., people were allowed only the use of the lobby, and even there were treated with contempt. At one low point in his career, Theodore Dreiser said he had been a resident of one of these charity hotels. The charge for a place to sleep and use of the public bath, with towel and soap provided, was 25 cents to 40 cents a day. A meal cost 25 cents. If a street person could not afford these payments, then he or she had to sink to "the Bowery, the hospital, and the river—the last, I think, the most merciful of all."[75]

To graduate from the street into a traveling minstrel troupe was undoubtedly the hope of many down-and-outs, particularly in the seventies and eighties, when minstrelsy was at its peak. From a dozen to sixty men made up one of these troupes. Chauncey Olcott said that in his early years he was fortunate to land a singing spot with a troupe and experienced all phases of the performance experience, from singing popular songs to counting the house. The thorough training prepared him for his stint in *The Old Homestead*, with Denman Thompson, and his later roles in operettas. Haverly's Minstrels, for which Billy Emerson won him membership, seated the singers in the front semicircle during a stage performance, with comics as the two end-men. Behind were the instrumentalists and, behind them, the drummers. Every performer had a specialty, but song and dance predominated.[76]

Around 1880, Eugene Field published a poem about these minstrels:

The Haverly Minstrels were boss in those days,
And our critics accorded them columns of praise;

They'd handsome mustaches and big cluster rings,
And their shirt fronts were blazing with diamonds and
    things.
They gave a parade, and a sweet music they made
Every evening in front of the house where they played.
'Twixt posters and hand-bills the town was a gog
For Primrose and West in their great statue clog.[77]

Barnstorming the United States with a minstrel troupe was never a carefree experience, according to a veteran, Ned Pedigo. He spoke of uncertain pay, giving a street parade on arrival in the teeth of a January blizzard, going around in blackface for a week because neither time nor facilities were to be had for washing, unbathed bodies smelling so strongly during performance that the audience complained, mishaps on trains and in hotels, and staving off grafters of every kind.[78]

Whether the musician was a member of a traveling minstrel troupe, variety show, medicine show, or circus, hardships had to be endured. Going from one one-night performance to another in the Midwest during the seventies, Corse Payton experienced exhaustion setting up props, distributing handbills, selling tickets, working as a stagehand, and filling in for any act that needed him. During these same years M. B. Leavitt traveled the western states; he spoke about the constant menace to train passengers of buffalo running across the tracks and the danger of attack by Indians or desperadoes.[79]

Twenty years later, in the nineties, the hardships on the travel circuit continued. Charles Leroy Whittier stated that hotel rooms went unheated in winter. No running water, let alone hot water, was available. Toilet facilities consisted of a slop jar. Freezing dressing rooms were the norm in theaters and, as a result the unmanageable grease-paint had to be held over lamp chimneys to soften it. Incredibly bad hotel meals were common; in one town, their three meals a day consisted only of beans.[80]

The street performance on arrival of a minstrel troupe or variety show, referred to in the Field poem and the Pedigo complaint, was designed to call attention to the evening's performance. Performers made use of the hotel bus transporting them from the train to their rooms. They sang and played "banjos, mandolins, fiddles, triangles, flutes, castanets . . . reinforced by a big bass drum on the roof," delighting the townspeople, upsetting the other passengers on the bus, and, more often than not, frightening the horses.[81]

George M. Cohan said that in the spring of 1889, when he was ten years old, his family went on the road as "The Cohan Mirth Makers, the

Celebrated Family of Singers, Dancers and Comedians with their Silver plated Band and Symphony Orchestra." The cast consisted of four people, the orchestra of eight. Cohan states:

> The street parade was the big feature. I was the drum major and led the band of eleven pieces—eight musicians besides the manager, property man and dad. The last three played the snare drum, bass drum, and cymbals. Mother and Josie followed the band in an open victoria draped with American flags. When the business was bad we'd discharge the band, cut out the parade, and give the show with a piano player.[82]

Some performers traveled as singles, joining one, then another variety circuit, and when their turn in the show arrived, they appeared alone onstage. Douglas Gilbert claimed that a surprising number of singles were men in blackface, and named J. W. McAndrews and Frank Bell as examples. Sophie Tucker said that after she began to perform as a single, she was advised by the veteran comedian George Le Maire to keep her act down to ten to twelve minutes so as not to "overfeed the audience." First, he said, she should sing a bright song to get the audience to like her; next, a dramatic song to rouse interest in her; third, a novelty to get them laughing; and last, a rag number so that everybody would keep time with her and thus prepare themselves to applaud loudly.[83]

Yet, two-person acts, normally of the song-and-dance type, were far more common—blackface, whiteface, double Irish, double Dutch (actually German), comic and straight man, man and woman, brothers, sisters. In 1903, while William Dean Howells was attending a vaudeville show, he became intrigued by a "twin sisters" act. Billed as "Refined Singers and Dancers," they came on the stage "in sweeping confections of white silk, with deeply drooping widely spreading white hats, and long-fringed white parasols heaped with artificial roses, and sang a little tropical romance, whose burden was 'Under the bamboo tree,' brought in at unexpected intervals. They also danced this romance with languid undulations and before you could tell how or why, they had disappeared and reappeared in short green skirts, and then shorter white skirts, with steps and stops appropriate to their costumes, but always, I am bound to say, of the refinement promised." Next, two brothers appeared "as 'Singing and Dancing Comedians' of the coon type." After the brothers came a man and woman in "The Singing Lesson." And later came a single: " 'Monologue and Songs' by a divine creature in lampblack, a shirt-waist worn outside his trousers, and an exaggerated development of stomach."[84]

Family acts were popular, among the most famous being The Four Cohans, who played variety theaters and dime museums during the eighties. If a child were involved, he or she could steal the entire show. Charles Leroy Whittier describes how his parents, in the late nineties, traveled to Chattanooga, Tennessee, to join a variety group and were told they would follow the Dufferins Trio. Whittier's father assumed they were acrobats, but found out they were a man, a woman, and a girl of five or six years of age. After the act was introduced by the orchestra, the parents sang a selection: "And could they sing! They rocked the house." Encore after encore followed. Then the little girl sang, while the parents harmonized: "The audience blistered their hands." His father, who was to go on next, felt sick. He was at last told to go on even though the applause was continuing, and was assured that it would cease when he appeared. But the audience ignored him and forced him to leave so that the Dufferins could return for another song.[85]

Male quartets were also popular. The traditional quartet, dressed similarly in dignified clothing, sang sentimental ballads in close harmony—the tenor taking the lead in Irish, and the baritone in mother, songs. The comic quartet included a straight man, a sissy boy, a dialect man, and a tramp bass, all dressed for their parts. Rough comedy was interspersed among their songs.[86]

In musical drama the singers assumed whatever roles were assigned them and, depending on the book, took on comic, romantic, ingenue, soubrette, or other characterizations suited to their singing specialty, age, and physical appearance, sometimes soloing, sometimes combining in various ensemble configurations. Although the songs they sang might or might not relate to the plot line, they were the principal reason for the audience's presence, and had to be sung.

5 UNDERSTANDING AMERICAN POPULAR SONGS

The real beginning of the American popular song was concurrent with the rise of Jacksonian democracy in 1829.[1] Its composers never intended to write a work of fine art—that is to say, an individual creation wrought with fastidious skill and exhibiting a refined perfection in its lyric and musical ordering. By the 1850s it was under attack from a few cultivated Americans like John Sullivan Dwight, who thought that all types of song should aim at goals above the commonplace. Dwight's taste, as revealed in his influential *Dwight's Journal of Music*, published in Boston from 1852 to 1881, ran to Germanic art music. He himself subscribed to transcendental philosophy that assigned an idealized and spiritual role to music, a role no native vernacular composition could possibly assume.

From the fifties on, the accusation of vulgarity was constantly levied against popular song, some years more loudly than others, some categories of vernacular music more censured than others. Critics decried the lyrics for their syntactical defects, excessive emotional display, or extreme coarseness in subject and language. The music, they said, was replete with compositional errors or had a vitiating sameness. Scarcely anywhere did a spark of originality reveal itself. Words and music again and again demonstrated the songwriter's usual ignorance of poetics or musical theory—so the criticism went.

What is more, some critics said the self-satisfied spirit of the bourgeoisie was reflected; others saw an aspect of herd comformity battened on by capitalistic exploiters; still others claimed popular song was a representation of debased culture sinking to the lowest common denominator of aesthetic discernment. Most of these criticisms, on balance, had some truth to them, especially when Tin Pan Alley thinking permeated the popular-song world after the 1890s.

In 1940, Douglas Gilbert, in his book on American popular music, could still describe popular song as consisting of gushy, moralizing, or humorous verse, of no import and usually awful, set to mawkish, nostalgic, or snappy tunes. In 1970, Max Morath, in an introduction to an anthology of songs from the 1890s, warned that 99 percent of these popular songs were "imitative and ephemeral," and "essentially a form of fashion, and as such," set "deadly traps" for anyone attempting their "premature evaluation as art."[2] One gets a strong sense of "let the buyer beware" from both statements.

On the other hand, Mark Twain insisted the disparagement of the American vernacular, as represented in his writing and in American music, was manifestly unfair. He wrote in 1890:

The little child is permitted to label its drawings "This is a cow—this is a horse" and so on. This protects the child. It saves it from the sorrow and wrong of hearing its cows and its horses criticized as kangaroos and work-benches. A man who is white-washing a fence is doing a useful thing, so also is the man who is adorning a rich man's house with costly frescoes; and all of us are sane enough to judge these performances by standards proper to each. . . . And the critic ought to hold himself in honor bound to put away from him his ancient habit of judging all books by one standard and thenceforth follow a fairer course. . . . You see, I have always catered for the Belly and the Members [the uncultivated classes] but have been . . . criticized from the culture-standard. . . . Honestly, I never cared what became of the cultured classes; they could go to the theatre and the opera; they had no use for me and the melodeon.[3]

John Kendrick Bangs, in *Leaves from a Lecturer's Note Book* (1916), defended the vernacular as follows:

> I can't be what Shakespeare was,
> I can't do what great folks does;
> But, by ginger, I can be
> ME!
> And among the folks that love me
> Nothin' more's expected of me.[4]

Many writers on American popular song have searched for foreign influences, particularly in those compositions deemed to have merit beyond the ordinary. They say that the English music-hall ditty, Viennese waltz, German folk song, and French romance were models for quite a few American songs. Because popularity, not originality, was a desideratum, utilizing what was in vogue, whatever its derivation, was a constant in popular entertainment. Transatlantic contributions to music, performers, and performance practices can be discovered at every moment of American cultural history. Yet, in most instances the contributions were adapted to suit American tastes and needs.

Further, this borrowing was never one-sided. American popular music, performers, and performance practices traveled abroad and influenced the popular music of various foreign nations, especially after 1850. Therefore, a stylistic feature, though directly European, might originally have come from the United States.

England, in particular, was receptive to American entertainment ideas. Informative in this regard is the statement of Michael Turner, a British publisher and investigator of Victorian popular culture. He stated that a two-way exchange in the latter half of the nineteenth century took place between the English music hall–type of song and American popular song. Moreover, he said, popular taste was becoming internationalized. Songs entering a new country were swiftly naturalized by changing old lyrics or writing new ones to go with the music. No sooner did a steamer dock in England than its cargo of American songs was hastily Anglicised and new editions rushed out to the British public:

> Many Britons now would be amazed to learn that "Daisy Bell,"
> the music-hall song that many took to be a satire upon the Prince
> of Wales's dear friend the Countess of Warwick, is in fact of Amer-
> ican origin, as are such completely "English" pieces as "Ta-ra-ra
> Boom-de-ay," "After the Ball," "A Bird in a Gilded Cage," "Silver
> Threads Among the Gold," and "Where Did You Get That Hat?"
> Even "Down at the Old Bull and Bush" derives from a tune by Tin
> Pan Alley's Harry von Tilzer.[5]

∙∙

THE UTILITY OF POPULAR SONGS

∙∙

Likes clothes ready-made and off the hook, like the new mass-manufactured goods with interchangeable stamped-out parts, the new popular songs of the postwar years also seemed to have come off the hook, as it were, and to contain interchangeable melodies, harmonies, rhythms, and verses. Inevitably, they had to modify the conveyance of any individual identity, offering instead a sense of fantasy, of music that could not be nailed down, of text that eluded specificity, especially in the chorus. They left an after-feeling of déjà vu and exuded a common familiarity extending from past songs, through present ones, and into future songs.

During the postwar period, many observers found popular song's uniformity becoming a matter of machinery, not humanity, of cutting things out mechanically and stamping them into rigid patterns. Yet, this uniformity in antebellum song provided entertainment for a diverse public unacclimated to or possibly uninterested in subtler works. This public, which inhabited widely scattered areas of the United States, had only moments of leisure, which were often unreposeful owing to the debilitative effects of long, demanding workdays. Moreover, like the American ax-handle and plough, products mass-produced, extensively advertised, and functional, song's shared designs could boast their own kind of serviceability and beauty. To be daring and innovative was out of place in this context. On the other hand, the composition had to sound *as if* its ideas were neither exhausted nor fatigued. A talent for freshening standardized verbal and musical statements was essential for songwriters, but the main attributes attached to a composition would be unchanged. For instance, a sentimental ballad of the seventies and eighties had to have a lyric marked by one intense, inwardly turned, melancholic expression, and music without danceable rhythms and quirky syncopations but with moderately slow, gentle curving, and stepwise-moving melody. Hence the stability and notion of order that inevitably accompanies the sounds of all popular pieces of the latter half of the nineteenth century.

Although many writers introduced some individual touches, these variables remained within the limits imposed by popular opinion. To transgress these limits invited public rejection. Only at those moments in American cultural history when society was in the process of accelerated change and needed a new category of song to reflect back what it was becoming did transgressed limits have a chance of acceptance. (Thus the somewhat rapid onset of coon songs and their quick progression to rag after the World's Columbian Exposition, held in Chicago in 1893. The fair attracted exhibitors from 72 countries and over 27 million visitors. "It produced an unparalleled surge of creative energy that had an important influence not only in architecture but also on the cultural values of the nation.")[6]

Song was a prominent part of "a people's culture," wrote Stuart Chase. It "is the sum of all the patterns of behavior" which "keep the group from flying into a thousand fragments, and helps it adapt to nature and survive its environment."[7] It mirrored American culture, explained postwar society, expressed commonly held values, and spoke for the millions who treasured it. Such a song is "Silver Threads Among the Gold" (1873). Eben Rexford's lyric exposes the piercing sorrow felt when the "I" as protagonist remarks "Darling, I am growing old," and, as if awakened to the contemplation of a common mortality, observes, with concern, a dearly loved spouse whose once-golden hair has turned silver white and once-rosy cheeks have grown dull. Yet, the "I" also insists that their love has neither changed nor grown dull and that such love takes primacy over aging and death. Apprehension about and defiance of what must be mingles with the comforting of the final verse:

> Love is always young and fair,
> What to us is silver hair,

Faded cheeks or steps grown slow,
To the hearts that beat below?
Since I kissed you, mine alone,
You have never older grown.
(Chorus)
Darling, I am growing old,
Silver Threads Among the Gold,
Shine upon my brow today,
Life is fading fast away.

The composer sympathetically conceived a melody that rocked back and forth in comforting two-measure half-phrases, down a ninth and up a ninth, over and over again. A song like this asked listeners to immerse themselves in an imaginary world that conjured up shared concerns and feelings. Besides, the completely diatonic melody is a haunting one in its own right.

A song like "Silver Threads Among the Gold" delivered what listeners required of it. However trivial and common it seems to a musical sophisticate, such a song did "take on new excitement" because the men and women who were making the demands apprehended it as a way "of transfiguring reality" into something inwardly meaningful.[8] Hence this popular song's utility.

"Silver Threads Among the Gold" addressed every person who, in Stephen Crane's words, had "a tongue of wood" but sang lamentably:

There was a man with a tongue of wood
Who essayed to sing,
And in truth it was lamentable.
But there was one who heard
The clip-clapper of this tongue of wood
And knew what the man
Wished to sing,
And with that the singer was content.[9]

Late-nineteenth century writers subscribed to the idea that the lay listener accepted the expression in popular song as his very own. Bertram G. Work, nephew of Henry Clay Work—of "Grandfather's Clock" (1876) fame—said that the true feeling of a people speaks through what they sing and popular song invariably gives the "most accurate expression of the popular mind." Charles K. Harris, composer of many sentimental ballads, stated: "I find that sentiment plays a large part in our lives. The most hardened character or the most cynical individual will succumb to sentiment sometime or other. In all my ballads I have purposely injected goodly doses of sentiment, and invariably the whole country paused." Harris recognized that, to men and women, "it is emotion that matters." Speaking in similar fashion, Ethelbert Nevin's father instructed his son never to fear sentiment: "We are all creatures of sentiment, we live and die by it, dispute it as we will, and it is the strongest force there is." Finally, sentiment did not mean sadness alone. Many a song was jolly and lighthearted, for as Phineas T. Barnum understood: "Men, women, and children . . . cannot live on gravity alone." They "need something to satisfying their gayer, lighter moods and hours."[10]

The frivolous text of "Ta-ra-ra-bom-der-e" (1891) gives this satisfaction:

> (Verse 2)
> I'm not extravagantly shy,
> And when a nice young man is nigh,
> For his heart I have a try—
> And faint away with tearful cry!
> When the good young man, in haste,
> Will support me round the waist;
> I don't come to, while thus embraced,
> Till of my lips he steals a taste!
> (Chorus)
> Ta-ra-ra-bom-der-e [sung eight times].

The appeal of the lyric is discreetly sensual; of the music, visceral. Many a young woman might empathize with the "shy" girl, and many a male might crave to be the "nice young man." The double-talking verse is sung to two rather deadpan melodic strains, which tease but give nothing away. Each strain, eight measures long, descends mostly in even eighth notes from the dominant to the tonic tone. A deceptive tranquillity prevails. Therefore, the wonderful exuberance of the tune in the chorus, whose effectiveness derives in large part from its rambunctious vulgarity, is unexpected. Each two-measure half-phrase begins as an eighth-rest pause plus three rather static eighth notes on "Ta-ra-ra," then produces a hammer stroke on almost every "bom" by means of a strong upward skip of a fourth to the tonic or dominant tone. The aroused listener wants to respond in energetic pantomime.

Yet, despite, my commentaries on "Silver Threads Among the Gold" and "Ta-ra-ra-bom-der-e," more often than not, the reasons for the success of an individual work remain intangible—which underlines the old saw "If I knew the secret for composing a hit song, I would not be writing about hit songs."[11]

Late-nineteenth century popular music did not form one immense, undifferentiated collection of musical pieces. It comprehended several genres between which the songwriters distinguished: the sentimental ballad, minstrel ditty, coon song, novelty number, comic piece, waltz song, rag song, and others. A song would strike the listener as beautiful not only because of its individual attractiveness but also because it effectively captured the essence of its genre.

The utilitarian value of popular song is evidenced in the variety of forms in which a song was made available. At most, an art song might be transposed to accommodate high or low voices; otherwise, tampering with it was forbidden. As a contrast, a copy of a very popular song, "Anona," published in New York by Feist in 1903, advertises: "This famous composition is also published as an Intermezzo—Two Step—for Piano, also for Band, Orchestra, Mandolin, Guitar, Banjo, Zither, etc." The song's key, tempo, and dynamics were also flexible, thus freeing the performer and making a winning presentation dependent on his or her interpretation. Distinct genres, each with a flavor of its own, the well-defined lyric and music of almost every song recognizable as belonging to a particular genre, and adaptable compositions reusable in various performance situations contributed to a popular song's utility.

Also contributing to a song's serviceability was the designing of its features in a way to promote immediate retentiveness in the mind. On a copy of the song "Absence Makes the Heart Grow Fonder," published by Witmark in 1900, is an advertisement for another song, "Sweet Matilda," which proclaims as one of the song's virtues: "Hear the chorus once, and you've got it." The banishment of ambiguity was fundamental to the design. Indeed, Horatio Parker, the most important American art-music composer of vocal works at the turn of the century, advocated directness of expression for all composers, popular and artistic. In 1899 he declared:

> Music is the art which comes nearest to the people and the one to which they can get nearest themselves. . . . There must be all kinds of music as well as natural creations! A hymn *must* be simple . . . but it ought not to be didactic, if it is for common use. What is true of hymns as poetry or literature is true in greater measure of tunes as music. They must be simple in rhythm, melody and harmony, not merely on account of the difficulty of things not simple, but rather because nothing other than simplicity will serve as a vehicle of expression for the feelings of a mass of people.[12]

LYRICS AND THEMES

The music generally follows a clear framework that delineates the parts of the song and frames the whole song. The melody unfolds in well etched phrases with simple curves. Each phrase compliments the verbal punctuation with an undeviating progression from beginning to cadential point. These phrases form musical strains, the counterparts of verbal sentences, which close with perfect cadences. The larger duality of verse and chorus is underlined by the combination of musical strains.

The verse's purpose was to particularize the subject and seek out the experience of a protagonist, normally speaking as "I." The chorus invited the public to share the experience, which is now generalized into a public utterance—the "I" understood to stand for "we."

During the latter part of the nineteenth century, the long-held image of private introspective man, whose destiny centered on God, family, and selfless love, gave way to the image of the public man of the world, whose experience, increasingly industrial and urban, weakened the ascendancy of God and family. Now fostered was the idea that all people, irrespective of family connection, were in the same boat together and shared a common predicament—the impingement of a real and amoral world upon previous assumptions about selfhood. While the former image held sway, the verse section, which individualized the subject, was song's dominant feature in words and melody, while the chorus section, which generalized the subject, became more or less an appendage. As the latter image gained prominence in song, the chorus section grew longer, its melody more independent, possibly reflecting the preeminence of public over private man in the public's thinking.

Interestingly, the late-nineteenth-century American composer of the art song more often than not chose to set lyrics that dispensed with the chorus, perhaps because within him the sense of a distinctive self remained strong and the intensity of individual feeling required less reconciliation with a public attitude. Such a creator resisted an identification with mass man except in a few songs, like Ethelbert Nevin's "Mighty Lack' a Rose" (1901), lyrics by Frank L. Stanton, and Carrie Jacobs-Bond's "Just A-wearyin' for You" (1901), lyrics by Frank Stanton, where a mantle of simplicity was deliberately donned.

Independently, a lyric may appear to explore its subject in an awkward manner or to rely on crude versification. In such cases, it falls upon the melody to provide the means for regulating and linking the words and polishing the metrical structure. Charles K. Harris once stated that although the lyrics may seem crude, the lyricist probably wrote words to fit a tune, making necessary allowances to fit the words with the music. Moreover, it is incumbent on the lyricist to write the text in such a way "as to give it that lilt or swing which makes for its popularity." No textual deficiencies, Harris said, would be evident during singing.[13]

The lyrics may operate as a self-dramatization, seeing and presenting the protagonist—a fantasied surrogate for the listener—as an actor in a drama. Some particular from everyday living is dramatized—domesticity, courtship, pastimes, celebrations, tragedies, work. The way contemporary people speak, dress, and behave figures in all songs. Fairly reliable information is provided on the tastes and attitudes of the mass of the American people. Reliability, however, is not complete, since the information is always reconstituted into a fiction.

Life situations, for instance, are overstated to help the listener to distinguish between them at first sight. All depictions are toward an end; song gives back and even alters the details of daily life in search of the kernel of personal meaning that is one of its reasons for being. Whatever else they accomplish, songs effect responses to the problems of life. They are not tales on how people actually live. In the lyrics an objective experience in itself provides little knowledge of why things happen as they do. The experience has been made over into an imitation of real life, executed with awareness that what matters is the aesthetic adaptation of ostensible reality so that it becomes an invented reality, one provided with a vitality of its own and with implications of universal import.

Ineptitude and lack of street wisdom, for example, are acted out by the simpleminded visitor to New York, portrayed in "The Bowery" (1892)

> (Verse 6)
> I struck a place that they called a "dive,"
> I was in luck to get out alive;
> When the policeman heard my woes,
> Saw my black eyes and my battered nose,
> "You've been held up!!" said the "copper" fly!
> "No, sir! But I've been knock'd down!" said I;
> Then he laughed, though' I couldn't see why!
> I'll never go there any more!
> (Chorus)
> The Bow'ry, the Bow'ry!

They say such things, and they do strange things on
The Bow'ry! The Bow'ry!
I'll never go there any more!

   The lyrics also may operate as an intensification of ordinary feeling
or behavior, the protagonist becoming each of us to an extreme degree
and through his or her experience revealing some human feature at the
peak of its special character, elevated or ridiculous. The highly sentimental "Love Me, and the World Is Mine" (1906) performs at one pole
of exaggeration:

> (Verse 1)
> I wander on as in a dream,
> My goal a paradise must be,
> For there an angel waits twould seem,
> Yet lo, dear heart 'tis only thee.
> Suns may shine to light my way, dear,
> Wealth be mine for aye dear,
> Queens may pledge their riches too,
> Yet the world would be lonely,
> With such virtues only,
> Life to me dear, means just you.
> (Chorus)
> I care not for the stars that shine,
> I dare not hope to e'er be thine,
> I only know I love you,
> Love me and the world is mine.

   Maurice Disher stated: "Soul was very much the Victorian songwriter's personal property. Other topics, from mothers-in-law to al-
coholism, might serve for comic relief, but the main entertainment had
to be soul no matter how many sideshows spiced it."[14] Although
written after the Victorian period, this American song and most other
sentimental compositions this book examines embody mankind's
emotional nature, or "soul." Possibly, sentimental songs were the
"main entertainment" of Americans in the sixties, seventies, and eighties; they became much less so from the nineties on.
   The preposterous "Budweiser's a Friend of Mine" (1907) occupies
the opposite pole. Here, human weakness provokes amusement. The
protagonist's pose is that of someone speaking with irreverent and
somewhat disingenuous candor of his sorrow, but the sorrow seems
related to a comment made by Emily Dickinson in 1877: "Sorrow is

unsafe when it is real sorrow. I am glad so many are counterfeits—guileless because they believe themselves."[15] The song begins as follows:

> (Verse 1)
> The Poets may sing of the friends who will cling to you,
> When you are gloomy and blue,
> But I have one friend who will stick to the end,
> Just the dearest friend I ever knew.
> When ever I'm sad,
> And the world treats me badly,
> Into some Rathskeller I stray,
> I fill up a stein with this old friend of mine
> And I dream all my sorrow away:
> (Chorus)
> Bud, Budweiser's a friend of mine . . .
> What care I, if the sun don't shine,
> While I've got Budweiser. . . .

Most songs have two or three verses plus a chorus heard at the close of every verse (similar to a refrain, since sheet music containing two-to-four part vocal harmonizations ceased soon after the Civil War). During the period under investigation, a few songwriters indicated that they wanted singers to reproduce all of the verses to a song. Concerning "After the Ball," Charles K. Harris wrote: "I tried to impress upon him [the singer introducing the song] that this ballad contained three verses and that it was essential for him to sing them all, otherwise the effect of the simple story would be lost."

The lyricist writes in any meter he feels like using, regular or irregular. Some songs cannot be scanned because they are quite irregular and impossible to accept without the music. Nor is precise rhyming always practised.[16] One notes in "Budweiser's a Friend of Mine" the uneven scansion—tetrameter followed by a trimeter, then two tetrameters. Inner rhymes occur in lines 1, 3, and 8, yet the rhyme scheme of the end lines is highly irregular, the asymmetric nine-line verse falling into two sections that rhyme *a a b a* and *c d e f e*. Note also the uneven metrical feet within each line. Line 1 starts on a weak stress, then goes on to four dactyls; line 2 contains two dactyls closing on an accent; line 3 starts on a weak stress, advances through four dactyls, and closes on an accent; line four contains an anapest plus three iambs, and so forth. Fortunately, the music imposes order. The entire verse is set to four musical phrases, each eight-measures long. Lines 5, 6, and 7 are gathered into phrase 3; otherwise, each phrase sets two lines of text. Each phrase begins on an upbeat, followed by the unvaryingly regular dactylic measures characteristic of waltz time.

An overview of song lyrics shows language is kept plain, graphic, relevant, and concrete. Abstract and unusual references are avoided. Generally, an informal conversational tone is adhered to, and subject and expression are kept recognizable for easier comprehension. The title evokes the chorus; the chorus summarizes the content of the verses. The sense of each line is normally complete; the end of each line comes to a natural stop before a new line is taken up. The change from verse to chorus is managed so as not to perturb the listener, the latter appearing as a reasonable epilogue to the verse that has come before.[17]

MUSICAL STYLE

A manifest charge placed upon the music was to set forth the lyric in an unforced, agreeable fashion, which the public readily perceived. A latent charge placed upon the music was to aid and abet expression while continuing to give a sense of order, about which the public was not necessarily aware.

Popular music was *the* contemporary music to a vast majority of the American public. It invariably demonstrated certain well-understood approaches to structure, rhythm, melody, harmony, and performance, whether vocal or instrumental. We should exercise caution in criticizing songs for features necessary for their utility, such as a prominent melody of limited range, a supportive and normally unadventurous harmony and predictable rhythmic organization, and little or no countermelodic activity. Note how F. O. Jones accounted for the significance of the songs by Will S. Hays: "The total number of copies sold of all Mr. Hays' songs must be several millions. Their extraordinary popularity is due to charming melodies, easy and effective accompaniments, and a genuine feeling. They were written for the masses and by the masses appreciated."[18]

At the same time, we must keep in mind that some arbitrariness enters into the historical periodization of musical events. Certainly, in popular more than in art music, swift stylistic change is rare and the history of musical events seems one seamless garment. To illustrate, rag song is sometimes written about as a radical departure from earlier vernacular compositional styles. Yet, if it is examined closely, its

antecedents are easily discovered in early British-American woodsmen's and boatmen's dance, in rural African-American dance, in
decades-old popular comic and minstrel song, in cakewalk, in coon
song, and, with the entry into Tin Pan Alley of songwriters of East
European Jewish ancestry, in Hasidic and Yiddish theater song and
dance.[19]

There is the danger, when determining the distinctive mark of a
period, of excluding whatever does not reveal that distinctiveness. If
we say that the music of the sixties and seventies remained diatonic,
with scarcely a secondary modulation evident, care must be taken not
to exclude a discussion of a song like Henry Tucker's "Sweet Genevieve" (1869), which blossoms with chromaticisms though the music
remains mainly in the key of B-flat major. Seventy-five percent of its
thirty-three measures are altered by sharps or flats.

The same holds true for summations of an individual composer's
style. John McCabe, the biographer of George M. Cohan, stated that
Cohan's songs were almost always in a major key, spirited and
happy, simple and sounding as natural as a person speaking. Flats
and sharps were absent, as was variety of notes. He quoted Cohan as
saying: "As a composer, I could never find use for over four or five
notes in my musical number."[20] Nevertheless, a glance at one of
Cohan's important compositions, his dispirited "Life's a Funny
Proposition After All" (1904), reveals a song that often veers into a
minor key, is made melancholic with the knowledge that "all we
seem to know is we're born and live a while and then we die," and
emphasizes chromatic alterations in the music. Only in the limited
range of the melody, a sixth, is the song in accord with McCabe's
summation.

No one song, or small group of songs, can exemplify an entire
genre. A song said to be typical can never truly embody the concept of
the genre to which it belongs, but can give only an imperfect idea of the
entirety. Therefore, in this book typical means that within certain
loosely specified years the author is conscious of a dominant musical
design composed of similar traits, which differs perceptibly from a
previously dominant musical design and which will be supplanted by
another musical design at some time in the future.

In most popular songs written in the years under examination
there was an isorhythmic structure with reiterated rhythmic patterns
regulating phrases whose melodic contours were dissimilar. There
was also an isomorphic organization in which different sections of a
song conformed with each other in shape and size. Before 1890, both
verse and chorus might share one isoform; after 1890, the verse was
most often given one, and the chorus another, isoform. Hart Pease

Danks's "Amber Tresses Tied in Blue" (1874)* is isorhythmic throughout, and its isomorphism is revealed in constant two-measure half-phrases, four-measure phrases, and eight-measure strains, with a melodic half-phrase organization of (verse) *a b c d e b c d* and (chorus) *e b c d*, and with interactional phrases alternating between a close on a half cadence and one on a full cadence. Joe Howard's and Ida Emerson's "Hello! Ma Baby" (1899)* utilizes one two-measure isorhythmic pattern in the verse and another four-measure pattern in the chorus. The melody of the verse moves in two-measure half-phrases, four-measure phrases, and eight-measure strains, with a half-phrase structure of *a b c d a e f g*. The isomorphic linking of half-phrases is found in the consistent melodic half-step alternations between two tones heard in every half-phrase save the last, and in the half-phrases alternating between a close with a downward skip of a fourth, and another with a movement upward. The entirely different melody of the chorus moves in four-measure units: *h i h j*. Yet, there is an interactional connection with the verse's tune. Instead of the previous half-step alternation with the tone below, each melodic unit now has a whole step alternation with a tone above; also, the skip of a fourth down for a phrase ending, followed by a movement upward in the next phrase, continues.

From everything that has already been said, one must conclude that the popular mind unquestionably recognized the melody given the singer as the most important musical feature of any composition. Finley Peter Dunne once described an evening's amusement among ordinary urban dwellers. A Mrs. Donahue glanced at the family's parlor piano, saying: " 'Tis a mel-odjious instrument. . . . I cud sit here be the hour an' listen to Bootoven and Chookooski." A Mr. Cassidy asked: "What did thim write?" The answer came from Mr. Donahue: "Chunes . . . chunes. Molly . . . fetch 'er th' wallop to make th' gentlemen feel good."[21]

E. M. Wickes wrote that, for a song to achieve popular success, it is essential that it be inviting and singable at sight, harmonized plainly, and given a purely supportive accompaniment. Various parts of the tune should open in identical or similar fashion, which causes the music lover to accept the song owing to the ease of memorization. He advises that "lesser known combinations" of sound be introduced judiciously and secondarily. In like manner the singer Henry Clay Barnabee wrote:

> Melody is the heart, brains, and soul of music. Harmony may be
> thought "as expressed in a succession of rhythmical chords, and so

---

* Asterisk indicates that song is reproduced in the Anthology of Songs at the end of the book.

related together as to form a musical whole . . . at once pleasing to the ear and characteristic in expression" . . . but melody, pure and simple, is the life-giving blood which quickens its flow and sends it on and on and forever on. Without it there is nothing but the technical and endless repetition and manipulation of phrases which leaves nothing to remember and will be heard again and again without leaving an enduring impression.[22]

A word should be said about the relation of the music, especially the melody, to the lyrics. Heard by itself, the music cannot honestly be said to indulge in a display of bathos, unbuttoned hilarity, or any other exaggerated feeling. Indeed, as often as not, the composer had created a melody as music alone, with the lyrics added later, sometimes by a different hand and with next to no discussion of the composer's intended expression, the only clues being how characteristic the melody was of a particular genre. In this regard, popular song was far removed from the art song's world, where a composer selected a poem of at least some literary quality for setting, then sensitively shaped melody, harmony, and accompaniment to realize the general expression of the text, changed his music to accommodate changing poetic sentiments in different stanzas, and gave special musical treatment to certain individual words.

In contrast, the music of a popular song in some measure had to provide it with a needed aesthetic distance from the lyrics' sentiments. Its expression remained unspecified, thus moderating the overstatement of the text. As words gave direction to and particularized the feeling, music acted as a kind of lubricant, removing the possible emotional friction and easing the process of acceptance of the text. This is a very different responsibility from that given to the music of many an art song.

With the above in mind, we can appreciate Theodore Dreiser's comment about his brother Paul's sentimental songs as consisting of

sighings over home and mother and lost sweethearts and dead heroes such as never were in real life and yet with something about them, in the music at least, which always appealed to me intensely, and must have appealed to others, since they attained so wide a circulation. They bespoke . . . true poetic feeling for the mystery and pathos of life and death, the wonder of the waters, the stars, the flowers, accidents of life, success, failure.[23]

Assuredly, without the buffering action of the music, the sentimentality of the words might have become oppressive and poetic feeling nil.

6 CONSERVATIVE SONGS

After the American Civil War a period of reconstruction followed, lasting through 1877, during which major readjustments in political, economic, and social life took place. Feeling secure only in what had been and apprehensive over what was coming to be, many Americans held "despairingly yet to the models departed." American society waited "unform'd" and "Between things ended and things begun."[1]

If not pushed to extremities of destitution or oppression, ordinary people tend to be more conservative than not, accepting innovation slowly, bit by bit, and making sure one small segment is integrated into their lives before accepting another. Change, to be sure, is inevitable. However much Americans living in the late nineteenth century longed to preserve the status quo, they would have to accept the dissolution of old values and the intrusion of the new. This was an inevitable aftermath of a physically and spiritually exhausting war. The principles, ideals, and cultural expressions that would take the place of what had gone before were as yet unsettled during the several years immediately after the Civil War. So long as the direction the nation might take remained murky, most men and women preserved whatever fragments they could of the life that once had been. Their state of mind was conditioned by the still predominantly rural and small-town ways of thinking. These descendants of the original settlers, mostly from the British Isles, wanted to believe that their American society continued to be largely homogeneous, Protestant, possessed of shared habits and activities, and buoyed by traditional beliefs that would restore mental and spiritual direction and a consciousness of stability within each individual.[2]

Inevitably, their holding action was reflected in most songs composed in the late sixties and throughout the seventies. According to Charles Hamm, the popular songs originating in the years of Reconstruction were usually written by northeastern or northwestern songwriters; hardly any by southern ones. The writers did not attempt to confront realistically the vexing questions of the day, choosing instead to invoke the emotions attendant on idealized love and romanticized yearning for a return to an irrecoverable past.[3]

Song styles originating in the forties and fifties were maintained in the sixties and seventies. Much of the popular music, like the Americans sponsoring it, resisted innovation and change. This conservative type of song did experience some modification, but more often it showed a concern for cultural stability and continuity. Its content revealed the longing to perpetuate the physical and spiritual environments of an older America and alarm over the flight from the familiar in the emerging new America. As in antebellum song, its text expressed faith in a harmonious social system prescribed by God and in the compatibility and legitimacy of well-worn and tested ways of life, the "tried and true." Conservative song bolstered trust in the family circle, authority of parents, identity with a community (usually nonurban), obedience to the behests of religion, and correct conduct and moral behavior. Committed and everlasting love as something one freely gives and receives, with no conditions attached, loomed large in these songs. The old-time rural farmer and village artisan were idealized as having fulfilled lives; the new-time industrial worker and the city dweller were depicted as forever unsatisfied and incomplete, finding fulfillment only when they could exchange their soulless environment for a more innocent and pastoral place.

The music of these songs was also retrospective in style. Taking its cue from antebellum compositions by Isaac Woodbury, Marion Dix Sullivan, Stephen Foster, and George Root, the music of these songs maintained similar procedures and expressions. The melody usually remained on one level of feeling, without mounting drama, without a passage where increasing loudness and a climax on a high note gave dramatic force to the entire work.

A quintessential songwriter of the Reconstruction period was James Bland. As Tom Fletcher stated, this African-American composer wrote music so similar in style to that of earlier songs by Stephen Foster that Foster was often credited as the composer of Bland's songs. Interestingly, when the nostalgia-ridden Virginia Conservation Commission recommended in 1940 that Bland's "Carry Me Back to Old Virginny" be accepted as the official state anthem, several members of the commission assumed that Foster had composed it.[4]

....

HOLDOVER SONGS OF SENTIMENT

....

The subjects of old-style songs, from one point of view, demonstrated cultural regression. They allowed the music lover to arrive at compromise answers to predicaments that were otherwise unresolvable. Contemporary stress was met with reversion to cultural characteristics of an earlier, and what was thought to be a simpler, era.

When Jennie Lindsay's "Always Take Mother's Advice" (1884) recommended the remembrance of a mother's teachings when faced with a moral dilemma, she echoed the earlier advice given in Septimus Winner's "What Is Home Without a Mother" (Philadelphia: Lee &

Walker, 1854). When Thomas P. Westendorf lived distant from his wife for a time and yearned for her presence, he was said to have expressed his feelings in "I'll Take You Home Again, Kathleen" (1876), which both David Ewen and Sigmund Spaeth state was modeled after Arthur French's and George W. Brown's "Barney, Take Me Home Again," issued earlier in the same year.[5] The subject was also much used in earlier songs, in which men and women were perpetually returning home after years of sadness, whether back to a previous arcadian home or to heaven as home.

James Bland ostensibly wrote "In the Evening by the Moonlight" (1879) after he visited a Virginia plantation and observed African-Americans peacefully strumming banjos in front of their cabins.[6] The piece, however, calls to mind hundreds of prewar songs about fictionalized African-Americans leading contented lives in a fantasized American South.

The composers of these pre–Tin Pan Alley songs wrote uncomplicated works of the heart-and-hearth variety: "Sex problems, gilded vice, and various other phases of the life of today had little or no place in their song perspective. Patriotism came in for its share of attention, but a patriotic song in those days was a thing inspired, and not a story entwined with the American flag from commercial motives."[7]

In general, the songs of sentiment depicted humanity as having a dimension nurtured in an innocent childhood phase and, after the corruptions of adulthood and the real world, redefinable through supernatural agency. The subject matter was permeated by an awareness of the immeasurable mystery of a spiritual world that exists beyond the limitations of our senses. This was a dependable, coexistent world paralleling the world of reality, with all its changeability, harshness, and suffering. The songs accept the existence of guardian spirits of dead loved ones, of custodial angels, and of a God who would eventually set things right—where those of a later age were more apt to recognize physiological and mental disturbances and the operation of nurture and chance for either good or evil.

Tinging the texts of the conservative songs of sentiment is what Ernest Tuveson speaks of as Christian alienation. This implies that the "close relationship of affection, family, friendship, or another close tie has been broken, often with detrimental effects on the psyche." Tuveson states that disorganization of the self, loss of identity, the breaking of close bonds between people are familiar themes, but to the Christian, "man by his sin and indifference may similarly alienate himself from a loving Father." Redemption comes with return to God the Father and arrival at the heavenly home. In a sense, alienation is necessary to establish a "new and perhaps deeper relation of God to man." Our nightmare world, with all of its dissatisfactions, "is the dark before the light." This makes the message ultimately an optimistic one, in contrast to the view that later prevailed—that mankind remains permanently alienated, with difficult solutions or no solutions to one's problems.[8]

In Septimus Winner's "Whispering Hope" (1868), darkness, connoting the present life of gloom and distress caused by suffering, is supplanted by blessed light, and angels' voices breathe optimism however afflictive one's circumstances:

> (Verse 2)
> If in the dusk of the twilight,
> Dim be the region afar,
> Will not the deepening darkness,
> Brighten the glimmering star?
> Then when the night is upon us,
> Why should the heart sink away,
> When the dark midnight is over,
> Watch for the breaking of day.
> (Refrain)
> Whispering Hope, oh, how welcome thy voice,
> Making my heart in its sorrow rejoice.

Turning to other examples from the songs, Samuel Mitchell's lyrics to "Amber Tresses Tied in Blue" (1874) describe a narrator's pure and guileless beloved who dwells in the carefree arcadia of his innocent youth. He has departed for both because " 'Twas decreed." (In songs of this type, the constantly depicted departure from an arcadian beloved and home should be taken as a rite of passage into adulthood.) Yet, he sees her "in ev'ry vision." She is "far away in sunny meadows,/ Where the merry sunbeams played," and he knows she will be "ever faithful, fond, and true." In J. E. Carpenter's lyrics to "Her Bright Smile Haunts Me Still" (1868), the narrator has not seen his beloved for years. Yet wherever he is, her smile haunts him and "her spirit comes at will"—whether "on the seas," or " 'neath alien skies," or leading a "reckless life" full of danger. He has tried to forget her but cannot, for she has turned into an unshakable guardian spirit who remains with him whether he wishes it or not. The lyrics of "Sweet Genevieve" (1869), written by George Cooper, are about a beloved from the "lovely past" and "my early love" who, in the contentious world of the present, returns to him "in ev'ry dream" and in all of his waking thoughts." Her glance "is in the starry beam"; his heart will "never rove,/ Thou art my only guiding star."

When not a beloved, it is usually a mother, less often a father or grandparent, who stays in memory. Moreover, if the vision of the person once loved and now dead has faded, a surrogate replaces it, as in "A Lock of My Mother's Hair" (1877), text by Frank Dumont, and in "The Old Wooden Rocker" (1878), text by Florence Harper.

The lyrics of "Little Footsteps" (1868) by Michael Bennett Leavitt tell of a dead loved one whose spirit footsteps the male protagonist hears "in this weary world of woe." He says: "She sleeps . . . by the golden river's shore [heaven]" and although his heart "yearns with sadness," he hears angels caroling tidings from his loved one to him, and she "still does hover" above him and will always be his "guiding star."

Earlier in this book the still-predominantly-rural and small-town ways of thinking have been mentioned. The guardian spirit (angel, mother, or beloved), which was a manifestation of this thinking is mentioned in *A Marsh Island* (1885), a novel about rural Maine life by Sarah Orne Jewett. She reminds us that many Americans of later generations continued to believe as did their forefathers, even though others experienced an abatement in their religious faith. [Examples of later songs that adhere to older modes of thinking include William J. Scanlan's "Peek-a-boo!" (1881), Jennie Lindsay's "Always Take Mother's Advice" (1884), Effie I. Canning's "Rock-a-bye Baby" (1886), and Rida Johnson Young's words for "Mother Machree" (1910).]

The Jewett novel has Richard Dale, a town dweller who is knowledgeable about the world, telling Doris Owen, a farmer's daughter, that in this life "all sorts of powers and forces [are] doing what they please with us." He clearly represents those Americans who felt permanently alienated, aware of no solutions to their problems.

Doris Owen replies: "We are taught to believe that one power is, aren't we? But always for our own good."

When Dale wonders if the "notion of our having guardian angels . . . is true," Doris Owen, who believes "in a spiritual guardian," answers: "It always seems as if there were one angel who follows me all the time, and tries to keep me back when I am going to do wrong, and is set to take care of me. . . . I wonder if we don't have friends in the unseen world?"[9]

No one should feel abandoned and alone, even in moments of great suffering. William Shakespeare Hays's "Nobody's Darling" (1870) is about a parentless, friendless, and unloved beggar child "out in this cold world alone." Although starving and freezing from the cold, the waif recalls the mother's smiles of time past. During prayer, a vision of "mother and heaven" arrives and the child affirms with conviction that "Heaven will merciful be./ There I am somebody's darling,/ Somebody cares for me."

Hays's child, like the usual adult of sentimental song, may live in a present shrouded in blackness, but human beings are only sojourners in the present. Life in a future arcadian home, often more precisely defined as heaven, is promised. Hays portrays another anguished beggar in "Driven from Home" (1868). Although "driven from home," the beggar has the expectation that "The Friend of all friends who rules earth and sea,/ Will look with a pitying eye upon me,/ I'll wander about till his messenger comes/ To lead me to father and mother at home."

"Sweet By and By" (1868), words by S. Fillmore, describes a protagonist looking forward to a heavenly home; he will meet all of his loved ones again "on that beautiful shore," an image similar to the "golden river's shore" of "Little Footsteps," mentioned earlier. A more vaguely defined home is referred to in Thomas P. Westendorf's "I'll Take You Home Again, Kathleen" (1876). The protagonist promises to take her home again, over the wild ocean (a frequent symbol for earthly adult existence) to a land without "pain or grief" (possibly heaven), where "laughs the little silver stream,/ Beside your mother's humble cot,/ And brightest rays of sunshine gleam" (an arcadia). Later songs adhering to this kind of imagery include Joseph P. Skelly's "Why Did They Dig Ma's Grave So Deep?" (1880), Arthur J. Lamb's and Henry W. Petrie's "Asleep in the Deep" (1897), and Mrs. Jessie Brown Pound's (text) and John S. Fearis"s (music) "Beautiful Isle of Somewhere" (1897). This last song was sung at the funeral of the assassinated President William McKinley by the Euterpean Quartette.

All of the songs discussed above serve to underline Richard Sennett's contention that many nineteenth-century bourgeois families "attempted to preserve some distinction between the sense of private reality and the very different terms of the public world outside the home." He points to a quality in this life "all too easy to forget—its essential *dignity*. There was an effort . . . to make distinctions between realms of experience, and thus to wrest some form out of a society of enormous disorder and harshness."[10]

In a vast majority of these songs of sentiment, the speaker "I" is usually a male or, if the gender is not stated, presumably male. The man was still seen as the one who acts, the doer, or the contemplator of some ideal, therefore more suited to be the "I." The woman was usually seen as the one acted upon, a passive agent, and an embodiment of deep feeling or an ideal. For this reason, few songs present the words of a feminine "I"; a few present a neutral and genderless narrator who is personally uninvolved with the scenes and people described.

"Amber Tresses Tied in Blue" is typically the narration of a masculine "I." In contrast, Joseph P. Skelly's "My Pretty Red Rose" (1877) has a feminine "I" who begins her narration with "He gave me a pretty rose,/ While rambling tonight o'er the lea." However, she remains a passive recipient, not the one taking action.

A genderless "I," in "Driven from Home," laments about being "Out in this cold world, out in the street/ Asking a penny of each one I meet,/ Shoeless I wander about thro' the day,/ Wearing my young life in sorrow away." Because the protagonist is the afflicted one who experiences acute suffering, a feminine "I" cannot be excluded. The verse of "Why Did They Dig Ma's Grave So Deep?" is narrated by an unidentified observer of a bereft young woman, who begins: "Poor little Nellie is weeping tonight,/ Thinking of days that were full of delight,/ Lonely she sits by the old kitchen grate,/ Sighing for mother, but now 'tis too late." However, the chorus refrain contains the words of Nellie herself. Keening over the grave, she asks: "Why did they dig Ma's grave so deep,/ Down in the clay so deep?/ Why did they leave me here to weep—/ Why did they dig Ma's grave so deep?" Here Nellie becomes the personification of emotion strongly felt, an appropriate feminine image.

A song of sentiment is frequently described as a "ballad" on the title page of the sheet music. Just as frequently it is stated to be a "song and chorus," a ubiquitous designation meaning that each stanza contains an individual verse text to be sung by a soloist, followed by a refrain text, labelled "chorus." The latter is given a four-part harmonization for soprano, alto, tenor, and bass voices—although it can also be sung by the soloist alone. Some songs are designated as a "ballad" on one page and a "song and chorus" on another page. "Amber Tresses Tied in Blue" provides an example of the usual "song and chorus" setup. Occasionally, a song may lack a refrain, as in "Her Bright Smile Haunts Me Still." Or an individual plan is followed. In "My Pretty Red Rose," for instance, the refrain in each stanza is stated twice: first by the soloist, then in a soprano-alto-tenor-bass harmonization.

In an overwhelming number of instances, the words of the verse do not lead into those of the chorus. The verse ends; without an intervening transition, the chorus enters in the guise of an epilogue. Hardly ever is a song found that attempts to smooth the connection between verse and chorus. For this reason, "We Parted by the River" (1866) by Will S. Hays is quite exceptional in that after the verse closes with a period to end the sentence and a tonic chord to end the musical strain, the word "Oh!" is immediately sung over a dominant-seventh chord. The "Oh!" serves in a double capacity: as a comment on the sadness permeating the verse and as the introductory word of the line that opens the chorus. The unstable seventh harmony requires resolution in the tonic harmony that introduces the chorus.

No consistent approach to the employment of a title in the lyrics can be detected. The title is not specifically designed, as it will be in the songs written after 1890, to give "punch" to a composition—that is to say, to be an effective device for catching attention and putting a song across, both in its appearance as a banner head and in its musical setting within the song itself. The title may open the verse, as it does in "We Parted by the River," or open the chorus, as in "Sweet By and By." It may be the first line in both the verse and chorus ("Little Footsteps"), the last line of the chorus ("Driven from Home"), or the first line of the verse and the first and last line of the chorus ("I'll Take You Home Again, Kathleen"). Several songs, like Hays's "Mollie Darling" (1871), bury the title in various parts of the text. In the Hays song, the title is tacked onto the end of text lines 1, 3, and 6 of the verse and the end of line 3 of the chorus, and always appears in the middle of a musical phrase (the conclusion of the first half-phrase), thus diluting its punch.

The number of stanzas in the lyric are generally either two or three (42% have 2, 53% have 3), and infrequently as high as four or five (5%). Most lyrics (50%) have eight lines in a verse stanza and four lines in the chorus stanza. Again, exceptions are few. "Sweet By and By" is four and four; "Little Footsteps" is twelve and four. Three end-rhyme patterns for lines predominate. Yet, songs are found that adhere to one rhyme scheme only for a quatrain, then switch to another. (See Table 6.1.) Four trochaic stresses in a line is normal, although now and again an irregular line of five or three stresses may occur. (See Table 6.2.) However, it is not unusual to have a free introduction into a line of a metrical foot or two at variance with the prevalent one. Moreover, the composer's musical setting often imposes one or more different melodic patterns of accented and unaccented notes that supersede the metrical stresses contained in the lyric.

In most of the sentimental songs of the Reconstruction period, a major tonality occurs, thus in some measure relieving the sentimental excess that may reside in the lyrics. Sixty-five percent of the key

TABLE 6.1   End-rhyme patterns in a quatrain

abab	cdcd, etc.	32% of the songs
aabb	ccdd, etc.	26% of the songs
abcb	defe, etc.	26% of the songs
Variable from quatrian to quatrain		16% of the songs

TABLE 6.2   Poetic meter

Trochaic	(/ -)	33% of the songs
Iambic	(- /)	27% of the songs
Dactylic	(/ - -)	20% of the songs
Anapestic	(- - /)	20% of the songs

signatures call for the flat side of the circle of keys, F to A flat. (See Table 6.3.) Sixty-five percent of the songs are in a relaxed 4/4 meter and 22 percent in 3/4 time. Occasionally, an unusual time signature occurs. One such, Henry C. Work's "Come Back to the Farm" (1867), is in 6/4 time—but the music is really in 3/4 time with half the bar-lines missing.

Songs of sentiment are moderately slow in tempo, not so slow that they seem to drag and cease to flow nor so fast that they lose dignity. Several of them have no tempo indication at all. (See Table 6.4.) Interestingly, few if any indications of expression or dynamics occur in the body of the music itself, the songwriter undoubtedly feeling the meaning of the text was the best guide to the manner of interpretive performance. Note how the song "Amber Tresses Tied in Blue" is prefaced by *Andante* but has no other dynamic or expressive indications. When these indications occur, they are inserted sparingly, as in "The Old Wooden Rocker," which opens *Moderato e semplice*. The dynamic *p* appears three times: at the beginning of the prelude, the verse, and the chorus. The only other modification is a *poco rall.* just before the chorus.

Simplicity is evident in the melody as well. In a great majority of the songs, the tune is entirely diatonic or altered by one or two accidentals, often in the form of a raised fourth or fifth tone of the scale, to accommodate a brief passing modulation of V of V to V, or V of vi to vi (lowercase letters indicate a minor chord). A tone altered by an accidental is normally stated as a neighboring note, in the configura-

TABLE 6.3   Tonality in songs that look backward

A-flat	major	15% of the songs
E-flat	major	8% of the songs
B-flat	major	38% of the songs
F	major	4% of the songs
C	major	15% of the songs
G	major	12% of the songs
D	major	8% of the songs

TABLE 6.4   Tempo indications

Moderato	28% of the songs
Andante	22% of the songs
No tempo indication	17% of the songs
Andantino	6% of the songs
Allegretto	5% of the songs
Only "Espressione" or "With Expression" given as an indication	17% of the songs
Other	5% of the songs

tion of a diatonic note descending to the raised note below and back to the diatonic note, or as a passing tone from a diatonic note to the same note raised or lowered by a sharp or flat to the adjacent diatonic note a half-step above or below. The soloist is not asked to sing a single altered tone in "Amber Tresses Tied in Blue." The tenor part of the chorus, however, does show a raised fourth note as part of a neighboring tone group.

Simplicity and ease of singing are also found in the management of the melody, which moves stepwise (between adjacent notes) or triadically, in comfortable small skips, thus enhancing its lyrical effect. This gives the song gravity and poise—the melody may sound like a hymn but scarcely ever like a dirge. F. O. Jones, for example, describes "Sweet By and By," whose melody is completely diatonic and moves mostly stepwise and by small skips, as sounding like a sacred tune: "A simple melody and refrain, composed by J. P. Webster, an American composer, but of whom little is known. It is one of the most popular religious tunes ever written, and is sung in every civilized country of the world."[11]

The melody in John Rogers Thomas's "Eileen Allanna" (1873) moves almost entirely stepwise. Danks's "Don't Be Angry with Me, Darling" (1870) moves stepwise and, less often, in small triadic skips. Hays's "Driven from Home" is unusual in its high number of repeated tones and small skips at the expense of stepwise progression. Also unusual is another melody by Hays, that of "Nobody's Darling" (1870), which twice skips downward a diminished fifth from the tonic tone to the raised fourth tone and later skips upward a minor third, from the tonic tone to the lowered third tone.

Melodic range also aids ease of singing. The preponderance of melodies remains within an octave or ninth, with *d'* or *e-flat'* as the lowest tone and *d''*, *e-flat''*, or *f''* as the highest. Assuredly, a tune sung slowly and without strain contributes an unassuming serenity to the expression. Some anomalies exist. "I'll Take You Home Again,

Kathleen" is exceptional in its calling for the low tone *c'* and range of a tenth, to *e'* '; "A Lock of My Mother's Hair" also has a range of a tenth, *d'* to *f'* '; and "We Parted by the River" goes from *f'* surprisingly up to *g'* '.

The melody of the verse is normally sixteen measures in length; that of the chorus, eight measures. In most instances, the structure of the song's melody is built upon two to four different melodic phrases, each of four-measure length, resulting in constructions like the following [the strokes ' or ' ' indicate a variation on the basic phrase]:

(Verse) A A' B B' / (Chorus)   B'' B'' ["Eilleen Allanna"]
     A A' B C /   D C [Harry Kennedy's "A flower from mother's grave" (1878)]
     A A' B A' /   C A' (This is the most commonly met with melodic form, as in Henry C. Work's "Lillie of the snow-storm" (1866); also the form of "The old wooden rocker" and "My pretty red rose.")

As can be seen from the above, the chorus always reproduces at least one of the phrases from the verse, and both verse and chorus continue to present the complete melody.

Instrumental preludes of four-measure length that reproduce all or one-half of the first melodic phrase of the verse are most commonly found in these songs (60 percent); those of eight-measure length are found in 27 percent of them; preludes with independent melodies are found in 13 percent of them. It is also normal, but not the rule, to find a four-measure postlude (33 percent of the songs); less common is an eight-measure postlude (21 percent). Forty percent of the songs have no postlude at all, and only 6 percent have an independent melody as a postlude. Instrumental interludes, in contrast, are extremely rare. An interesting use of an interlude is found in "Interlude after Chorus," which behaves very much like a postlude, in the song "Amber Tresses Tied in Blue." Its four-measure-long prelude utilizes only two measures of the opening verse melody; the "Interlude" reproduces the last four measures of the chorus melody.

In keeping with the distinctive simplicity and clarity of the usual sentimental composition, harmony is mostly confined to the essentials: tonic, subdominant, and dominant: (I, IV, and V). The endings of four-measure phrases are indicated by conventional formulas: the half cadence of I to V or V^7, meaning a partial close and an unfinished statement, and the authentic cadence of V or V^7 to I, meaning a full close and a complete statement. For example, "Amber Tresses Tied in

Blue," whose phrase structure is A B C (which somewhat resembles A) B / C B, cadences on V^7, I, V^7, I / V^7, I.

Such a song continued the emphases of popular music from before the Civil War, which had adhered to diatonicism, rock firm tonality, and a limited harmonic vocabulary concentrating on a key's major triads. The configuration I-IV-I-V (or V^7)-I crops up again and again in the holdover songs of sentiment. There was a contradictory yet circumspect tendency even in the conservative postwar songs—increased use of secondary dominants, a home tonality elaborated through a few passing modulations, and a modestly enlarged harmonic palette employing mediant, submediant, and supertonic triads and the variety of colorations offered by augmented-sixth, diminished-seventh, and nondominant-seventh chords. Henry C. Work's "Agnes by the River" (1866) introduces several supertonic triads. "Her Bright Smile Haunts Me Still" also employs the supertonic triad and in addition has passing modulations to the submediant (V^7 of vi to vi). Most unusual, in "Nobody's Darling" and in "We Parted by the River Side," is the sudden appearance of the major triad on the lowered submediant. The use of these harmonies created a feeling of greater instability and tension.

The accompaniment for piano included in the sheet music is also quite simple. Single or octave quarter notes separated by rests in the left hand and easy eighth-note arpeggios or reiterated chords in the faster-moving right hand are the norm. For the most part, the tune does not appear in the accompaniment, except sometimes in the accompaniment to the chorus, in which the pianist's music may coincide homophonically with the soprano-alto-tenor-bass vocal parts (see "Amber Tresses Tied in Blue"). There is no hint of dance rhythms in compositions in common time, and only weak references to waltz rhythms in those in triple time.

BUOYANT SONGS OF REMEMBRANCE

Sung alongside sentimental compositions were more uplifting songs full of life and resiliency of spirit. They were performed in song-and-dance acts, comic skits, staged musical comedies, circus interludes, medicine-show entertainments, and minstrel shows. During the period of Reconstruction, the minstrel show was the primary vehicle for these songs.

Minstrel performers and their pseudo–African-American dialect songs began in the 1820s. By the forties, scores of all-male minstrel troupes were traveling the entire United States. In the fifties sentimental ballads also figured prominently in their repertoire while the dialect element in the minstrel lyric abated. In fact, it was not uncommon to publish a song in both dialect and nondialect formats, to sing a minstrel composition altogether innocent of dialect, or to present vocal music of nonminstrel origin.[12] After the war, the trend was to huge minstrel companies like Leavitt's Gigantean Minstrels and to the introduction of women minstrels.

According to Clayton W. Henderson, some troupes began to abandon blackface, and African-American subjects were supplanted by such topics as women's suffrage, American Indian stereotypes, and caricatures of recent immigrants. Furthermore, African-American minstrel troupes—such as Callender's Original Georgia Minstrels—began to be formed. Henderson also stated: "Minstrels began to rail against the decline in morality and warn against the evils of city life; a yearning for a return to the simple, 'good old days' was a common theme."[13]

A dialect song featuring an old-time comic minstrel subject complete with its usual inconsequential observations and nonsense words is "Good-bye, Liza Jane" (1871), arranged by Eddie Fox. Note to what extent dialect is absent from the following excerpt:

> (Verse 2)
> Behind the hen house on my knees
> I thought I heard a chicken sneeze. . . .Twas nothing
> but a Rooster saying his pray'rs [sic]
> And giving out a hymn Such a getting up stairs.

The last line makes reference to an 1830s comic minstrel song, "Such a Gitting Upstairs," which was full of grotesqueries and little else. George Willig, Jr., of Baltimore published an undated version of it as "sung by Mr. Bob Farrel, the original Zip Coon."

In similar comic vein is "Sweet Mary Ann" (1878), lyrics by Edward Harrigan. It also harks back to antebellum minstrel song, but without the dialect. In stanza one, Mary Ann is a teacher made ridiculous for all her learning—she speaks all sorts of languages, including Timbuctoo, Hindustan, and Jerusalem. In the second stanza she is a lady who is an astute gambler and a whiz at cards. In the third stanza she is a virtuosic dancer of the allemande, mazurka, polka, quadrille, reel, jig, schottische, and a "shuffle in the sand," but also such a "heavy stepper" "she'd break up all the lumber that you'd lay down on the floor."

Several popular minstrel songs, like many sentimental songs, extol an arcadia, usually located in the South, that is bountiful, well-ordered, and uncomplicated, and praise it in terms similar to those in antebellum compositions like Dan Emmett's "Dixie" and a host of Stephen Foster's dialect works.[14] Will S. Hays's "The Little Old Log Cabin in the Lane" (1871) features a few of the clichés from the fifties. An African-American sings of a dead "ole massa an' ole miss's" from a time long ago, in an arcadian rural South, where he and his friends had danced, sung songs, played banjos, and been happy. But all of this is past—the creek has dried up, the old mill has tumbled down, and only his old faithful dog remains (a mix of the subjects in Thomas Dunn English's and Nelson Kneass's "Ben Bolt" [1848] and Stephen Foster's "Old Dog Tray" [1853]). Fortunately, angels watch over him and he will soon join them in heaven.

The idealized beloved in an idyllic arcadian locale is the subject of the nondialect minstrel song "Love Among the Roses" (1869), lyrics by William H. Delehanty, music by E. N. Catlin. The protagonist adores his Matilda when he sees her among the roses. Fractured sentences deliver the message of the text:

> She had a novel reading
> Just as I was passing by. . . .
> She smiled as I approached her
> And I begged her to excuse.

He approaches her, not for the sake of a temporary liaison but to make her his wife, "dear as life."

In 1871 the Jubilee Singers of Fisk University conducted their first fund-raising tour of northern cities in the United States and soon became the rage among white Americans because of their moving rendition of African-American spirituals. Songwriters associated with minstrel performance, who were quick to take advantage of the spiritual's popularity, set themselves the task of shaping a new type of minstrel piece combining traditional popular features with those of the spirituals. Songs of a simulated religious nature were the result.[15]

Will S. Hays's "Angels, Meet Me at the Cross Roads."* (1875) is a dialect minstrel "song and chorus," according to the title page. The protagonist, employing symbols common to the traditional songs of sentiment, desires Gabriel to call him to his heavenly home, located "on de toder shore." As additional guidance, he asks that angels meet him "at the cross roads," which *Webster's Third New International Dictionary* defines significantly as a "central meeting place," a "crucial point especially where a decision must be made." The "I" makes clear his total disgust with a life in which he "can't get used to" the "weepin' tears" it constantly calls forth.

James Bland's "Oh, Dem Golden Slippers!" (1879) employs the old-time minstrel symbol of the protagonist getting ready to ride "de chariot in the morn" to a place (a heavenly paradise) "Whar de rain don't fall or de wind don't blow, / And yer ulster coats, why, yer will not need." The golden slippers that he has donned to get there "must be nice and clean" for wearing when he at last walks "de golden street." He adds, "What a great camp-meetin' der will be dat day," when he is seen riding and wearing golden slippers and white kid gloves. Bland's "In the Morning by the Bright Light" (1879) speaks of going to a Baptist camp meeting; its music has the vigor of a revival song, complete with hallelujahs. From the evidence of Monroe H. Rosenfeld's successful "Johnny, Get Your Gun" of 1886 it can be presumed that the lively revival type of song retained its popularity for several years. The song fails to make complete sense, but the main point of its message is the need for readiness to successfully shoot down a soon-to-arrive Satan and thus ease one's way to heaven.

What was said earlier about the format of the text in the traditional songs of sentiment also applies to the buoyant songs in minstrel shows, with a couple of exceptions. For example, two-stanza lyrics are fewer, three-stanza lyrics characterizing over 70 percent of the songs (some lyrics go as high as four or five stanzas). Further, much greater use is made of trochaic meter.

"Angels, Meet Me at the Cross Roads" has five stanzas, each composed of a four-line verse plus a soprano-alto-tenor-bass chorus, also in four lines but with the first line repeated twice. Each line receives four stresses in trochaic meter. The end rhyme is *a a b a / c c c d*. The gender of the "I" is not indicated, but one could assume a male protagonist. The title is heard three times in the chorus. In contrast to most other songs of the time, which do not bother to connect verse with chorus, a verse-to-chorus transition of sorts is evident in "Angels, Meet Me at the Cross Roads," on the word "O!" sung above a V^7 chord.

As for the music to the songs, duple time is almost always found and tonality veers toward the sharped keys. (See Table 6.5.) In contrast to the sentimental songs, melody is more inclined to remain diatonic and harmony to adhere to tonic, subdominant, and dominant harmonies (I, IV, and V chords) with little or no modulation, even of a passing nature. For example, "Sweet Mary Ann" has no modulations whatsoever, remains diatonic throughout (save for one raised fourth tone

TABLE 6.5 Tonality

E-flat major	8% of the songs	
B-flat major	16% of the songs	
F	major	25% of the songs
C	major	9% of the songs
G	major	34% of the songs
D	major	8% of the songs

stated as a lower neighboring tone), and employs only harmonies on the tonic and dominant (I and V) from beginning to end. On the other hand, "Good-bye, Liza Jane" has a verse in the key of D major, a chorus entirely in the key of B minor, and a return to D major in the postlude. Also unusual is the chorus of "Love Among the Roses," with chromatic slides in the melody and several passing modulations in the harmony.

Tempo is moderately fast, normally *Allegretto*. When tempo is indicated as *Moderato*, it means moderately fast, not the moderately slow of a sentimental ballad. Bland's "De Golden Wedding" (1880) opens *Allegretto*, the chorus calls for polka time, and the postlude sounds in march time. These different tempo headings do not indicate changes in speed. All three designations call for a moderately fast speed but indicate changes in the character of the music and the manner of performance. The polka had arrived in the United States around the mid-forties, and its sturdy two-stresses-a-measure pulse had swiftly been associated with the march. However, characteristics similar to those of both polka and the military quickstep had already appeared in the minstrel songs of the 1830s, whose antecedents were the dances and dance-songs brought to the United States by settlers from the British Isles.

Several of these songs have independent dances as instrumental preludes or postludes. Note the "dance" that closes "Angels, Meet Me at the Cross Roads." "Love Among the Roses" has two different eight-measure dances: one forms the prelude, the other forms the postlude. In addition, the entire music of each of these songs enjoys a rhythmic propulsion that is dancelike. This quality distinguishes such songs from the sentimental works. Moreover, it provides a degree of expressive energy and excitement and an impetus that unify each of these compositions and make up for their frequent lack of narrative logic. No new experimentation with rhythm is apparent. What syncopation there is reflects practices already well known in the thirties (see, for example, the second, fourth, sixth, tenth, twelfth, and fourteenth measures of the concluding dance in "Angels, Meet Me at the Cross Roads").

The melody of "Shew! Fly, Don't Bother Me" (1869), written by Frank Campbell and arranged by Rollin Howard, constantly resorts to a similar shifting of metrical accent. A piece of this sort, with its dancelike qualities and mild syncopations, appealed to the popular taste of the postbellum years. Witness the comment of James Ford, who labels the ditty a "lyrical scourge which swept through the country as no other song has before or since. It was whistled, sung, played and hummed, even by those who could neither play nor sing, in a manner possible only to a song written on a few notes."[16]

It follows that the vocalist's melody is far less lyrical and more rhythmic than in sentimental song. Its roots continue to be in British-American traditional song and dance. In this regard, a statement made in the *London Musical Times* of 1880 is informative. The writer offered conjectures about American ministrelsy, then popular in England. He found the tunes to derive from British ones, "slightly modernized and banjoized." The more pathetic songs resembled the Episcopalian chants, which crossed the ocean with the English immigrants: "They come back to us in one changed rhythm or another, but their spirit and origin no twang of the banjo can overcome." British jig and hornpipe, the article stated, were the antecedents of the African-American comic dialect songs.[17] The remarks in the *London Musical Times* could as easily have been applied to the antebellum minstrel songs.

Charles Hamm said that whether in the songs of Bland or of other African-Americans, there is no more influence of music from black sources than is seen in compositions of white Americans like Hays. Black music, he correctly observed, will truly effect popular song only at a later date.[18]

Repeated tones and skips abound, and stepwise motion is secondary. Phrases proceed mostly in eighth notes (making much less use of the quarter notes and half notes so often seen in the sentimental ballads), and sixteenth notes are frequently introduced. The incidence of gapped tunes, which employ mostly or only five or six of the scale tones, is much greater. The effect is one of brisk, self-assured perkiness. Certainly the accompaniment adds to this effect, especially when it typically resorts to a constant "stride" leap from bass note or octave upward to an offbeat chord, as in "Angels, Meet Me at the Cross Roads."

"Angels, Meet Me at the Cross Roads," designated a "song and chorus" on the title page, is in 2/4 time, E-flat major key, and *Moderato* tempo—obviously meaning moderately fast. The prelude contains a single *mf*, the chorus a single *f;* otherwise, expression and dynamic indications, as in so many of these songs, are absent. Both prelude and postlude present dances unrelated to the tune, while the tune of the verse has a remarkable resemblance to that of "Zip Coon," which is known to have been sung by the minstrel Bob Farrell as early as 1834. Although the vocalist's melody has a unique range, from b flat to e flat' ' (an eleventh), it is otherwise true to type in its use of repeated tones and skips, lack of chromaticisms, and strong suggestion of a gapped tune, one that avoids the fourth and seventh tones. Only the dance at the end has a raised fourth tone, which passes by so fleetingly it is barely heard. Nor does harmony ever budge from the home key in any portion of the song.

Unique for the time, and a forecast of things to come, is the melodic-phrase structure—(verse) A B C D / (chorus) E F E F—in which no phrase from the verse recurs in the chorus. Each phrase is two measures long. An identical melodic-rhythmic pattern is heard in each of the verse's phrases, thus giving a sense of unity to the verse. Another identical melodic-rhythmic pattern is heard in each of the chorus's phrases. Unique also is the employment of only tonic and subdominant harmonies in the verse, which closes on a held submediant minor chord (with its decidedly modal implications). This is then followed by a dominant-seventh linkup to the chorus.

All of the songs discussed in this chapter suited the temper of the times. They comforted and heartened Americans. Even the most pathetic of these conservative compositions promised an eventual surcease to present pain. Somewhere in the future was happiness. Not least, they introduced musical beauty into people's lives, which was in itself a consolation and a delight.

7 SONGS FOR A CHANGING SOCIETY

Although many postwar songs continued to adhere to the subject matter and musical styles that had evolved in the 1830s and 1840s, others began to look forward to the markedly different compositions of the turn of the century. During the sixties and seventies, and especially in the eighties, compositions started to appear that were altered in some individual details but not so differently from the norm that they were transformed into something entirely new. By the beginning of the nineties only a minority of songs held the line against some sort of modification. The increasing number of altered works established beyond doubt that, along with the gradual conversion of American society from a rural, agricultural, and homogeneous populace to an urban, industrial, and variable one had come a redirection of cultural expression.

Swift expansion to the west, stepped-up immigration, and accelerated industrial growth were three important factors in shaping a new national society. The settlers of the western territories brought home the truth of survival of the fittest, not of the most idealistic. The 15 million people arriving from abroad between 1867 and 1910, who found work in the mines, mills, and factories, did not care about the old mythology and images in traditional song. They were not aficionados of the music, nor of the professional formats, such as the minstrel show, that introduced songs to the public. East European Jews, Mediterranean peoples, Slavs, and Hungarians (along with immigrants from Ireland and Germany) flocked to the American cities. They formed a large part of the urban entertainment audience, entered show business, and introduced their tastes into popular compositions. Belching chimney stacks, grimy boardinghouses, and unverdant streets belied the picture of arcadian peace, beauty, and bounty and necessitated a new form of expression for the new experiences of daily living.

Innovative technological advances in transportation, communication, and manufacture lessened localism and operated to produce one immense national market for goods. A new class of wage-earning industrial laborer—one not rooted in a particular locale—appeared. The new aggressive middle class was intent on material advancement, consciously scheming to promote self-interest, and ready to claw its way to greater wealth and position.[1]

The admonition to love one's neighbor clashed with an opposing principle, that mankind's instincts were to do in one's neighbor before he did you in. The influential writings of John Stuart Mill and Charles Darwin cast doubt on immortality and hope for betterment in a future life and suggested that instead one ought to attempt to avoid pain and win satisfaction in the present life. In like manner, William A. Madden stated, the arts commenced to show a rejection of old principles and a skepticism in which "each man was an island unto himself; the 'facts' of experience were seen as a series of impressions which the individual memory would store and the individual imagination could rearrange, but from which no rational or objective or common knowledge could be inferred."[2]

Adherents of the antebellum point of view could not reconcile themselves to the changed outlook. Walt Whitman, writing in 1871, saw the American democracy as overly stressing material success and failing "in its social aspects and in really grand religious, moral, literary, and esthetic results." He sensed a "hollowness of heart," with "genuine belief" lost and the "underlying principles" of America no longer "honestly believed in." Thinking along similar lines, Emily Dickinson states: "Science will not trust us with another world. Guess I and the Bible will move to some old fashioned spot where we'll feel at Home."[3]

A different kind of American novel—one that espoused vernacular realism or dissected the social conflicts of industrial America—began to appear: Mark Twain's *The Gilded Age* (1873), coauthored with Charles Dudley Warner, Twain's *The Adventures of Tom Sawyer* (1876), and *The Adventures of Huckleberry Finn* (1884), which explored themes of political corruption, racial prejudice, and moral blindness; William Dean Howells's *A Modern Instance* (1882) and *The Rise of Silas Lapham* (1885), which examined the problems of personal ethics and commitment in the new industrial society; Stephen Crane's *Maggie: A Girl of the Streets* (1893); and Theodore Dreiser's *Sister Carrie* (1900), in which poverty and life in an urban jungle defeat innocence and humanity. "Neither Howells nor I believe in hell or the divinity of the Savior," wrote Mark Twain. Theodore Dreiser observed that in an earlier era Americans had traditions and ideals reflected in and "created by song and romance," as seen in Stephen Foster's works. Foster's music embodied "the spirit of rural America, its idealism, its dreams. . . . The very soil smacked of American idealism and faith, a fixedness in sentimental and purely imaginative American tradition, in which I, alas! could not share." He had witnessed the craft, cruelty, and brutalizing effects of city streets and could no longer subscribe to the older traditions.[4] The poems of Edwin Arlington Robinson, written in the nineties, deromanticized past, present, and future. Robinson rendered severe sketches of humans with all their contradictions and absurdities, their anxieties and nonfulfillment: Richard Cory, a gentleman who "put a bullet through his head"; Miniver Cheevy, full of rose-colored nostalgia for the "days of old" but "born too late"; and old Eben Flood, alone among strangers, singing "For auld lang syne" and seeking solace in his jug since "there was not much that was ahead of him."[5]

The collapse of Jay Cooke's financial empire in 1873 precipitated a national panic that lasted through 1878. An oversupply of goods, excessive expansion of industrial capacity and railways, and monetary inflation killed off the postwar prosperity. Industrial laborers found themselves out of jobs or working for less-than-survival wages. Debt-laden farmers rose up against depressed agricultural prices.

Economically weakened entertainment troupes were compelled to cease operations, join other troupes, or change their formats altogether. Many a minstrel organization suffered bankruptcy, yielding place to the upstart variety show, which at that time boasted greater flexibility and control over costs. Surviving performers sought to refurbish their repertoires with more up-to-date subjects to attract an illusory audience.

The public for popular song was different from the antebellum one. Rich, educated, and sophisticated Americans, and those men and women aspiring to ascend the ladder of prestige, often divorced themselves from native vernacular music and became devotees of European art music, whether symphony, opera, or chamber work. When this level of sophistication was beyond them, they turned to semiserious musical imports. Those Americans with money to pursue a musical education normally went to Germany for their advancement. Thomas Ryan of Boston stated that around 1889 he visited the master-violinist Joseph Joachim at his Berlin music conservatory (the *Hochschule*): "I heard the pupils play symphonies and difficult concert overtures,— also cantatas with solo singing and chorus. Perhaps one fourth of the 'string' performers were young ladies, and several were Americans whom I knew. . . . There was also a number of young men from America."[6]

The simpler and more melodious music brought to Americans by European immigrants proved attractive to native Americans, as did the sound of English, French, and Viennese operettas. English music-hall ditties and strophic songs of Central European origin executed by nonnative singers were very much a part of the American popular scene. In particular, Gilbert and Sullivan, Offenbach, and Johann Strauss provided fresh musical attractions that proved irresistible to Americans from all walks of life. It was to be expected that American songwriters would commence paying attention to this fashion trend in entertainment. In Septimus Winner's "Whispering Hope" of 1868, the influence of the Austro-German folklike waltz, which had been well cultivated by transatlantic song composers like Carl Friedrich Zelter (1758–1832), was already evident.

The incentives for change in popular music were many. This change was always evolutionary, not revolutionary. As Stuart Chase stated in 1948: "A culture is a process of gradual change, without beginning or end. . . . Individuals are born and die, the cultural pattern slowly shifts under the pressure of climate, new invention, internal need. . . . No reform can ever bear fruit unless it is grafted successfully to the living tree of culture." Or as William James had said, some forty years earlier: "We patch and tinker more than we renew. The novelty soaks in; it stains the ancient mass; but it is also tinged by what absorbs it. . . . More usually it is embedded . . . cooked, as one might say, or stewed down in the sauce of the old."[7]

Little by little, new elements emerged in the text and music that were not clearly discernible in any of the popular songs that had come before. Nevertheless, on the whole, they were small alterations that took on added significance owing to their placement within a solid bedrock of traditional procedures. With such placement, minor subtleties contrasted, sometimes glaringly, with the commonplace. A vernacular work operated within certain prescribed limits of structure, method, and style. Whereas within an artistically complex composition a modest alteration might have seemed to be of no consequence, it was of importance within the relatively simple, abbreviated, and stock context of a popular song.

THE MODIFICATIONS IN SERIOUS SONGS

The songs discussed here are invariably sentimental, but they normally direct their theme in a direction different from the traditional. The designs of the text and music may also differ in certain noticeable traits. For many Americans, the economic and social problems they inherited as an aftermath of the seventies had resulted in intractable fears and tensions arising from psychological conflict. These found expression in songs in which feeling was honed to razor sharpness. Central to an understanding of the lyrics was the evident need for men and women to feel something deeply, if only to assure themselves that they were sentient beings still capable of emotional involvement, still more human than robotic in their dealings with their surroundings and fellow beings.

Harry Kennedy's "Cradle's Empty, Baby's Gone" (1880) seems only superficially to invoke a metaphor of established usage—a dead baby who has gone to the "golden shore,/ O'er the silv'ry waters" and joined the angels. However, the words are overly artificial in language and imagery ("My heart doth sadly moan") and milk a pathetic situation for itself alone, with no connection made to an overall structure. Every line is given a different emotional twist in order to call forth tears and allow the audience to indulge in excessive sentimentality. The sense of artificiality and lack of deeper meaning encouraged parodies of the song to be written, like Tommy Tucker's "Bottle's Empty, Whiskey's Gone" and William Delaney's "Empty Is the Bottle, Father's Tight."[8]

C. F. Wood's "Somebody's Grandpa" (1880) provides a second instance. Again, sentiment has become detached from a hitherto prevalent symbol system and exploits a pathetic situation for its own sake. (An earlier song would have fitted the situation into a grand, God-given design.) The subject is an aged drunkard whose life has been filled with sadness, taunted by "rude, thoughtless boys." A virtuous girl intervenes, exclaiming, "He's somebody's grandpa! Don't hurt him." To excite increased sympathy, the scene shifts to a cold, barren attic room, where a suffering granddaughter, Bessie, waits. " 'I'm hungry," she whispers, 'starving for bread,' / Then silently turns to the wall and cries, 'Why don't grandpa come?' " Additional emotional indulgence is encouraged when the old man staggers up to the garret and finds Bessie murmuring "her last earthly words, 'I knew you'd come, grandpa, God answered my prayer.' " Finally comes the moral that however one may have sinned, "there still may be hearts to whom he is dear." The subject, claimed to be based on a story appearing in the *New York Tribune*, is certainly designed for maximum sentimental effect. Other songs of similar sentimentality are Bobby Newcomb's "There's a Light in the Window" (1885), Paul Dresser's "The Letter That Never Came" (1886), and William Devere's and W. S. Mullaly's "The Mottoes That Are Framed upon the Wall" (1888). The Dresser song describes someone who has for years awaited the arrival of a letter ("was it from a gray-haired mother, A sister or a brother?"). He "moans his fate" and "murmured, surely she must sometimes think of me." At last he dies, leaving a note asking: "Should a letter come, please place it by my side . . . but the letter that he longed for never came." Not even hinted at, as it would have been in the older type of song, is an after-death resolution of his problem, when he sheds his mortality to enter another world. Also disquieting is the warning about the undependability of existence in the present world and the illustration of daily frustrations never assuaged.

Surrogate objects lose the meanings previously attached to them.

In Henry Work's "Grandfather's Clock" (1876), the clock is not portrayed as a symbol of a grandparent, nor seen as eliciting the personal emotional involvement and commitment of the grandson, as would have been the case in the older songs.[9] Instead, it is described as having been a sort of domestic attendant of the grandfather ("My grandfather said that of those he could hire,/Not a servant so faithful he found") and to have no implications at all for the grandson. The "I" is portrayed as an observer of a phenomenon outside of himself. On the other hand, the "I" of Joseph Murphy's "A Handful of Earth from My Dear Mother's Grave" (1845) emotes over the idyllic homeland, Ireland, and the mother he has left behind. Yet, the mother died *before* he has left arcadia, no reason for leaving is suggested, and no mention of rejoining the mother is made. The handful of earth is a remembrance of former times, but his sorrow is not connected to anything beyond "Erin, my home" and the grave of his mother. The song makes no idealized references, nor does it give any descriptions of the qualities attributable to the mother figure. The handful of earth does not stand as a surrogate for the mother, as it once might have, and therefore fails to call forth the rich number of inferences once derivable from that sort of symbol.

The evanescent quality of anything connected with happiness and beauty is stressed as never before. John J. Handley's "Sleep, Baby, Sleep" (1885) gives a traditional assurance: that a mother and angels will watch over the sleeping babe. However, there is also the disturbing message that soon childhood will pass, like "Life's springtime so sweet." Because childhood "soon fades away," the babe is advised to continue "dreaming while you may," before the inevitable rude awakening arrives. "Twelve Months Ago To-night" (1887), lyrics by John F. Mitchell, states that over a year ago, friends met, laughed, sang, and drank to a future bright and without sorrow. But where are now the friends "who sang the songs of gladness, / And spent an hour in Paradise?" Death has visited them: "Some of them lie in foreign lands, while others sleep at home." The carpe diem subject is not new, but to say one can have only a mite of happiness after which comes unwelcome death (or its equivalent) is! Sigmund Spaeth writes that Mitchell was dying of tuberculosis when he wrote the words and reflecting on a convivial gathering held a year earlier.[10]

Existence apprehended introspectively as a series of life situations and the individual functioning in an unpredictable and aimless world run as threnodies through the compositions of the eighties and foretell the predicament of Americans in the late twentieth century. American cultural conventions, we are told a hundred years later, construe one's identity, deeds, and ultimate objectives in ways that keep the individual paralyzed in his fearsome sense of aloneness. There are encumbrances that have grown out of our culture, and they indicate the ways we have been thinking over many decades.[11]

The star, once the symbol of steadfast direction to right thinking and final safety, becomes the name of a foundering ship in Henry Work's "When the 'Evening Star' Went Down" (1866): "A light was put out, in dread, in doubt [!],/ When the 'Evening Star' went down." The protagonist's encounter with his dead beloved enshrouded in darkness in Work's "The Mystic Vision" (1875) is heartrending. He is filled with uncertainty that the vision is true. "Tell me, tell me truly is it you, love?" he pleads. "Is it really your sweet voice?/ Answer now, if only by a whisper." But blackness blots out the silent apparition and the "I" is left alone and uncomforted. The "veil" continues a curtain that cannot be parted.

Where was religion, God? Note Emily Dickinson's comment in a letter to Mrs. J. G. Holland in May 1877: "Vinnie rocks in her Garden and moans that God won't help her—I suppose he is too busy, getting 'angry with the Wicked—every Day.' He loves too homogenously for Vinnie's special mind."[12] Discussing the 1870s, Ann Douglas stated a hundred years later that the hold of traditional religion upon family morals, civic responsibility, and social functions was disappearing. A more liberal and sentimental creed showed greater concern for increasing church membership and attendance than for strengthening and putting into practice one's beliefs.[13]

Ties to God, loyalty to parents, right conduct, and connection with one's best self had less hold on youthful minds. Gertrude Atherton wrote of growing up in liberal California, in an openminded community that no longer strictly observed orthodox forms of behavior. When sent to her uncle's family in Lexington, Kentucky, in 1875, she and other young people were intent on rejecting what they perceived as the strictures of their less-enlightened Kentuckian elders: "I found congenial spirits in my cousins, who were in a constant state of rebellion."[14] More than before, youth wanted to make its own mistakes whatever the consequences.

The other side of the coin was the avoidance of responsibilities once taken for granted. Henry Work's "Come Back to the Farm!" (1867) portrays a distant son refusing to come to the aid of a burdened father who is ill, feeble, lonely, and needs him. The father begs: "Come, bring us the light of your presence,/ Come give us the strength of your arm;/ That we may once more see joy, as of yore,/ Sit smiling upon the old farm." The symbols of traditional arcadia (family, farm), so consistently associated with caring and trust in the old songs, acquire an unlooked-for emptiness, since they are set into a real world of experience, of sorrow and suffering, not the ideal world of uncontaminated joy and well-being.

George L. Catlin's lyric for "Over the Hill to the Poor House"* (1874) reads like a contemporary person's *King Lear*. An old, helpless father and his wife, now dead, have loved their children selflessly. He has given his children the deed to the family farm and they repay him by driving him out of his home and forcing him to enter a poorhouse. The unfaithful and unloving sons and daughters depicted in this composition were scarcely to be discovered in the antebellum songs. Other deviations from the meaning of the old imagery stand out. For example, the descriptions of blooming flowers, sweetly singing birds, and brightness of day that once would have been properties of arcadian happiness and innocent love become taunting accompaniments to the elderly parent left alone in the cold, where he will be allowed "to perish."

The nobility discoverable in ordinary individuals, so often the subject of antebellum ballads, is less in evidence. Work's "Lillie of the Snow-storm" (1866) deals with a drunken father who treats his wife and daughter cruelly. His "Sweet Echo Dell" (1876) has a parent wondering about a son thought to live but who has died: "Is he laden well with gold? / Does he bring me wealth untold? / Why then does he linger? / Say can you tell?" Although more elevated sentiments occur elsewhere in the verse, this interest of a parent in money, unseemly in earlier works, would have sullied the spiritual values attributed to the home and its residents. Work's "The Song of the Red Man" (1868) is not about the noble savage of Rousseauistic proportions, which appears so consistently in earlier song. Here he is wronged by "false traders," crazed "by their fire-water," and incited into destructive bloodshed. In all probability the unrelenting struggle of whites with western Indians, which peaked in the post–Civil War years, impacted on songs like this one.

Most of all, it was the concept of the glorified woman dear to a man's heart and the quality of the love felt for her that was redefined in song. Throughout the seventies, but particularly in the eighties, an ever-more-militant women's suffrage movement developed. At the same time that the right to vote was demanded by a small yet very vocal group of educated women, a larger number of the less educated found they had to work to supplement family incomes. Although neither group might agree with the other, both provoked a debate over the changing role of women that had an influence on song lyrics. Moreover, even the women whose careers centered on their households found their domestic duties becoming less onerous owing to improved and more efficient means of refrigeration, food preservation, laundering, cooking, and housecleaning. Fewer women died in childbirth, and some were electing to bear fewer children. No longer satisfied with domesticity, a new woman was seen more in public. By 1879 the editor of *The Clipper* was observing: "Now, and very properly too, our fair ones turn out in numbers second to none" in order to attend minstrel and other entertainments, especially if they promised "clean amusements."[15]

In 1886, Henry James noted that the new woman was sweeping away old stereotypes. Among the reasons he gave for writing *The Bostonians* was the following: "I wished to write a very *American* tale, a tale characteristic of our social conditions, and I asked myself what was the most salient and peculiar point in our social life. The answer was: the situation of women, the decline of the sentiment of sex, the agitation on their behalf."[16]

The next year, Sarah Orne Jewett gave an account of the new woman in her novel *A Country Doctor*. Her feminine protagonist turns down love and marriage in favor of a career as a physician. A constant thread throughout the book is the contrast of a fading old morality as seen in traditional Maine village life and the arrival of a new set of values as the village expanded into a town and acquired factories. It was a situation that could not help but affect women's lives and attitudes. Because the old-fashioned village of Oldfields grew very slowly and with extreme deliberation, it seemed to have a delightful completeness as opposed to the "towns which are built in a hurry [factory towns]" that

> can be left in a hurry without a bit of regret, and if it is the fate or fortune of the elder villages to find themselves the foundation upon which modern manufacturing communities rear their thinly built houses and workshops, and their quickly disintegrating communities of people, the weaknesses of these are more glaring and hopeless in the contrast. The hurry to make money and do much work, and the ambition to do good work, war with each other.

Jewett spoke of "poor humanity" that now "has to grope its way through a deal of darkness," amid "failures and miseries." She predicted: "There will be more and more sorrow and defeat as population increases and competition with it. . . . To excel in one's work becomes more and more a secondary motive; to do a great deal and be well paid for it ranks first."[17]

The nature of love between the sexes also had to change. Martin Cyril D'Arcy stated that since ancient times a threefold division of love has existed, defined in terms of self-interest or its absence. The lowest form was selfish love; next, love as pure enjoyment; and highest, a committed love for another, for that person's own sake. Then D'Arcy makes a fourth distinction: Christian love, agapé, which involves charity.[18] Traditional song had steered clear of the first form of love and cautiously dealt with the second, preferring to laud self-giving human commitment and divine love. New songs began to assume an opposite view.

Already in "You Naughty, Naughty Men" of 1866, lyrics by T. Kennick, music by G. Bicknell, the shy, innocent maiden ready to render pristine affection to some fortunate man has been replaced by the worldly-wise female who says that professed love is a cloak that hides the deceiving and scheming of men:

(Verse 3)
And when married how you treat us, and of each fond wish
   defeat us,
And some will even beat us, oh! you naughty, naughty men.
You take us from our mothers, from our sisters, and our
   brothers,
When you get us, flirt with others, oh! you cruel wicked men.

In addition, the song was sung by Millie Cavendish in the hit stage entertainment *The Black Crook*, where what the production lacked in dramatic logic it made up for in the sexual suggestiveness of the half-clad women who paraded on the stage.

Some songs refer to women whose love is mercenary, temporary, or fleshly. C. F. White's "Marguerite" (1883) is a young woman quite willing to forget the man who adores her. She chooses instead "The festive dance, the rich, the gay,/ So dif'rent from our home." Beyond the means of the man loving her is "this bright world" that he wishes "were all of mine to give." Paul Dresser's "The Outcast Unknown" (1887) portrays a young woman not as an idealized beloved but as an erring human who has come to grief and has died cast off by society. Monroe H. Rosenfeld's "With All Her Faults I Love Her Still" (1888) delineates feminine love that is neither dependable nor everlasting.

The makeup of the lyric was also changing, particularly during the eighties and in those songs that veered away from traditional subjects. Two stanzas prevail, although one or two songs employ as many as five. While the term "Chorus" is still used, a majority of the choruses are actually one-part refrains. Home entertainment had decreased, primarily in urban areas, owing to the increase in affordable professional performances. It might as well be that because amateurs were less versed in part-singing, the public was less interested in or in need of choruses with soprano-alto-tenor-bass harmonizations. That segment still interested might very well have improvised the vocal parts, since choruses in the main continued to exhibit fairly standardized harmonizations. ("Over the Hill to the Poor House" has an exceptional length of five stanzas but a typical one-part "Chorus.")

Most stanzas continue eight lines to the verse and four to the chorus, but irregularities do occur, such as the eight plus six line division in "With All Her Faults I Love Her Still" and the ten plus six line division in "The Letter That Never Came." Irregular and individual rhyme schemes are far more frequent, two songs rarely being alike. Often the stanza displays a different rhyme for every quatrain. Scarcely a lyric adheres to the regularity of "Over the Hill to the Poor House"—*a b c b d e f e / g h i h.*

Also appearing with increased frequency are internal rhymes—that is to say, rhymes within a line. For example, "A Handful of Earth from My Dear Mother's Grave" has a sixteen-line stanza with no chorus. Lines 5, 9, 11, and 13 have inner rhymes. In addition, although the iambic foot and the four-stress line (or 4 + 3 couplet) are seen with some frequency in the songs, the usual stanza can freely introduce differing metrical rhythms within a line and from line to line. An explanation can be suggested. More specialized popular-song lyricists increasingly wrote texts to fit the melodies given them or to suit the requirements of popular-song composers. They expected that music would provide rhythmic regularity.

Two other differences from traditional song are apparent in the lyrics. One is the uniform tendency to have the title appear in the chorus; the other is the surprising number of compositions that defer to the increased prominence of women and pass up a male orientation. Unmistakably, the symbol of the ideal woman was changing. Around one-third of the lyrics center on an "I" of unspecified gender, and one-quarter of the lyrics adhere to a feminine perspective.

The design of the music is also different from that of traditional song in several significant particulars. Most noticeable is the increase in triple time; around one-half the songs are written either in 3/4 or 6/8 time. The change was attributable to the European works in triple time that were currently popular. Furthermore, songs tend to move at faster tempos; fewer *Andantes* appear, more *Moderatos* or faster indications. Apparently the pulse of the new American society was quickening; so also was it music. Although duple-time piano accompaniments remain unchanged on the whole, those in triple time may acquire a dancelike lilt, which helps to ameliorate the saccharine flavor of some texts. The pathetic "Over the Hill to the Poor House," in 6/8 time, sounds dancelike in the prelude and chorus. In common with a surprising number of other songs veering away from the traditional, it has no postlude.

Harmony tends to be richer and more varied, modulation more conspicuous. In "Over the Hill to the Poor House," the progression II–V of V–V in the first melodic phrase may be more or less commonplace in many songs of the seventies and eighties, but the modulation into the key of the submediant in the third melodic phrase is more typical of the breakaway songs, and the occurrence of a nondominant augmented-sixth chord under the word "my" is quite unusual.

• •

PORTENTS OF CHANGE IN THE LIVELIER SONGS

• •

The most salient feature to affect the direction of the livelier songs was the gradual demise of minstrelsy and its characteristic songs. The growth of the usual troupe to gigantic proportions, coupled with the financial straits of the seventies, was the beginning of the end. Mostly male casts and stereotyped formats added to mistrelsey's difficulties. Mark Twain stated in the late 1870s that although the minstrel show had delighted audiences in the antebellum years, it bored them in the seventies and found it could not compete with variety theater, even when it tried to parallel the presentations of the variety stage.[19]

Edward Marks and Brander Matthews gave a similar explanation, though Marks stated that minstrelsy remained somewhat strong into the nineties and added that the American manners and courtesies emphasized in the minstrel show had become a thing of the past, therefore no longer pertinent to people's lives. Both said that the public demanded greater diversity in entertainment, including the appearance of attractive female performers. When, in 1908, George M. Cohan organized, wrote for, and produced what was known as the Cohan and Harris Minstrels, which contained around eighty singers and dancers, he lost over $100,000 and learned "that American minstrelsy was a dead issue with the theater-going public."[20]

As a matter of course the number of minstrel songs featuring a pseudo–African-American dialect declined. One of the most popular, William H. Delehanty's cheery "I Hope I Don't Intrude" (1877), sub-captioned a minstrel "song and dance," provides one such example. Its text is altogether free of dialect. Delehanty paired with Thomas Hengler to form one of the most popular blackface minstrel teams of the time.

Moreover, the number of lively songs that satirized themes once respected or venerated had increased. Stephen Foster's revered "Old Dog Tray" (1853) is metamorphosed into the ridiculously exaggerated "Widow Nolan's Goat" (1881), lyrics by Edward Harrigan and music by David Braham in the Harrigan and Hart show *Squatter Sovereignty*. Widow Nolan fawns on her former husband's goat: "Come back to my bosom, my own darling Billy." The goat attends her at the breakfast table, proves to be a trustworthy companion because he has been carefully reared, and is ever ready to fight off strangers while exhibiting the utmost gentleness toward neighbors. Two years later, Harrigan and Braham produced "My Dad's Dinner Pail" for *Cordelia's Aspirations*, a staged comic sketch. The song savages older, overreverential compositions like Samuel Woodworth's "Old Oaken Bucket" (ca. 1833) and George Morris's and Henry Russell's "Woodman! Spare That Tree!" (1837). "Preserve that old kettle so blacken'd and worn, / It belong'd to my father before I was born," exclaims the absurdly fervent protagonist, who then informs us: "Me he would wale / If I just put a finger on Dad's dinner pail." A tongue-in-cheek demand ensues: "Go fill it wid porter, wid beer, or wid ale, / The drink would taste sweeter from Dad's dinner pail." Water obviously will not do. Nor will the alcoholically weak beer and ale of the earlier "Little Brown Jug" (1869) of Joseph E. Winner. In the Winner song, a husband and wife are anything but an idealized couple: "She loved gin, and I loved rum." The humble home is slyly invoked: "My wife and I lived all alone, / In a little log hut we called our own." And what deserves the most ardent love? The answer is given in the chorus: "Ha, ha, ha, you and me, / 'Little Brown Jug' don't I love thee!" Finally, the mocking caricature of Joseph J. Sullivan's "Where Did You Get That Hat?" (1888) was heightened in actual performance by introducing the singer with a trumpet flourish by Richard Wagner.[21]

Many sentimental songs had praised the modest, simple, and honest life that is somehow ennobling. Changing values are evident in Henry Work's "Dad's a Millionaire" (1867), in which poverty is nonsensical, wealth is better, and money brings joy. The daughter buys the most fashionable clothing and drives in a stylish carriage; the son dashes out to acquire the best "trotting nag" available; the father builds a mansion and invests in "some mammoth farm out West." The daughter, with an eye for a future husband, announces: "We'll invite none but the 'upper ten'" to a party, where "dukes and lords and nobles" will also be present. Values given respectful treatment in traditional songs are turned on their head.

Without money, debts mount. Friendship is anything but everlasting, especially if you owe a few dollars to a so-called friend. These are the themes in Harry Kennedy's "I Owe $10 to O'Grady" (1887). The protagonist complains about the little money he earns. He explains that he has gone out on strike for better wages. But his friend O'Grady, who will not wait for his ten dollars, urges him to steal his girlfriend's piano and pawn it. A fistfight results, along with the vow that O'Grady will have to wait a long time for his money. Harry Kennedy's "I Had $15 in My Inside Pocket,"* published two years earlier, tells of a "gang" of acquaintances who have played the protagonist for a sucker. On Saturday night the gang promises to make him an alderman, and he celebrates by drinking with them. The next day he finds he has been bilked of his $15.

Slice-of-life fragments of actual experience, with no cosmic implications, fill out many of the livelier songs. Harrigan and Braham were outstandingly popular purveyors of this type of composition. Their "The Babies on Our Block" (1879) describes tenement life in New York City. Their "Paddy Duffy's Cart" (1881) recalls the urban past of the protagonist, when as a boy he used to meet with friends on his street during the evening. He then informs us that one has become a senator and two have been killed in war. No sentimental embellishments are attached.

Many a song dismisses the lofty, unphysical love that was highly lauded by American songwriters of the first half of the nineteenth century and deals instead with what actually seems to exist. Such a treatment of the theme of affection had occurred in a few antebellum songs, but after the Civil War they proliferate. Possibly the prolonged conflict, the sundering of ties owing to long separations, the increase of "Dear John" announcements, and the inevitable cynicism that is an aftermath of war had some influence. Whatever the reasons, songs looking at the realities of the amatory state were far more evident immediately after peace was restored and soldiers returned home.

C. W. Webb's lyric to "Croquet" (1867), ostensibly a topical song on a contemporary game rage, describes the affection of a young man and woman for each other in terms of warm kisses and encircled waists, not necessarily censorious activities but ones heretofore rarely described. Bobby Newcomb's "The Big Sunflower" (1867) states that a young woman may at first reject a young man who has looked her over and found her attractive. Later she may change her mind, not so much because she has learned to love him as much as to offer consolation: "She said she really felt quite sad / To cause me such distress." Henry C. Work's "The Buckskin Bag of Gold" (1869) has a young woman falling in love with a man for his handsomeness and money (neither tests of nobility, honesty, or morality guide her), then discovering he has robbed her father's bank. A dialect-minstrel song, "Susan

Jane" (1871) by Will S. Hays, revives the grotesque comparisons common to the genre during the 1830s; his beloved's mouth is like a "cellar," her foot like a "ham," and eyes like an "owl's at night." The theme of the song, however, is betrayed trust and the ensuing pain when the fickle beloved bestows her affections elsewhere: "I'll never love another, / To cause me any pain; I've trusted her, and all the girls / Are just like Susan Jane"—thus does the lyric rebut the claims made in "You Naughty, Naughty Men."

The similarity of text design to that in the lively songs dealing with traditional subjects is surprising. The number of stanzas to a song, lines to a stanza, rhyme patterns to a quatrain, and use of metrical feet in a line seem unchanged. It is as if there was a greater urgency to modify the subjects of the lyrics before turning attention to their formats. The male point of view predominates in a vast majority of the songs. A possible reason may be that these songs were customarily performed by men. Usually, no particular section receives a special treatment so as to arrest attention. Therefore, the punch given the opening of the chorus in "I Had $15 in My Inside Pocket" is exceptional, where the verse closes plaintively in the key of the relative minor and the chorus suddenly opens, boldly and *forte*, on the title phrase and in the major home key.

For the most part, the music also is like that of the lively traditional songs. Slightly more frequent is the incidence of 6/8 time (not 3/4 time!), the favoring of the sharp side of the circle of keys, and the use of accidentals in the melody and of minor triads, secondary dominants, and temporary modulations in the harmony. Nevertheless, the music of many a song has at least one peculiarity. That of "I Had $15 in My Inside Pocket" has already been cited. To give two other examples, the verse in "The Big Sun Flower" moves into the dominant key, then into the submediant, and next returns to close in the dominant key; the chorus opens on a dominant ninth in the home key. William Gooch's music to "Reuben and Rachel" (1871) has a prelude that commences in the relative minor key, then moves into the major home key; the verse is introduced with a vamp, which may be repeated until the vocalist is ready to sing—a practice common from the nineties on but most unusual (that is to say, in prescribed written form) in the seventies.

Several of the songs with music by David Braham are given prominent tunes in the chorus. They are distinctly different from, and of equal if not greater importance than, those in the verse. "The Mulligan Guard" (1873) and "The Skidmore Fancy Ball" (1878) provide two instances. They presage the practices in the songs of two decades later.

As should be evident from the discussion in this chapter, what important differences there were between traditional and nontraditional songs, slow and serious or fast and comic lay mostly in the themes they treated. Text design and music showed fewer dissimilarities. This was especially so in the livelier songs, less so in the sentimental ballads. Furthermore, the songs written in the decade of the eighties demonstrate the greatest inclination for change, whether in subject, text format, or music. Not until the nineties do songs differing from the traditional types become standard.

8 ACKNOWLEDGING THE INCONSTANT HUMAN CREATURE

Between 1890 and 1910, the urban population of the United States grew to constitute almost one-half of all Americans. In the northeastern section of the nation it was over 80 percent; in the Middle Atlantic states, around 70 percent; in the Pacific states, over 50 percent. At the end of the two decades, not only had many new cities come into existence, but so had twenty-five huge metropolitan areas.[1] The onset of predominantly urban living had not only social and economic but also psychological significance. Writers, artists, and composers would no longer reflect predominantly rural American values: "The shift from [John Greenleaf Whittier's poem] 'Snowbound' to [Edwin Markham's] 'The Man with the Hoe,' from Cooper's [novel] *Oak Openings* to Garland's [stories] in *Main Travelled Roads*, was not merely literary. When the farmer ceased to 'reign like kings in fairy land, Lords of the soil . . .' and became, instead, a hayseed—or just a headache—a revolution had occurred in American thought."[2]

The body of publishers, song composers, lyricists, arrangers, and retailers of popular music that came to be known as Tin Pan Alley shared in the new psychology. The base for the popular-music world's activities was New York City. Here also the performers and theaters that purveyed popular songs were concentrated. For the first time in American history, a composition might possibly sell millions of copies if it were a big hit. Charles K. Harris's "After the Ball," when it came out in 1892, proved this.

The New York City of these years was arresting in the variegated picture it presented. It exhibited a diversity of peoples, a variety of experiences, and great social contrasts of astounding poverty and beggary versus opulence. Composers, lyricists, publishers, and theater managers still knew each other personally; their common meeting ground was Manhattan. From this center started the most important vaudeville performers, traveling the nationwide circuits organized and controlled by management firms like Keith and Proctor and Klaw and Erlanger.[3]

The two decades starting in 1890 and ending in 1910 witnessed a high tide in live musical-stage entertainment, before motion pictures and radio began their encroachments. The division between high and low musical culture, aesthetic stimulants for the culturally sophisticated and simpler amusements for the masses, was still not as clearly defined as it would be fifty years later. Whether gentlemanly or plebeian, musical taste ran to the offerings of variety, now called vaudeville, and the lighter drama-cum-music productions.

The urban picture captured the imagination of those busy with the creation of popular songs. Thus, "Maggie Murphy's Home" (1890), by Edward Harrigan and David Braham, deals with the modest tenement life of New York City and, for that matter, almost any other of the teeming cities of the nation. It provides an up-to-date alternative to the bucolic scene in Stephen Foster's "Old Folks at Home" (1851). "The Bowery" (1892), by Charles H. Hoyt and Percy Gaunt, and "Forty-five Minutes from Broadway" (1905), by George M. Cohan, look askance at the rural folk who were once eulogized in popular songs like "The Village Blacksmith" (1857), music by Willoughby Hunter Weiss to the poem by Henry Wadsworth Longfellow.

Various writers felt the need to adapt to and describe the new America that was coming into being:

> "We're a gr-reat people," said Mr. Henessy, earnestly.
> "We ar-re," said Mr. Dooley. "We arr-e that. An' th' best iv
> it is, we know we ar-re."[4]

The marches of John Philip Sousa and popular songs of composers like Paul Dresser, Charles K. Harris, George M. Cohan, and Harry Von Tilzer captured the confidence, vitality, colorful contrasts, and often the sadness found in turn-of-the-century America. The United States was a nation more than ever characterized by ceaseless change, inconstancy, and a new ordering of things, both in public and private life. In what seems an elaboration on the Mark Twain comment quoted earlier, Theodore Dreiser wrote:

> The significance of scenes in general which hold and bind our lives for us, making them sweet or grim according to the sharpness of our perceptions, is a wonderful thing. We pass among them every moment. A new arrangement is had with every move we make. . . . The fact significant is that every scene possesses that vital instability which is the charm of existence. It is forever changing. . . . Great forces are at work, strong ones, and our own little lives are but a shadow of something that wills activity and enjoys it, that wills beauty and is beauty.[5]

"New arrangements," "vital instability"—these are phrases exemplified in the songs of the time. The titles of the songs alone, whether those that won a local or a national following, point to the mutability of the age and the different American then aborning: "Mariutch (Mak-a the Hootch-a Ma kootch) Down at Coney Isle" (1908) by Andrew B. Sterling and Harry Von Tilzer; "I Love My Steady, But I'm Crazy for My 'Once-in-a-while' " (1909) by Irving Hinkley and Allan W. S. Macduff; "Come, Josephine, in My Flying Machine" (1910) by Alfred Bryan and Fred Fisher.

William James stated it was a time of relentless inquisitiveness and experimentation, and secularism had arrived. With the 1890s, unity gave way to multiplicity, certainty and faith to a search for empirical understanding. Now, James asserted, only those who were tough-minded could feel comfortable with the persistent concern for uncovering facts, not forging principles. Truths had to take reality into account, including, James wrote, sensations over whose "nature, order and quantity we have as good as no control. *They* are neither true nor false; they simply *are*. It is only what we say about them . . . that may be true or not."[6]

The essence of the new popular song was the depiction of the sensations over which the individual had little or no control (mindless violence, driving passion, self-protective friendship, and so forth) and the situations, even predicaments, in which they placed the individual. At a critical point in America's cultural history, popular song reached the decisive climax toward which it had been moving during the seventies and eighties. Vivid emotional experiences were now portrayed. In a majority of instances they predicated an unfriended individual, a powerless or ineffective God, or a society characterized more and more by amorality.

The subject of most songs was the protagonist who found himself going it alone. He is less the spunky survivor figure of earlier song but more the fatuous mannequin existing for no reason at all, who may have to resign himself to whatever life allots him. He cannot take command of his fate, however much he may fight to do so.

Many song lyrics are pervaded by an existential uncertainty about right and wrong, good and bad. A person's actions might have consequences that could not always be foretold. Few lyrics promise a permanent termination to incertitude and sadness or an endless continuation to confidence and joy. Whether essentially decent people or not, the men and women of the song lyrics try to cope as best they can with different forms of insecurity and sudden or radical change. They make tentative attempts at altered ways of living: social, economic, psychological, and personal. Somewhere in most lyrics occurs a reference to lost serenity, innocence, morality, or connection with others. The present sense of loss did not remain delimited, as it had been in older compositions, with arcadian paradise at one boundary and a land of promised redemption at the other. True, many a song overgeneralized and lacked specifics; yet, this was a virtue since it allowed the depicted situation to apply to a greater number of Americans.

Nevertheless, still found among contemporary song themes were the steadfast love, humble contentment, religious devotion, innocent enjoyment of simple pleasures, and contentment with virtuous living that had been featured in the antebellum songs. The demand for them continued at a much lower but steady volume. Several were extremely popular. For example, Harry Kennedy's "Molly and I and the Baby" (1892) breathes the old sentiments and was an undoubted hit:

(Verse 1)
I've a neat little cottage and in it does dwell
Molly and I and the baby,
And I'm sure that for comfort no king can excel
Molly and I and the baby.
. . . .
(Verse 2)
Now we care not for riches or palaces grand,
Molly and I and the baby,
For I'm sure we'd not change with the best in the land,
Molly and I and the baby.
. . . .
(Verse 3)
Every bright Sunday morning to church we will go,
Molly and I and the baby,
As we walk down the street all the people they know
Molly and I and the baby.
Now Molly's a girl that you'd all like to meet,
Her ways are so charming, her smile is so sweet,
If you chance to be our way just drop in and greet
Molly and I and the baby.

Other songs on older themes that achieved great popularity include "Say 'Au Revoir' But Not 'Good-bye' " (1893) by Harry Kennedy; "When You Were Sweet Sixteen" (1898) by James Thornton; "Mighty Lak' a Rose" (1901), words by Frank L. Stanton and music by Ethelbert Nevin; "In the Shade of the Old Apple Tree" (1905), words by Harry H. Williams and music by Egbert Van Alstyne; "Love Me, and the World is Mine"* (1906), words by Dave Reed, Jr., and music by Ernest R. Ball; and "Honey Boy" (1907), words by Jack Norworth and music by Albert Von Tilzer. (The citing of additional titles here and elsewhere are intended as further substantiation of what is stated and as guides for further study.)

However, more often than before, love and optimism were surface sentiments that allowed doubt and dismay to peek through, as in "Will

You Love Me in December as You Do in May?" (1905) by J. J. Walker and Ernest R. Ball:

> (Verse 1)
> Now in the summer of life, sweetheart,
> You say you love but me,
> Gladly I give all my heart to you,
> Throbbing with ecstasy.
> But last night I saw while a-dreaming,
> The future old and gray,
> And I wondered if you'll love me then dear,
> Just as you do today.
> (Chorus)
> Will you love me in December as you do in May,
> Will you love me in the good old fashioned way?
> When my hair has all turned gray,
> Will you kiss me then, and say,
> That you love me in December as you do in May?

The reference to loving in "the good old fashioned way" is significant as opposed to the new-fashioned way of fair-weather love. The song had grown out of the anxieties and disillusionments of the times, represented in Mark Twain's *The Man that Corrupted Hadleyburg* and *The Mysterious Stranger*, and in Thomas Bailey Aldrich's lament:

> The oldtime fire, the antique grace,
> You will not find them anywhere.
> Today we breathe a commonplace
> Polemic, scientific air.[7]

The new American was restless, energetic, clear-witted, skeptical, and possibly weak in faith. If a member of the urban masses, he wanted to make the most of the one free day a week available for leisure and recreation, even if that day were Sunday. " 'Where is the city in which the Sabbath day is not losing ground?' asked one sad voice. 'To the mass of the workingmen, Sunday . . . is a day for labor meetings, for excursions, for saloons, beer-gardens, base-ball games and carousals!' " William James referred to a Professor Starbuck of California, who taught the psychology of religion, and said that this academic told him of once receiving a letter from a writer whose views were embraced "by a multitude of our contemporaries," whether they were trained in science or merely conversant with popular science. The writer found religion meant nothing to him, and the religious people he knew were hypocrites. Religion, the writer stated, taught us "to rely on some supernatural power, when we ought to rely on ourselves." Instead of religion, he would "just as lief, yes, rather, die with a hearty enjoyment of music. . . . Lively songs and music . . ." because "wishy-washy hymns are my destination." The writer describes his temperament as "nervous, active, wide-awake."[8]

One is reminded of George M. Beard's description of what he saw as the major disorder afflicting Americans in the late nineteenth century. In his book *American Nervousness* (1881), he calls it neurasthenia, a group of symptoms that produce worry, depression, fatigue in mind and body, nervousness, anxiety, headaches, loss of sleep, and digestive difficulties. The cause was the constant drive to improve one's position and to prove one's worth through a series of successful achievements. With this drive came an attendant dissatisfaction, restlessness, and ceaseless clashing with others who were also striving.

Not surprisingly, contemporary popular music exhibited a greater liveliness and nervousness than before, even when intended to go along with sentimental lyrics. As Isaac Goldberg wrote, many songs were raffish and rakish both in words and melody, seeking out novel rhythms. He cited pieces like "My Best Girl's a Corker" (1895) by John Stromberg and "I Don't Care If You Never Come Back" (1897) by Monroe Rosenfeld. "Vigor, novelty, musical daring remove them from Europe," wrote James T. Mahar of songs like "You've Been a Good Old Wagon, But You've Done Broke Down" (1895) and "Mister Johnson" (1896), both by Ben R. Harney, and "Some of These Days" (1910) by Shelton Brooks.[9]

Max Morath stated that between 1892 and 1904 two important national fairs, the Columbian Exposition of Chicago and the Louisiana Purchase Exposition of Saint Louis drew all sorts of black and white musicians and entertainers. Here, he claimed, were sown the seeds of syncopation, planted in Chicago and maturing into ragtime in Saint Louis. New things were seen: electric lights, phonographs, kinetoscopes, automobiles, cameras, flying machines, telephones. The fairs were symbols of America's coming of age, "unique and painfully different," with a population that was "polyglot, energized, on-the-make."[10]

This chapter will discuss the basic themes to be discovered in the lyrics of the songs. The design of text and the nature of the music will be taken up in the next chapter.

. . . .

ACCEPTANCE OF REALITY

. . . .

Never mind the arcadia that might have been and the paradise to come, tell us about the now, which may be all there is to life—this is the disconcerting imperative that quite a few songs tried to answer, as did novelists and poets. Mark Twain mirrored his age in world-wise stories in which laughter mingled with irony and satire that was sometimes bitter. However much he might laugh at it, life to him was serious, unpredictable, and likely to deal out body blows.

When Mark Twain's much-loved daughter Susy died, he wrote to his friend William Dean Howells, on January 22, 1898:

> Look at those ghostly figures. I used to write it "Hartford, 1871."
> There was no Susy then—there is no Susy now. And how much lies
> between—one long lovely stretch of scented fields, & meadows &
> shady woodlands, & suddenly Sahara! You speak of the glorious
> days of that old time—& they were. It is my quarrel—that traps like
> that are set. Susy & Winnie [Howell's daughter Winifred, who had
> also died] given us, in miserable sport, & then taken away.[11]

This was life as it was truly lived. Here was heartbreak: the tragic irony of receiving a wondrous gift, his Susy, and then having her snatched away. His experience taught him that there was no concerned God "who giveth and taketh away" and promises that ultimately things will be set right. And there was irony even in trying to set things right, since the harm was done and nothing could undo it—the theme of his bitter *The Tragedy of Pudd'nhead Wilson* (1894).

Forward-looking lyrics, in their own way, also dealt with practical experience and not with representations that stood for facts. The rites of passage and the idealized relationships once overtly pictured or implicit in the lyrics of serious antebellum songs have much less importance. The former comic hero as confident survivor, full of his aliveness and valiantly coping with whatever confronts him, often changed into a blustering knave more brazen-faced than brave. Those fellows once created to satirize the excesses of society now exalted in their excesses, implying that everybody is self-indulgent and out to get their own, so why not me. Alluded to again and again are the deficiencies in the way life has been depicted: of formerly glorified symbols now seen as rigid and empty; of moral precepts whose practice can have untoward results; of feelings true today and false tomorrow.

Moreover, as in Twain's writing, many a situation is found to have its ironic aspect.

First to be noted is the dismissal of the traditional symbols of earlier song. In "The Sunshine of Paradise Alley" (1895), words by Walter H. Ford and music by John W. Bratton, a scoffing irony resides in the meaningless street name. The alley is a "little side street . . . not very wide, and it's dismal beside." In "Down by the Old Mill Stream" (1910) by Tell Taylor, "The old oak tree," which traditionally stood for eternity, the connection between past, present, and future, here "has withered, and lies there on the ground."

"Don't Take Me Home" (1908), words by Vincent Bryan and music by Harry Von Tilzer, has a lyric that devastates the once-honored symbols of the protecting home and the faithful, loving, and compassionate wife. Nor is the protagonist, Augustus J. McCann, an exemplary husband. The "henpecked" McCann has fought with his wife ever since the beginning of their marriage. When run over by an automobile, he begs not to be taken home: "Do, have a little pity, I'm a poor married man, in search of peace I roam." Released after six months in jail for brawling, he again begs, "in fear," not to be taken home. He escapes from his wife by enlisting as a soldier, finds himself wounded but pleads not to be taken home. To increase the irony of the message and point up the difference from the old meaning, the song's prelude quotes the last melodic phrase of the tune to "Home! sweet home!" (1823)

The lyrics were in accordance with the observations of the famous Mr. Dooley about the contemporary stage play:

> Nobody's married in th' modhern play, Hinnissy, an' that's a good thing, too, f'r anywan that got married wud have th' worst iv it. In th' ol' times th' la-ads that announces what's goin' to happen in the first act, always promised ye a happy marredge in th' end and an' as ivrybody's lookin' f'r a happy marredge, that held the aujeence. Now ye know that th' hero with th' wretched past is goin' to end with th' couples prettily divorced in th' centher iv th' stage. 'Tis called real life an' mebbe that's what it is.[12]

Irony turns into sarcasm in the mocking illustration of Charles Darwin's *Origin of Species* (1859), entitled "Down in Jungle Town" (1908), words by Edward Madden, music by Theodore Morse. Upton Sinclair's *The Jungle* (1906), with its brutal struggle for power, may also have influenced the lyricist. Monkeys, after *The Descent of Man* (1871), are stand-ins for humans; the message: one has to fight for what one wants. To be nice and idealistic is to lose everything. The king of

Jungle Town finds that "another beau" desires his girlfriend and "won't let go." Immediately, the "king got sore, then softly swore 'His tale of love I'll cut' / First he bit him, then he hit him with a coconut." After the rival is vanquished, the king is acclaimed by his subjects: "Hail to the King! He's Jungle Town's real thing." He has proved his machismo by demonstrating supernormal strength, and therefore he is entitled to power.

This was a time of "coarse leadership" and "crudely exercised power," wrote Robert Wiebe, when democracy was seen by workers as synonymous with injustice, when every protest was met with violence. "I have always had one rule," a contemporary New York employer said. "If a workman sticks up his head, hit it."[13] Indeed, survival of the fittest was very much in the air in the year that "Down in Jungle Town" was published. In that same year, Winston Churchill published *Mr. Crewe's Career*, in which occurs the following passage:

> "Life," observed the Honourable Hilary, unconsciously using a phrase from the "Book of Arguments," "is a survival of the fittest."
> "How do you define 'the fittest'?" asked Austin. "Are they the men who have the not unusual and certainly not very exalted gift of getting money from their fellow-creatures by the use of any and all weapons that may be at hand? who believe the acquisition of wealth to be exempt from the practice of morality?"[14]

Survival of the fittest, brute force, and the solemnization of physical power form the theme of several novels of the time: Jack London's *The Call of the Wild* (1903), and Frank Norris's *McTeague* (1899) and *A Man's Woman* (1900). The young Dreiser sorrowfully observed that wealth and success now take precedence over love: "When it came to wealth and opportunity, how poor I seemed. No girl of real beauty and force would have anything to do with a man who was not a success."[15]

The self-centered dandy does not get his comeuppance in "Bill Bailey, Won't You Please Come Home?" (1902) by Hughie Cannon. Bill Bailey believes in the acquisition of material things no matter who is hurt. He knew that lessons of morality are empty and God metes out no justice in the world of reality. The overweening parasite on gullible females reigns supreme; Bill Bailey owns a magnificent automobile, wears a huge diamond, has servants to attend him. He has exploited his girlfriend and bled her of her possessions. After she has thrown him out of her house, she sees him arrogantly driving by, still living in affluence. Apparently he has found other women to prey upon. After his own unscrupulous fashion, he gets money and achieves a success of sorts. Ironic is the opposite result achieved by the girlfriend's action.

The moral: right may be on her side but she is the loser. Unbearable isolation is her lot, so she pleads:

(Chorus)
Won't you come home, Bill Bailey, won't you come home?
She moans de whole day long;
I'll do de cooking, darling, I'll pay de rent;
I knows I've done you wrong;
'Member dat rainy eve dat I drove you out,
Wid nothing but a fine tooth comb?
I knows I'se t blame; well, ain't dat a shame?
Bill Bailey, won't you please come home?

In actual existence, the test for a moral principle is what happens to you in this life. She has lost out, therefore she is wrong, she is to blame. A second song whose theme is similar to that of "Bill Bailey" is "Alexander" (1904), words by Andrew Sterling, music by Harry Von Tilzer.

A likeness to Bill Bailey may also be discerned in the ragman of "Any Rags" (1902) by Thomas S. Allen. Without any compunction he will steal anything he can get his hands on—your furniture, your wife; "If he'd steal from his friend, he'd steal yer life." No conventional morality affects him. Note the cynical quip in "Any rags, any bones, any bottles today, / It's the same old story, in the same old way."

Some lyrics suggest scaled-down expectations so that one will not fail to receive what is desired. Nellie, in "Wait 'Till the Sun Shines, Nellie" (1905), words by Andrew B. Sterling, music by Harry Von Tilzer, has little desires: the pleasure of the sun shining, a new gown, a trolly ride during which she can show off her gown. The ordinary person in "Bon Bon Buddy" (1907), words by Alex Rogers, music by Will Marion Cook, is happy to get a modest satisfaction out of life, like a nickname that is less offensive than most. Surely, implied irony hides in the derisive sarcasm that permeates the lyric. The protagonist knows others with nicknames like "stubborn Phil," "ugly Will," "dummy Smith," "Baby Blue." He feels he has had it "soft" because he has been given the innocuous sobriquet of Bon Bon Buddy:

Bon Bon Buddy, the chocolate drop, dat's me,
Bon Bon Buddy is all that I want to be
I've gained no fame but I ain't shame
I'm satisfied with my nick name.

A sad irony resides in the results achieved by the young woman Madge in "Just Tell Them That You Saw Me" (1895) by Paul Dresser.

A state of affairs exists that is the opposite of what was anticipated. Although not clearly stated, one surmises that Madge had left her home healthy, full of hope, and high in spirits for the promise of the city, and probably those of a lover who has since deserted her. She catches sight of the narrator, who comes from her small hometown. Quickly she turns away as he consoles her with "Don't turn away, Madge, I am still your friend." She looks ill, depressed, and in need of help. Madge begs the narrator to report that she looks well and loves her mother as before. "Pride alone," she says, is "keeping me away." This is the final irony: whatever is keeping her away, it certainly is not pride alone.

Madge "had done that dreadful thing that everybody deprecates and everybody likes to do—left the country and come to live in the city," to quote George W. Cable.[16] Her misfortunes may have been compounded by inexperience in urban manners and usages. Whether she is a "fallen woman" or not is a matter of conjecture. On the other hand, there is no conjecture about the person portrayed in "She Is More to Be Pitied Than Censured" (1898) by William B. Gray, which describes a woman who has "fallen to shame" and walks the streets of the Bowery. Again, as with Madge, she is pitied and not censured, quite an up-to-date concept. Both songs deal with a reality scarcely ever touched on before the late nineteenth century, women who have gone to the city, have lost their virtue, and are viewed as gullible individuals and not moral monsters.

Writing about Dresser's pathetic songs about lost women, Ellen Moers said that the subjects are real, not false. Whatever the melodrama, it mirrors the actual conditions of life in end-of-the-century America.[17]

In keeping with the new perception of what can happen to people and why, one sympathizes and tries to understand, not grow self-righteous and condemnatory. About people's changed view of themselves in this period, Joseph Wood Krutch stated: "If Darwin seemed to deprive man of all credit for the upward evolution of himself as an organism, Marx and Freud seemed to relieve him of all blame for his sins and his crimes as well as for his follies." The message in a poem of Stephen Crane, written at the end of the nineteenth century, is clear in this regard:

> "It was wrong to do this," said the angel.
> "You should live like a flower,
> Holding malice like a puppy,
> Waging war like a lambkin."
> "Not so," quoth the man
> Who had no fear of spirits;

> "It is only wrong for angels
> Who can live like flowers. . . ."[18]

If you are streetwise and know what you are doing, the city is the place to be, not the "sticks," is a theme frequently found in the song lyrics of George M. Cohan. Dismiss impractical fancy, deal with things as they are, and urban existence may offer you a variety of pleasures. If you are a greenhorn (like Madge), then your expectations will be defeated for sure. "Give My Regards to Broadway" (1904) is not a paean to an city but to the actual New York of his experience—Broadway, Forty-second Street, Herald Square, and the "gang" to be found in this area. "Forty-five Minutes from Broadway" (1905), scornful of rural simplicity, demolishes what was once valued in song. Here, irony comes in the form of a gibe, a portrayal of naïveté as seen in awkward rustics who react to the city in unsuitable and unwise fashion. Unflatteringly, Cohan's lyric describes "rubes" and "jays," with "whiskers like hay," who live as close to the city as New Rochelle. "Bunco men," that is to say, swindlers, find them easy marks when they come into town. Country people are so out-of-date and unsophisticated, they will laugh at the hoariest jokes. Yet, they are to be pitied, since the places where they come from boast no cafés or elegant restaurants.

Some songs exhibited a form of irony perhaps not consciously intended by the lyricist but perceptible to the listener, that of romantic overstatement—hyperbolic exaggeration that was the opposite of things as they are, because the characters depicted are so absolutely contrary to what might naturally be expected. "Arab Love Song" (1908), words by George V. Hobart, music by Silvio Hein, provides an example. The lyric is an assemblage of clichés and misdirection. A nomadic Arabian chief speeds through the Egyptian night, singing to the stars of his all-consuming passion for a "gypsy maid" who lives by the Pyramids. Then, on the next day, the lovers meet in the shade of a banyan tree. Fiction has reached its extremity. Everything and everybody described can exist only in fantasy.

"The Sidewalks of New York" (1894), by Charles B. Lawlor and James W. Blake, also reveals the same sort of irony. It paints an urban landscape in never-never land. Ethnic Americans (Irish, German, and Italian) live harmoniously together, sit on tenement stoops on summer evenings, singing and dancing, "while the 'Ginnie' played the organ." Hyperbolic fiction is found in:

> They would part with all they've got-
> Could they but once more walk,

> With their best girl and have a twirl,
> On the sidewalks of New York.

The reality was opposite—constant resentment and fighting between ethnic groups. Some first-generation and more second-generation ethnic Americans disliked the slums they lived in and would have been glad to leave. Teenage gangs were busy guarding their own "turf" from each other, not waltzing together! What Italian would have waxed nostalgic about the insensitive allusion to the organ-playing "ginnie"?[19]

Hyperbolic exaggeration is also found in "Budweiser's a Friend of Mine" (1907), words by Vincent Bryan, music by Seymour Furth. It was one of several songs praising beer drinking that came out in the first decade of the century. Budweiser is a better friend than humans, and it alone provides comfort when the "world treats me badly," states the protagonist. Nor does the drink talk back or get angry like a wife does. Nor does it preach to you: "Some friends like to tell you why hard luck befell you, / Budweiser is wiser than they. / . . . . What care I, if the sun don't shine, / While I've got Budweiser; / That's the reason I feel so fine." (As an amusing aside, on the cover of the sheet music is the statement: "Compliments of the Anheuser-Busch Brewing Assn.") An earlier song, "Under the Anheuser Bush," words by Andrew B. Sterling, music by Harry Von Tilzer (1903), had celebrated billing and cooing and Budweiser:

> Come, come, come and make eyes with me,
> Under the Anheuser Bush.
> Come, come, drink some "Budwise" with me,
> Under the Anheuser Bush.

The recognition of sexuality as an instinct shared by women as well as men grew in the 1890s. Although the nubile and uninhibited female may be the focus of this kind of song, the sexualization of humans is understood to involve both male and female. The theme is not so much the new woman of the late nineteenth century asserting herself in politics and economics as it is any woman, like her male counterpart, becoming aware of heretofore suppressed bodily urges and taking pride in whatever physical charms she can command. In short, sexuality is a shared attraction, impelling men toward women and women toward men.

After the Civil War, the female body had been constricted as never before. Women coped with bustles, stays, viselike corsets, distortive poke bonnets, and ugly shoes. Then suddenly, with the nineties, the bustle was ousted and skirts fitting tightly over the hips became the rage. Color and a new exuberance in dress took over. Silk petticoats swished invitingly. Marcelled hair and increased use of cosmetics added to women's charms. Showing off one's physical attractions was no longer as taboo as it had been. At the beginning of the nineties, Edward Harrigan wrote an article on the changed moral outlook, which now permitted near-nudity on the stage, and themes and language that once had been forbidden. Harrigan stated that the staged presentation of "unchastity and vice" was constantly on the increase."[20]

"Betsy's the Belle of the Bathers" (1907) by Richard Carle illustrates the relaxed moral tone that came in with the turn of the century. Betsy dresses deliberately and provocatively in a tight bathing suit, showing off her bodily curves to the admiring males on the beach. Of course, "Women are jealous of Betsy, / Hate even hearing her name./ For Betsy has charms, and not one of those qualms, / To stop her from showing the same."

As in the previous song, conduct showing an awareness of sexual urges or a desire for sexual gratification is frankly described. Moreover, the link between certain popular songs and the brothel are clearly established. For example, the Dreiser family was once supported financially in Evansville by the madam of a bordello, Sal, who was the mistress of Theodore's older brother, Paul Dresser. Furthermore, according to Vera Dreiser, her uncle Paul played the piano and sang in Sal's house while appearing with a local stock company. Eventually, Sal and Paul quarreled and parted, but the relationship did produce one of Paul Dresser's most important songs, "My Gal Sal" (1905).[21]

Several of the most well-received songs of the 1890s had connections with houses of prostitution. "All Coons Look Alike to Me"* (1896) was said, by its black author Ernest Hogan, to have a tune that he had picked up in Chicago's red-light district. In St. Louis, Babe Connor's freewheeling nightclub showcased the musical performances of Mama Lou. Henry J. Sayers heard "Ta-ra-ra-bom-der-e" sung here and liked the song. After rooting out the objectionable language in the lyric, he issued the piece under his own name in 1891. From Babe Connor's also came "May Irwin's 'Bully' Song," which Charles E. Trevathan put his name to and May Irwin featured in the musical *The Widow Jones*. The song involves a protagonist who must prove his masculinity by facing the bully with ax and razor in hand, in order "to carve him deep" and "lay him down to sleep." Theodore Metz may have heard "A Hot Time in the Old Town" for the first time at Babe Connor's, although Old Town, Louisiana, is also the possible origin of the tune. Metz then asked Joe Hayden to write lyrics for the tune and had the song out by 1896. Ostensibly about a religious meeting, the lyric's second verse refers to the ample supply of sexually attractive young women. One is described as "dressed all in red," therefore possibly lacking moral restraint, whom the male protagonist has just hugged and kissed. Furthermore, she promises him "a hot time in the old town tonight."[22]

In the 1900s allusions to the libido were commonplace. Updating Millie Cavendish singing "You Naughty, Naughty Men" in 1866, Lottie Gilson sang "Coax Me" (1904), words by Andrew B. Sterling, music by Harry Von Tilzer, in a manner calculated to arouse the desire of the men sitting close to the stage. In "Meet Me in St. Louis, Louis" (1904), words by Andrew B. Sterling, music by Kerry Mills, Flossie without warning takes her dresses and all of her husband's "rings and the rest of his things" to the fair. She leaves a note for "poor Louis," asking him to meet her at the fair, where she'll "dance the Hoochee Koochee" with him and prove that she is still his "tootsie wootsie." The implications are obvious.

Another song, "I Love My Wife, But Oh, You Kid!" (1909) shows that a husband's desires are no longer expected to focus only on his wife. The title was a catchphrase of its time. A year later came "Any Little Girl, That's a Nice Little Girl, Is the Right Little Girl for Me," words by Thomas J. Gray, music by Fred Fisher. It concerns an empty-headed groom married to a flirtatious young bride, with no real love between them:

> Miss Newly wed, to hubby said,
> In a Pullman parlor car,
> "I'm going out, to look about
> Just sit right where you are."
> She did not come, he said, at one,
> "Please, porter, find my bride."
> "She left you flat, who shall I get?"
> Then Newly wed replied.
> (Chorus)
> "Any little girl, that's a nice little girl,
> Is the right little girl for me."

The lyrics of "Some of These Days" (1910) suggest that libidinous gratification is what the protagonist has to give and, it refused by a lover, will be sorely missed. The message is unequivocal in "Do Your Duty, Doctor!" (1909), words by Irving Berlin, music by Ted Snyder. Eliza is "suff'ring" from a love-attack. She is in physical pain and needs a man to doctor her. When the "doctor" arrives, she tells him it is his duty to love her up and so he "started lovin' Liza good and strong." The lyric shows an analogy to the typical salacious joke told in male company.

THEMES OF ISOLATION

Confidence in one's own efforts and abilities was a long-standing American tradition that had already been recognized in Ralph Waldo Emerson's "Self-Reliance" of 1841. Yet, to take responsibility for oneself had ramifications at the close of the century that Emerson had failed to anticipate. When self-confidence was tempered with the idea of a survival-struggle, it encouraged an aggressiveness that was not so much owing to perversity as it was a tendency to react under the stress that such a combination produced.[23] Moreover, to be all-virile and aggressive in appearance made the protagonist capable of being wounded. His bravado rested on unsubstantial foundations. This knowledge inhabited the recesses of the protagonist's mind and encouraged psychotic apprehension over an outside world that never ceased threatening to inflict harm if he failed to act first. The pitiless and uncontrolled wilderness of the anti-self could be encountered as close as the next block, where there might be strange people, strange landmarks, strange ways of speaking, and perhaps an assassin who had the protagonist's number. Or the same lack of control could apply to an irrational inner self, which responded impetuously, even rashly, on an emotional level. The response could be self-protective; it could also be self-destructive. One had to go it alone, and one had to be ready for anything—these are ideas at least hinted at in several of the songs already discussed.

Alexis de Tocqueville had warned in 1835 that as social conditions were equalized in the United States, more and more Americans would feel they owed nothing to and expected nothing from each other. They would begin to feel that each of them stood alone and their destiny depended on themselves alone.[24] As the lyrics of popular songs attest, this state of affairs was coming to pass in the 1890s. In addition, Henry Steele Commager saw the decade as one of uncertainty, of doubt: isolated individuals were finding the old securities gone and insecurity taking over.[25] Increasingly in the song lyrics are found a self-absorption and a search for (or a denial of) self-gratification, aspects of narcissism that withdrew "love from any kind of commitment, personal or social."[26]

The result could be self-inflicted suffering, as in "After the Ball" (1892) by Charles K. Harris. The protagonist discovers his sweetheart kissing another man, will not listen to her explanation that the man is her brother, produces two broken hearts, his and hers. He is revealed as responsible for his own action. He has behaved willfully in response to an irrational ego. Without question, he could have done something about the situation but has chosen not to. Years go by. He becomes an old man and remains alone, isolated from happiness. Thus, the protagonist has turned into a contemporary symbol of unconsummated love, narcissistic misery, and gnawing loneliness. The poignancy of the lyric was found deeply affecting by contemporary Americans.

A similar theme emerges from "Absence Makes the Heart Grow Fonder"* (1900), words by Arthur Gillespie, music by Herbert Dillea. The lovers have parted because the protagonist has spoken harshly and caused his beloved pain. Now, in his loneliness, he longs for her and inflicts misery upon himself by obsessively dwelling on the question— does she love me still, is she still true to me? As in "After the Ball," his suffering is owing to a self-willed action. And reconciliation does not seem to be in the offing.

"Dear Old Girl" (1903), words by Richard Henry Buck, music by Theodore M. Morse, recognizes that a faithful and shared love has existed for years in the past. But the situation dwelt on is the lot of the protagonist denied his beloved, who has died. He is devastated because left alone, forever weeping, forever crushed by grief. Nowhere is grief lessened by the promise of an eventual reunion.

"Can't You See I'm Lonely" is the cry of the protagonist in the song of the same title, words by Felix F. Feist, music by Harry Armstrong, published in 1905. The self-centeredness is obvious: "Today has been a sad one, / I've been all alone . . . / So listen while I plead, / It's company I need . . . / Say that you'll be mine." Here is another side to aloneness, an undesirable condition that is to be alleviated not by a giving of self but by a taking from someone else's self. A similar concept permeates "Carrie" (1909), words by Junie McCree, music by Albert Von Tilzer. Harry feels free to flirt with other girls. Yet, when he reconsiders, he decides Carrie is the only girl for him: "Carrie, I am feeling very blue, / Lonely as can be, won't you speak to me, / I'm so sorry I offended you." He wants Carrie's company and love, although he has forfeited both through his own actions.

The protagonist is constantly throwing love away, discovering unbearable loneliness, then living perpetually with his loss or trying to regain what he once treated lightly by inducing his girlfriend to give to him, and by his selfishly taking from her, a love he in no way deserves but which he finds he needs.

THE NEW WOMAN IN SONG

The new woman was depicted as sharing the problems of her male counterpart. She wanted equal rights with men; she wanted respect for her individuality. More often than in the past, she was self-supporting. If marriage failed her, she wanted the right to be free of her husband, through legal separation, and, increasingly, through divorce. But her behavior could also be egocentric and fickle; her lot could be abandonment by others and an existence accompanied by unbearable friendlessness. Two songs already mentioned, "Bill Bailey" and "Alexander," point to this conclusion. Yet, because the lyricists were almost always men, the sentiments expressed were not always sympathetic with or sensitive to the problems women were confronting in their daily lives.

Finley Peter Dunne gave voice to the popular mind's recognition of the growing liberation of women in *Mr. Dooley in Peace and War* (1898): "Molly Donahue have up an' become a new woman! . . . Ol' man Donahue [has] . . . seen her appearin' in th' road wearin' clothes that no lady shud wear an' ridin' a bicycle; he was humiliated when she demanded to vote; he put his pride under his ar-rum an' ma-arched out iv th' house when she committed assault-an-batthry on th' piannah. . . ." Hearing this, Molly counterattacks with: "Th' new woman 'll be free fr'm th' oppression iv man. She'll wurruk out her own way, without help or hinderance. She'll wear what clothes she wants, an' she'll be no man's slave. They'll be no such thing as givin' a girl in marredge to a clown an' makin' her dipindent on his whims."[27]

In 1896 the lyric to "All Coons Look Alike To Me" discarded the idea of the traditional woman ever faithful and loyal to her man, replacing her with the image of an untrustworthy gold digger, as if to say she had liberated herself from virtuous love. She allows herself the freedom to act unilaterally, with no consideration for the other person involved. Certainly the song represents the evaluation of unsympathetic men puzzled and alarmed by the societal changes then taking place. The unshackled Lucy of this song without hesitation abandons one lover for another who is a bigger spender. Money is the only criterion that guides her selection of a beau. The male protagonist bitterly complains: "If I treated her wrong she may have loved me, / Like all the rest she's gone and let me down." A similar young woman is portrayed in "The Bird on Nellie's Hat" (1906), words by Arthur J. Lamb, music by Alfred Solman; the derisive theme: "Love's young dream all wrong." She takes her boyfriend for all he is worth, a diamond ring and his money, then drops him. She has liberated herself from moral scruples.

The subject may be as old as song itself. However, its burgeoning incidence in compositions published after 1890 is novel in American cultural history. In the song above, the man is the victim. Nevertheless, in many songs, the woman is the victim—as she is in "Bill Bailey" and "Alexander." One song, "Beautiful Eyes" (1909), words by George Whiting and Carter DeHaven, music by Ted Snyder, claims feminine shallowness makes her a victim. Baby talk and slang is the language allowed the young woman: "Papa's little ducky dear, who loves oo till oo die." She is foolishly infatuated by a pair of beautiful and romantic eyes. No longer guided by traditional strictures, free to follow her own dictates, she finds that her emotions of the moment carry her away. She hands money and jewelry to the man she desires, and is deserted at the end.

"Mother Was a Lady," words by Edward B. Marks, music by Joseph W. Stern, came out in 1896 and puts forth a viewpoint not uncommon in the period under discussion. The lyric reveals two traveling salesmen insistently flirting with a waitress. Upset, she points out that she is not the new unconventional female. Her mother was a lady; her brother Jack will vindicate her. One salesman, a friend of Jack, immediately understands that she has been gently reared and is therefore worthy of marriage. She is not the now frequently encountered coquette who has an eye out only for the main chance.

Love in the above song seems too swiftly conceived to be lasting. In another song, "The Moth and the Flame" (1899), words by George Taggart, music by Max S. Witt, what love there is also appears superficial. An emancipated young woman, asserting her right to change her mind, has rejected a former suitor in order to marry somebody else. At the last minute, she learns that she is about to wed a person already married: "She flutter'd away just in time." Back with her first lover, she returns to what was, the lyricist claims, her true love. One cannot help remaining skeptical.

An individualistic daughter rejects parental authority in "Anona" (1903), by Vivian Grey [Miss Mabel McKinley]. She is an Indian girl who chooses to elope with her lover, a mere warrior and not a chief, even though her father has threatened to disown her. Two years later she returns with a "papoose" and wins her father's forgiveness. The refusal to do a parent's bidding and running away from home with the intention of marriage are acts almost inconceivable in older popular compositions. She has acted independently, for her own reasons, not those of her father. That the ending is a happy one is surprising, since in most contemporary songs, especially those more inclined toward sentimentality, the feminine eloper is expected to end up alone and in misery. Although "Just Tell Them That You Saw Me" and "She Is More to Be Pitied Than Censured" have already been cited as examples of an ironic defeat of expectations, they could also serve to illustrate the more common outcome for an unconventional woman who gives in to passion without considering the possible consequences.

Independence not only from parents' but the entire community's values is declared in "I Don't Care" (1905), words by Jean Lenox, music by Harry O. Sutton. The feminine protagonist is determined to go her own way, not caring what people think of her. They can dislike her, treat her with disrespect, say she is crazy and conceited, she does not care. If whatever she turns her hand to proves unsuccessful, she won't worry. She is her own person, alone, ready to face the world.

Some songs show a young woman cautiously approaching her independence, not certain what she should do with it. The following quatrain occurs in "Don't Be Cross with Me" (1908), words by Will M. Hough and Frank R. Adams, music by Joseph E. Howard:

> It's a great big world and it's new to me,
> And I don't quite understand
> Why I shouldn't say when I meet a man,
> "Won't you kindly hold my hand?"

"Are You Sincere?" (1908), words by Alfred Bryan, music by Albert Gumble, reveals the young woman as uncertain, wondering about her real relationship to a young man. In self-centered fashion, he says: "Linger near me, cheer me, / I like you much better, sweetheart, ev'ry day." But she queries him: "Are you sincere? / . . . What you mean, mean what you say." She is trying to come to terms with a modern world where deception is met everywhere.

A MISCELLANY OF FRESH THEMES

Giving advice to songwriting novices of the early years of this century, E. M. Wickes suggested using up-to-date objects like automobiles and telephones as foils for human players. Together, object and humans could provide the basic theme around which a lyric could be built. A big tragedy, like the *Titanic* sinking (an event that produced several songs), rarely proved to be the kind of occurrence that could be transmitted into a hit song. Hardly anybody desired to be amused by the subject. The same went for large issues like eugenics and votes for women—they had no serious place in popular music: "As a rule people taken up with these subjects have very little time for singing light ditties or ragtime. The masses have a general idea of these national issues, but forget all about them once the hours for pleasure and amusement arrive."[28]

Lyrics on newsworthy topics of the day or utilizing objects that demonstrated the latest technological developments achieved a popularity greater than any known before. Already mentioned was Edward Marks's and Joseph Stern's collaboration on "The Little Lost Child" (1894) after they had seen a newspaper item on a lost child found by a police officer who discovers he is the long-separated father. Racial questions, including segregation and discrimination, were in the news and induced the publication of "Stay in Your Own Back Yard" (1899), words by Karl Kennett, music by Lyn Udall. The lyric dealt with the way one black mother and child faced this reality, giving it a localized and emotional dimension: "Now, honey, yo' stay in yo' own back yard, / Don't min' what dem white chiles do." When newspapers were reporting on the increase of women and children as workers in factories, Jean Havez composed "Everybody Works But Father" (1905), where the issue was humanized and made acceptable for light entertainment.

The utilization of recently invented objects as part of modern human situations to which sentiment is ascribed is seen in "Hello! Ma Baby" (1899) by Joseph Howard and Ida Emerson; "Hello, Central, Give Me Heaven" (1901) by Charles K. Harris; "In My Merry Oldsmobile" (1905), words by Vincent Bryan, music by Gus Edwards; "Take Me out to the Ball Game" (1908), words by Jack Norworth, music by Albert Von Tilzer; and "Come, Josephine, in My Flying Machine" (1910), words by Alfred Bryan, music by Fred Fisher.

The exploitation of some ethnic identity was also very much in the fore. Throughout the nineteenth century, Irish characters had appeared in many well-received lyrics, and they continued to be popular. Witness "The Irish Jubilee" (1890), words by James Thornton, music by Charles Lawlor; "Molly O! (Mavourneen)" (1891) by William J. Scanlan; "My Wild Irish Rose" (1899) by Chauncey Olcott; "Arrah Wanna" (1906), words by Jack Drislane, music by Theodore Morse (where an Irishman woos an Indian maid!); and "Mother Machree"

(1910), words by Rida Johnson Young, music by Chauncey Olcott. However, the new trend was to downplay the comical fighting-and-drinking Irishman and stress serious sentiment. Most Italian-American song characters were treated comically and spoke in broken English, as in "My Mariuccia Take a Steamboat" (1906), words by George Ronklyn, music by Al Piantadosi, and "Cavalier' Rustican' Rag" (1910), words by Harry Williams, music by Egbert Van Alstyne. Jewish-Americans were featured in "Sadie Salome, Go Home" (1909), words by Edgar Leslie, music by Irving Berlin, and "Goodbye, Becky Cohen" (1910) by Irving Berlin. A highly imaginary Chinatown is conjured up in "Chinatown, My Chinatown" (1910), words by William Jerome, music by Jean Schwartz.

Another fresh theme centered around the life of children. Already in 1883, G. Stanley Hall was writing about child psychology, in *The Contents of Children's Minds*. He insisted that children were not little adults. To them, lying was a form of play. Naïveté and quick anger characterized them. Adult morality was like a straitjacket to them. A parent should allow a child to utter his or her true feelings, preferably in childish slang.[29] By the 1890s, these different concepts about children were very much in the air. In addition, children were appearing as vaudevillian performers; mothers brought children to matinee performances. In addition, not a few adults wanted to leave behind the cares of the day and for a moment escape into childhood. Of course, the way children thought and talked would figure in popular songs. Undesired were boys and girls who behaved like adults. "Daddy Wouldn't Buy Me a Bow-wow" by Joseph Tabrar was an 1892 hit; "I Don't Want to Play in Your Yard," words by Philip Wingate, music by H. W. Petrie, was an 1894 hit. "Hoo-oo! (Ain't You Coming Out Tonight?)" (1908) by Herbert Ingraham seemed an epitome of childhood.

The mixture of various themes, topical, ethnic, and child-oriented, just mentioned, establishes how alive the just-being-born Tin Pan Alley was to the goings-on of the day and how it labored to reduce them to more manageable, intimate, and personal dimensions, where emotion could be focused and thus have an enhanced effect on the public. Given a likeable melody, the composition might well be a hit.

9 TEXT AND MUSIC IN THE NEW SONGS

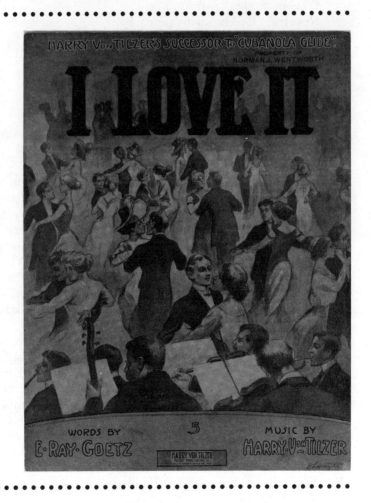

This chapter examines the manner of expression that characterized popular songs written from 1890 through 1910. Its purpose is to discover the distinctive technical ways that songwriters disposed elements of words and sound to build a musical composition.

What were the categories of song that the contemporary music world recognized? In 1907, Jerome H. Remick Publishers issued "Ain't You Glad You Found Me," words by Harry Williams, music by Egbert Van Alstyne. On the verso of the cover are listed the following divisions, and a song-example of each, that were offered for sale by the firm:

Ballad: "The Tale the Church Bells Tolled"
Cowboy Song: "San Antonio"
Novelty: "Be My Little Teddy Bear"
Irish Comic: "Patsy Dear"
Coon Song: "Yo' Eyes Are Open But You're Sound Asleep"
Indian Love Song: "Iola"
Waltz Song: "Somebody's Waiting for You"
Topical Song: "Traveling"
Sentimental Ballad: "Sweet Julienne"
March Song: "Alice, Where Art Thou Going?"
March Ballad: "So Long, Joe"

The list has shortcomings. A ballad, Indian love song, sentimental ballad, and often the waltz song, march ballad, and topical song of these years may all have a high sentimental quotient. Cowboy, novelty, and topical songs can easily be confused with the march song. Coon and rag song are often identical in sound. Some march songs make use of the syncopations that serve to identify the rag song. A few rag songs are innocent of syncopation and musically are really march songs. Examined more closely, the Remick categories sometimes refer to subject or emotional content and sometimes to the basic musical meter.

E. M. Wickes, in his advice to popular-song novices, warned that there were no clear-cut categories of popular song. Considerable overlap between types was the rule. Yet, he distinguished between two general kinds of song: the *ballad*, which included "the Semi-high-class, March, Rustic, Irish, Descriptive, and Mother" songs; and the *novelty song*, which included "Flirting, Juvenile, Philosophical, Comic, Irish, Production, Stage, Suggestive, and Ragtime" songs. Language helped guide Wickes's twofold division. Under ballad he would include subjects of import set forth in serious language, with American idioms allowed, and accompanied by dignified music. Under novelty, he undoubtedly meant to include songs having little weight, containing a great deal of current slang or comically fractured English, and featuring lively music. The exceptions here were possibly philosophical and stage songs. Older types of rustic ballad, Wickes states, had been in waltz time but immediately after the turn of the century were mostly in march time and featured some novelty in their rhythms. Waltz ballads, he said, were musically quite conservative.[1]

For purposes of study, the songs are grouped into five genres: (1) normally slower sentimental compositions of serious intent, many of these designated as "ballads"; in some examples, the music may resemble the waltz or march song; (2) artistic and semiartistic songs; (3) waltz songs; (4) coon and rag songs; (5) march songs and other pieces (often called novelty songs) in animated tempos. That the grouping is not arbitrary will be established in the ensuing discussion. In all instances the characteristics of music and lyrics have aided in the classification.

Speaking of the songs in general, Wickes claimed that the American South was a preferred location for their subjects because it was connected with romance. On the other hand, "Names like Oregon, Nebraska, Michigan, and Dakota suggested adventure, cold, and commerce." All names appearing in a text had to be euphonious. Massachusetts was a hopeless name to use. New Hampshire had appeared successfully in one song, "My Old New Hampshire Home" (1898) and Indiana in another, "On the Banks of the Wabash" (1897). Easier to boost into a hit were titles like "She Was Bred in Old Kentucky" (1898), "so long as one can blend a pretty southern love song with a catchy melody."[2]

One new feature in the design of most songs in these two decades was the equal if not greater importance of the melody in the chorus as opposed to that of the verse. As Charles Hamm observed, the "chorus" was for a solo voice. He surmised that the changeover from minstrel to variety show left the singer to perform alone, since a chorus was no longer available. Beginning in the 1890s, the chorus was of equal or longer length than the verse. Hamm made a perceptive analogy between the verse-chorus of popular song and the recitative-aria of opera.[3] Nevertheless, the verse's music was genuinely melodic, and only after 1910 did it grow more declamatory.

Was Edward Marks correct in saying, "The verse doesn't matter. Nobody ever remembered it anyhow"?[4] In a way, this was true. It was memorable melody that emblazoned words on people's minds, and increasingly the more memorable melody was that of the chorus. But lyricists and composers continued to put out songs that included the verse, despite the lesser significance of its melody. One reason can be suggested. However Marks might dismiss the verse's importance, the public wanted it included in the song's structure; otherwise, Tin Pan Alley would have banished it. The chorus contained a song's "presenting" or overt message; the verse contained the "hidden" or underlying message. The verse set up the chorus, acted as a foil to it, and gave it a reason for existing. The verse dealt more specifically with the song's preoccupations. Together, verse and chorus suggested completeness. Moreover, only a little effort is required to establish an organic connection between the music of the verse and chorus, which often do share peculiarities of melody, rhythm, and harmony.

A strophic setting was suited to the uncomplex lyrics, because the typical text hewed to one expressive mood from stanza to stanza. This approach accommodated the construction of a fine independent tune. Thus, the vocalist who sang the tune was expected to predominate, while the accompanist remained just that, cautious about calling attention to himself or herself.

Increased chromaticism is found in the melody and harmony of compositions belonging to all genres save that of the waltz song. Secondary dominants, chromatically altered chords, augmented-sixth chords, ninth chords, and nondominant seventh harmonies increase. Key changes to the dominant, submediant, and subdominant, lasting for four to eight measures, occur. One is surprised to find the frequent references to the key of the supertonic, both in passing and in phrase-length modulations. Irregular chord resolutions and deceptive cadences are heard. The increased complication of the music is sometimes the consequence of a desire for heightened expression. More often it is the result of coloristic considerations, meant to add interesting and pleasing variety to the basic diatonic sounds. It also reflects an urban, cosmopolitan, and many-sided taste greatly removed from the more unassuming, homogeneous, folk-oriented, and close-to-the-soil sounds of antebellum America.

There is little word painting as such, since it might interfere with the wholeness and flow of the melody. In almost all instances, the music is far superior to the lyric. Indeed, one senses that most lyrics exist only for the sake of the music, not the other way around. The melody has to convey a sense of regular, effortless, and natural motion, punctuated by clear resting points. A definite rhythmic profile, both in the metrical pulsation and recurring melodic-phrase patterns, is normally seen. If the proper declamation of the words gets in the way of an attractive, smoothly unfolding tune, then the tune must come first. In fact, the music is frequently needed to ameliorate the awkwardness of the text, where defective rhymes, unevenness in the poetic meter, and lines that vary in the number of stresses they contain are more usually encountered than was the case in older songs.

The close links to British-American folk song are almost gone. No longer do most song composers have British-American antecedents. Thus, tunes based on gapped scales—that is to say, on less than the seven available tones of the diatonic scale—now become rare; the incidence of melodic motion involving the semitone increases. Links with the jig and hornpipe are much weaker. The modest syncopations resulting from the natural stresses of the English language, on words like "mother," are augmented with more artificially contrived accentual displacements. A persistent rhythmic device in more than a few of the newer melodies is a chain of dotted eighths followed by sixteenth notes, where once a similar articulation would have comprised even eighth notes.

It is necessary to mention the concept of "punch" that Tin Pan Alley composers began consciously to apply to their pieces. Punch to them signified something notable in the text and music, or both, that would drive home the point of a song and continue to command attention in the listener's memory. The hustle and bustle of turn-of-the-century American life and the many entertainment offerings that contended for the public eye and ear precluded any listener's giving careful consideration to the overall merits of any one musical composition. Something had to immediately attract his attention— the punch. That the concept was also applied to the published writings of the time is made clear in a comment by Theodore Dreiser, who referred to his publisher as having a middle-class and very American conviction about the need for "punch."[5]

Brett Page, in *Writing for Vaudeville*, insisted that all popular hits had real punch and that composers of popular songs tried to incorporate it into their music. To do so, they would select a few notes that would individualize a piece as *"the song."* This string of notes was then placed in the chorus. He advised repeating the string at least once, but always in natural and adroit fashion. Some composers, in order to give punch to a song, borrowed from an *"old* favorite." They made over its tune but kept the new one just enough alike so as to prove haunting. Perhaps Page had in mind the Westminster-chime tones that sound in "Say Au Revoir But Not Goodbye" (1893) by Harry Kennedy and "You're the Flower of My Heart, Sweet Adeline" (1903), words by Richard H. Gerard (Richard Gerard Hausch), music by Harry Armstrong. This "secret" of the popular-song trade was not really plagiarism, he stated, and the remodeling did not work if a melody from a recent song was used. Punch could also come from a line in the lyric.

The composer selected a simple but attractive phrase and inserted it into the chorus, especially at the end.[6]

E. M. Wickes said a good title can have punch and make the song into a hit. A title tag lingered in memory after one heard the piece; it conjured up related images and revived past recollections and associations. Some of the best titles were adverbial clauses, like "When the harvest days are over," "When the meadow lanes are green again," and "Where the sweet magnolias bloom." Titles connected to the events of the day were valuable because they received free publicity. At any rate, a fine title suggested or conveyed a definite idea. It helped to attract the attention of performers, especially if they were selecting songs to be sent to them from a catalog. Amateurs in a music store would ask to see and hear a song whose title caught their eye.[7]

Not surprisingly, the title was almost invariably used as a punch line by placing it in the first line and, less often, also toward the end of the chorus (see "Absence Makes the Heart Grow Fonder"). Nearly without exception, it was set to one of the most appealing melodic phrases, and in most cases the most winning phrase, of the song.

SENTIMENTAL SONGS

The texts of the turn-of-the-century sentimental songs are distinctly different from those of the older songs. They were created in years when life seemed increasingly rushed, time more of the essence. Impatience with length surfaced as never before. Half of the compositions are limited to two stanzas, each constituting an individual "verse" plus a reiterated refrain called a "chorus." (See Table 9.1). About 60 percent of the songs have a verse in eight lines; 43 percent of the songs have a refrain of four lines. Clearly, the prominence of the choral refrain does not result from an increase in the number of lines allotted to it. Most exceptional is the eleven-line verse of "Honey Boy"

TABLE 9.1.   Stanzas in songs

2	50% of songs
3	36% of songs
4	7% of songs
5	7% of songs

(1907), words by Jack Norworth, music by Albert Von Tilzer, and the five-line chorus of "Mary's a Grand Old Name" (1905) by George M. Cohan. (See Table 9.2.)

The iamb predominates (followed by the trochee) as the usual prosodic foot. Yet, now the irregularities are so many that, once the music becomes familiar, the listener finds that the music's meter must guide any scanning of the lines. End-rhyme schemes vary, with *a b c b* and *a b a b* still the ones most commonly encountered in a quatrain (58 percent and 33 percent respectively). However, in a majority of instances, no two quatrains in a stanza employ the same design.

Even more than the verse, the chorus is likely to have an individual rhyme scheme, for example, the *c c c d* of "Down by the Old Mill Stream" (1910) by Tell Taylor and the *a a b a a a c a* of "In the Shade of the Old Apple Tree," words by Harry H. Williams, music by Egbert Van Alstyne.

Notice the elimination of the separation between verse and chorus. Earlier, there was normally no lead-in from verse to chorus; now at least 85 percent of the sentimental songs give the verse an inconclusive ending, which serves as a musical introduction to the chorus. The typical verse with a lead-in requires completion in the chorus, closing with a phrase like "He said as he wandered" or "She cried out in pain," and the chorus supplying what is said or cried out. Thirty-five percent of the songs also have an inconclusive musical ending, mostly V^7 of V–V.[7]

Another change is in the gender of the protagonist. Most older sentimental songs had a male protagonist. Now less than half (46 percent) are clearly male in orientation; 15 percent are female. In quite a few (23 percent) the protagonist's gender is not clear; in 14 percent the narrator's gender is ambiguous. Possibly the neutrality was in recognition of the increased number of professional female performers of sentimental songs, and the practical need to fit the protagonist to either sex.

In "Absence Makes the Heart Grow Fonder," both verse and chorus are given eight lines each. The rhyme scheme is surprisingly regular,

TABLE 9.2. Lines in a stanza

Verse	Refrain	
8	8	33% of songs
8	4	25% of songs
4	4	18% of songs
Other		24% of songs

one of alternate lines throughout: *a b a b c d c d*, etc. There are four fairly regular trochaic stresses per line. A musical lead in, V^7 or $V–V^7$, closes off the verse and opens the way to the chorus. An ambiguously sexed "I" is the protagonist. As is usual in songs from the nineties on, the title forms the first line of the chorus and is set to an attractive melodic phrase—thus constituting the "punch."

The punch of "Dear Old Girl" (1903), words by Richard Henry Buck, music by Theodore M. Morse, is extremely effective. The song, with its many downward sliding chromatic semitones, quickly became a favorite with barbershop quartets. The punch at the beginning of the chorus consists of the title tag set to an attention-grabbing chromatic slide: *g' f-sharp' f'*, followed by the wide major-sixth skip upward and graceful return: *g' e'' d'' b' g'*. Also effective is the fleeting harmonic shift to the dominant of the lowered supertonic key to depict the phrase "my broken heart."

As in previous sentimental songs, duple time prevails, although a sizable minority has the verse in 4/4 time and the chorus in 3/4 time. (See Table 9.3.) The key signatures, as of old, tend toward the flat keys, possibly because woodwind and brass instruments in the pit band of a theater were most comfortable in these keys. Nevertheless, one-quarter of the songs are in the key of G. (See Table 9.4.) Tempi remain as before, most songs moving at an *andante* or a *moderato* pace. A few are in a dignified march tempo, and those whose choruses are in 3/4 normally go at a slow-waltz speed (indicated as *Valse Lento*).

Indications of expression and dynamics are sparingly inserted, although the typical composition contains more than heretofore had been the norm. Songs without any expression marks are much fewer than before (53 percent have fewer than four, 40% more than four). That songs continue to practice caution is seen in "Absence Makes the Heart Grow Fonder," in which the prelude has an *mf;* the verse a *p;* the chorus an *mf;* and prelude, verse, and postlude close on a *ritard.*

TABLE 9.3. Time signatures

Verse	Chorus	
4/4	4/4	46% of songs
2/4	2/4	5% of songs
4/4	2/4	5% of songs
4/4	3/4	27% of songs
3/4	4/4	5% of songs
6/8	6/8	10% of songs
Other		2% of songs

TALE 9.4. Tonality

A-flat major	8% of songs
E-flat major	4% of songs
B-flat major	17% of songs
F major	21% of songs
C major	13% of songs
G major	25% of songs
A major	4% of songs

The design of the prelude and the absence of interludes continue as before, although now almost 75 percent of the preludes are of brief, four-measure length and 25% are of eight-measure length. Fifteen percent of the songs now introduce a two-measure vamp, to be repeated until the vocalist is ready to sing, between the prelude and the verse; 85 percent have no vamp at all, while 15 percent have a two-measure vamp. What is interesting is the disappearance of the postlude: 90 percent have no postlude at all. As far as the public was concerned, once the vocalist was through, so was the song. When a consequent verse was to be introduced by the vocalist, all that was necessary was a couple of get-ready measures in the accompaniment—hence the increase in the use of a vamp, either written out or improvised. An exception is "Mother Was a Lady" (1896), words by Edward B. Marks, music by Joseph W. Stern. Although the expected prelude of four measures deriving from the tune of the verse does occur, the eight-measure postlude based on the close of the chorus melody is rarely encountered.

The great majority of songs assign different melodies to the verse and the chorus, which in most instances are of equal musical length—a striking deviation from time-honored practice. The verse's melody, effective as it may be, is the subordinate one. Thus, once a listener knew both verse and chorus of a song, he need only recall the verse and limit listening to the more engaging chorus if he so desired. Time could be saved, if necessary, or a short attention span conciliated.

Unconcealed borrowing of tunes from extant musical compositions increased somewhat. The advice given by Brett Page earlier in this chapter is followed with a vengeance in one song, the well-received "Red Wing" (1907), words by Thurland Chattaway, music by Kerry Mills. It is given a verse tune that directly plagiarizes the melody to Robert Schumann's "The Merry Farmer," from Album for the Young, opus 68 (1848).

Although the chorus no longer sports a soprano-alto-tenor-baritone harmonization, an unaccompanied vocal-quartet harmonization of this section is sometimes included in the sheet music to accommodate the many amateur and professional quartets, particularly male ones, active during these years. In instances where optional quartet harmonization is omitted, the possibility of improvised vocal harmony was probably assumed.

No prevalent melodic design is evident. However, the verse normally begins on the phrases A and A', each four measures long, then goes on to a B and C phrase, or a B and A phrase. Some are structured A B A' C. More than 50 percent of the chorus melodies are stated as A B A C. (See Table 9.5) "Absence Makes the Heart Grow Fonder" has the following design:

(Verse) A B A C / (Chorus, different melody) A B A C

Measures: 4 4 4 4   4 4 4 4

This song demonstrates that, consciously or unconsciously, the careful shaping of a melody of considerable charm distinguishes the best of the sentimental tunes, both those of the verse and of the chorus —however much the chorus melody is considered the more important of the two. The verse melody is given a rhythmic half-phrase pattern of six even eighth notes followed alternately by a quarter to a half note or by a half note and quarter rest. Measures 2 and 3 of the verse recall the Hart P. Danks melody to "Silver Threads Among the Gold" (1873).

One hears beauty and grace in the winding of the first half-phrase around the tone a', only to light on the tone below, g', sounding above the pianist's supertonic minor chord, thus giving a delicately mournful shading to the word "lonely" (in the second verse, to "dearer," producing an expressive implication the word would otherwise not have had). The answering second half-phrase mounts from c' to $b\text{-}flat'$ and now at last ends on the awaited a' over a tonic chord.

TABLE 9.5. Some typical melodic-phrase forms

Title	Verse	Chorus (different melody)
"Arab Love Song"	A A' B C	A B A C
"Asleep in the Deep"	A A' B C	A A B C D E
"Beautiful Isle of Somewhere"	A B	A B
"Dear Old Girl"	A A' B A'	A A B C
"Down by the Old Mill Stream"	A B A' C	A B A C
"Mary's a Grand Old Name"	A A C	A B A C
"My Gal Sal"	A A' B C	A B A C
"On the Banks of the Wabash"	A A B A	A A'

The next half-phrase, in its downward descent and close on *e'*, balances the previous one; and the fourth half-phrase first winding around *g'* and at last arriving back on *g'*, above the pianist's dominant chord, is a natural closing response to the first half-phrase. The fifth and sixth half-phrases duplicate one and two. The seventh half-phrase is a variant on the first and migrates more definitely to the key of the supertonic, while the last moves into the dominant key and ends the verse melody on its highest note, a *c''* over the dominant seventh of the home key. The music has been intentionally left up in the air and demands continuation.

The consistent rhythmic half-phrase pattern of the chorus melody is four eighth notes, then two quarter notes, followed by either two half notes or a dotted half note plus a quarter rest. The characteristic curve of each half-phrase is downward, usually ending alternately on a low median note, except in the fourth and seventh half-phrases, in which the closing notes are, respectively, first a high *c''* arrived at by an unexpected upward leap of an octave, then the highest note of the song, a *d''*, reached through an upward leap of a fifth. Balance is restored with the final descent from *c''* to *d'* and the conclusive finish on the tonic. Charming as the melody is, it grows from the same harmonic progressions as those in the verse, giving the effect of a chaconne to the whole. Obviously, more than passing thought was given to the forging of the music.

Vocal range in the sentimental songs remains the same as before, the span of an octave or ninth prevailing. Melody continues to move mostly stepwise, or through small triadic skips and two-note repetitions. Chromatic notes have increased, though still mostly in the customary raised neighboring tone below and the three-semitone-stepwise configuration. The first measure of the verse in "Absence Makes the Heart Grow Fonder" has a routine chromatically raised supertonic tone as part of a neighboring tone group; less routine is the melodic skip downward of a diminished fourth to the chromatically raised tonic tone.

Completely diatonic compositions are now quite rare. Nonharmonic tones increase, and passing and half-phrase and phrase-length modulations to the dominant, submediant, mediant, and subdominant keys are common. Sudden key shifts to the major key on the lowered mediant and submediant are more frequent than in earlier times. One example is found in the verse of "All That I Ask of You Is Love" (1910), words by Edgar Selden, music by Herbert Ingraham, where measure 5 unexpectedly darts from the home key of B-flat major into that of D-flat major. A new element is the fondness for allusions to the key of the supertonic minor. In "Absence Makes the Heart Grow

Fonder," note the verse's measures 1–2, 9–10, 13–14, and the chorus's measures 1–2, 8–10, and 13–14.

ARTISTIC AND SEMIARTISTIC SONGS

From 1866 to 1910, American composers like Edward MacDowell, Ethelbert Nevin, and Amy Beach, who created artistic songs normally, had a great deal of musical training, obtained abroad, usually in Germany, or at home in one of the new collegiate music departments or conservatories of music. Almost always the lyrics existed before the music, usually as written poetic verse.

These musical compositions were published on better paper than that used for Tin Pan Alley songs. Many works were given opus numbers and prefixed dedications. The music publishers issuing such compositions—Arthur P. Schmidt, Boston Music, and G. Schirmer, among them—devoted themselves to issuing mostly artistic compositions, like sonatas, concertos, symphonies, and operas, not what they regarded as ephemeral music for the mass market.

The more popularly oriented firms were not averse to publishing a few pieces aiming higher than the mass market, so long as there was hope that a sizable following might result. Songs of this sort, published from 1867 through 1910, are designated as semiartistic because, although technically well crafted and written by trained composers like Reginald De Koven and Ernest R. Ball, they were created with commercial intent. At the same time, they purported to be the tasteful expressions of individual imaginations. Two good examples are "Oh, Promise Me" (1889), words by Clement Scott, music by Reginald De Koven, and "Love Me, and the World is Mine" (1906), words by Dave Reed, Jr. music by Ernest R. Ball, which was published by Witmark and Sons.

Few semiartistic, and fewer artistic, songs became truly popular, but those that did were often found suitable for performance not only in the circumspect recital hall and sophisticated musical theater but also on the vaudeville stage. This was especially true in the twenty years beginning with 1890, when the crossover of schooled vocalists from opera and musical theater to vaudeville was in the ascendant. Moreover, vocalists appearing in vaudeville were instrumental in promoting songs like those of Carrie Jacobs Bond—"I Love You Truly" (1901), "Just A-wearyin' for You" (1901), and "A Perfect Day" (1910)—and of Ethelbert Nevin—"The Rosary" (1898) and the Irish-dialect

"Mighty Lak' a Rose" (1901). When Oley Speaks set Kipling's poem "On the Road to Mandalay" (1907) to music, a hit resulted because male vaudevillians with chesty voices enjoyed singing it and audiences loved the virile melody, steadfast but contagious rhythms, and vivid harmonies touching on secondary keys.

Those artistic and semiartistic songs that won wide followings shared several important characteristics with the pieces primarily aimed at a mass entertainment market. Shortly after "The Rosary" (1898), words by Robert Cameron Rogers, music by Ethelbert Nevin, came out, Madame Ernestine Schumann-Heink explained why she considered it a "perfect song." In an article appearing in *Bohemian Magazine*, she states:

> The critics may not all agree with me there. But the public is the best critic after all, and the public likes 'The Rosary'; not only the American public, but the German public. . . . The essentials of a really great song are heart interest and beautiful melody. Nobody will deny either to this song. The poem recites a soul tragedy to which the composer has achieved a musical setting, exquisitely conceived in the lyric mood and expressed with simplicity and directness.[8]

Edward MacDowell's "Thy Beaming Eyes" (1890), opus 40 number 3, words by William Henry Gardner; Amy Beach's "Ah, Love, But a Day!" (1900), opus 44 number 2, words by Nelle Richmond Eberhart; and Charles Wakefield Cadman's "At Dawning" (1906), opus 29 number 1, words by Robert Browning, are three other art songs that achieved public acclaim owing to "heart interest" in the words and "beautiful melody" as the most important element of their music. All of them evoked fullness of feeling through rich harmonies, supple rhythms, and apt accompaniments.

Assuredly, whether artistic or semiartistic, those compositions achieving popular acceptance had kinship to sentimental songs. Concerning semiartistic songs, Wickes stated that they almost always deal with love or, to a lesser extent, with some aspect of nature. But love is projected "in a chaste form—and the writers strive to employ phrasing that will appeal to educated persons, as well as to the little factory girl." Concrete scenes are absent in songs of sentiment, the writer letting the hearer's imagination take over. Indeed, the words may make no particular reference to a physical situation and the protagonist "just sings as if he were talking to his sweetheart, oblivious of his surroundings."[9]

Love was not the only fitting subject for this sort of song, but it was an extremely popular one. "Waiting!" (1867), words by E. H. Flagg, music by Harrison Millard, depicts a young woman longing for the evening appearance of her lover. Hearing his approaching footsteps, she prays that the stars will shine their brightest and the nightingale sing his sweetest to guide the man she loves to her waiting arms. "Oh! That We Two Were Maying" (1888), words by Charles Kingsley, music by Ethelbert Nevin, portrays the longing of one lover for an unsunderable joining with a beloved, during the joyous time of youth, during days when both become dreamers, and finally during death, when both are "at home with God." "Love Me, and the World is Mine" contains the impassioned thoughts of a lover to whom "All the joys the world may hold dear, / Lands and wealth untold, dear, / Seem as naught compared to you. . . . / I only know I love you, / Love me, and the world is mine."

The design of the text in the artistic and semiartistic songs is similar to that of the sentimental pieces. Yet, individual touches are more evident and set forms more in abeyance. In two respects, less irregularity exists—in the laying out of the prosodic meter and the end rhymes. Refrains are rare, employed only in some of those atypical compositions that affect vernacular speech or assume a folk tone. Notwithstanding that the punch is absent, songs immersed in emotion tend to communicate the equivalent of punch in their end-climaxes. These are approached by an ecstatically rising vocal line, a crescendo to f or ff, a stream of unstable chords, a thickening harmonic texture, and a *rallentando*. In this regard, note the climax in "Love Me, and the World Is Mine" on the phrase "I only know I love you."

Time signatures are mostly duple, in 4/4 time. However, eighth notes in triplet groupings are common, at times so persistent as to give the effect of 12/8 time (or a switch to 12/8 time occurs, as in the refrain of "Love Me, and the World Is Mine"). Keys tend even more to the flat side than they do in sentimental works, 10 percent of them in D-flat. Although versions of the songs dealt with in this section were issued in from two to four keys to accommodate different voice ranges, most versions remain on the flat side of the circle of keys. This places in abeyance the earlier surmise that the predominance of flat keys is entirely in response to the requirements of a pit band, since most of these songs were conceived primarily in terms of voice and piano. "Love Me, and the World is Mine," whose C-major version is reproduced in this book, is also available in the keys of B flat, E flat, and D flat; the vocal range is a tenth. As with this piece, the availability of different key transpositions is critical, since the typical vocal range of a song exceeds the octave, sometimes expanding to the thirteenth in "Waiting."

Preludes are always present; less often, postludes. Interludes may be inserted to connect the customarily written-out later stanzas of what are, in most instances, essentially strophic works. Expression indications inserted as symbols, words, and phrases show a marked increase. Those songs, like "Mighty Lak' a Rose," which hew to simplicity, in response to the nature of the text, deliberately eliminate almost all expression marks, as they do chromaticisms and elaborate accompaniment. Songs replete with strong emotion exhibit the full gamut of expressive directions. "Oh, Promise Me!" contains numerous dynamic modifications from *pp* to *ff*, accent marks, *crescendos* and *diminuendos, rallentandos*, and instructions like *pesante, semplice, con tenerezza, poco rubasto, con forza*, and the voice rises to an end-climax: *largamente e con passione*.

For the most part, one sees some increase in chromatically altered melody, more increase in the complexity and variety of chord formations and in excursions to tonalities other than the home one, and increased technical and interpretive demands made on vocalist and accompanist. "Love Me, and the World Is Mine" shows these changes. Nevertheless, the telling music evolves with a naturalness and sense of direction that establishes it as the result of both creative talent and craftsmanship. That it may not suit some late-twentieth-century tastes is neither here nor there. Sophisticated and unsophisticated Americans alike sincerely valued it at the beginning of this century, and critics should be careful of quality judgments based on a latter-day set of premises or ones betraying a European art-music orientation.

The musical design in these songs is so variable that it is not easily summed up. However, the most-favored one is a sixteen-measure, A A B C structure. "Love Me, and the World is Mine" has a sixteen-measure verse, A A' B B' in 4/4 time, and an eight-measure refrain stated in two different musical phrases in 12/8 time.

WALTZ SONGS

Up to the eighties, American songs in 3/4 waltz time were out of the ordinary. However, precursors to the waltz were written by composers like Will S. Hays ("Nobody's Darling," 1870) and Septimus Winner ("Der Deitcher's Dog," 1864, and "Whispering Hope," 1868). During the eighties, songs in 3/4 time increased. From 1890 to 1910 they constituted an important genre of popular music.

Beginning around 1780, the waltz was known as a Central European couple dance. In the nineteenth century Viennese musicians, especially Joseph Lanner and the Strauss family, urbanized the dance and were instrumental in its spread to all European countries.[10] Johann Strauss the Second was invited to the Boston Peace Jubilee of 1872 and conducted his waltzes in Boston and New York City before admiring American crowds. During the seventies, well-received operettas by Gilbert and Sullivan, Franz Von Suppé, Jacques Offenbach, and Johann Strauss the Second were mounted by companies that toured the principal cities of the United States.[11] Music in triple time was much in evidence.

The huge influx of German migrants, beginning in 1848, helped to further the cultivation of the waltz. Among them were musicians who immediately joined bands and orchestras as players and conductors—whether in symphony, opera, theater pit, or variety-hall ensemble. Their tastes influenced programming and, coupled with the preferences of German-Americans—who now formed an important segment of the audience—the increased performance of waltzes was ensured. The earlier songs in triple time by Septimus Winner were certainly indebted to the Central European waltz. The several popular American waltz songs in praise of beer drinking looked to Central Europe for their inspiration. A German brass band playing in the street is supposed to have influenced the writing of "The Band Played On" (1895), words by John F. Palmer, music by Charles B. Ward.

The extraordinary American popularity of "Daisy Bell" (1892), by British composer Henry Dacre, and of "After the Ball" (1892), by Charles K. Harris, encouraged a firmer fixation on songs in triple time. The verse of "After the Ball" is in duple time; the chorus alone is in waltz time. There is more than a casual connection between "Daisy Bell's" tune and that of "The Sunshine of Paradise Alley" (1895), words by Walter H. Ford, music by John W. Bratton. The Harris song, when its sheet-music copies began to sell in the millions and its triple-time chorus tune was on everybody's lips, encouraged other songwriters to produce hundreds of imitations.

From what has just been said, it should be evident that American musical traditions had slight connection with the waltz song. This is an important reason why the genre frequently seems to hark back to European antecedents, to show few of the quirks that distinguish the sound as American, and to remain cautiously within standardized parameters.

Like the sentimental songs, most American waltz songs written in the nineties and first decade of the twentieth century (63 percent) have two stanzas, each consisting of a verse and refrain, marked "Chorus";

32 percent have three stanzas. About one-half (47 percent) of the songs are given an eight-line verse and an eight-line chorus, a much greater number than in sentimental songs and indicative of the increased importance of the latter; 18 percent have an eight-line verse and four-line chorus, and 12 percent have a four-line verse and chorus. End-rhyme schemes, prosodic meter, and stresses per line are essentially the same as those in sentimental song.

On the other hand, a larger number of waltz songs, around one-third, have no lead-in whatsoever from verse to chorus, and only 45 percent employ the harmonic lead-in of V^7 of V to V^7.

A surprising one-half of the verses have a narrator of undefined gender, although the chorus may feature a male (11 percent) or female (7 percent) "I." Interestingly, this feature will also appear in the march song. (See Table 9.6.) The title-tag always appears in the chorus, in the first line and frequently in the last.

"Let Me Call You Sweetheart" (1910), words by Beth Slater Whitson, music by Leo Friedman, has the anticipated two stanzas, each a thirty-two-measure verse of eight lines and a thirty-two-measure chorus of eight lines. The protagonist, speaking in the first person singular, is of unidentified gender. The verse's end-rhyme scheme is *a b a b c c c a;* the chorus's, *a b c b d b a b* (the *b* of the chorus rhymes with the *a* of the verse). The title-tag opens and closes the chorus.

The music of the American waltz songs tends to be more conservative and adheres more to a norm than that of the other contemporary popular-song genres. It has the fewest syncopations, chromatics, and harmonic variety within a key. In addition, secondary-key allusions, expressive indications and dynamics, and accompaniments of more than blandly supportive significance hardly ever occur. Predictably, regular rhythmic motion and an unfaltering beat unrelieved by flexibility in melody or tempo enhance the great family resemblances from song to song. The worst examples sound dreadfully tedious. Yet, the music in the better waltz songs does have a dreamlike charm. Earthiness is kept at a distance. Monotony is

TABLE 9.6. Gender in songs

Verse	Chorus		
third person	male "I"	11%	of songs
third person	female "I"	7%	of songs
third person	third person	33⅓%	of songs
male "I"	male "I"	33⅓%	of songs
male "I"	female "I"	6%	of songs

replaced by hypnotic involvement, as if the listener were a participant in a formal ceremonial.

Choice of keys goes from A flat to A major. (See Table 9.7) The prevalence of the eight-measure prelude based on the verse tune and the absence of a postlude conform to what was seen in sentimental song. Eighty percent of the songs have no vamp before the verse. "Are You Sincere?" (1908), words by Alfred Bryan, music by Albert Gumble, is one of the few with a two-measure vamp. Several songs end their prelude on two measures that, although not so indicated, could be used as a vamp—among them, "After the Ball" and "I Don't Want to Play in Your Yard" (1894), words by Philip Wingate, music by H. W. Petrie. "Let Me Call You Sweetheart," in B flat, has an eighth-measure prelude based on the verse tune, no vamp or postlude.

Most pieces are in a *"Tempo di Valse"* throughout and include hardly any indications of expression. A fairly consistent feature is the repetition of the chorus, performed first *piano* and then *forte*. "The Band Played On" is unusual for its prelude in 4/4 time marked *"Marcia,"* verse in 2/4 time marked *"Allegretto,"* and chorus in 3/4 time marked *"Valse."*

"I Don't Want to Play in Your Yard" asks that its 3/4 time be performed in the *"Tempo di Mazurka."* This reminds me of a comment once made by Allan Dodsworth, the outstanding dance master of late-nineteenth-century America, that the American version of the dance, known as the Boston waltz, may have descended from the Bohemian *redowa*, a dance very much like a mazurka but much "subdued." Philip Richardson, who reproduced Dodsworth's observation, also stated that the "Boston" version was an important subdivision of the waltz and well known in Europe. He quoted from *Punch*, as follows:

What our Waltzing is coming to:

Distinguished Foreigner: "Voulez-vous me faire

TABLE 9.7. Tonality in songs

A-flat	major	6% of songs
E-flat	major	6% of songs
B-flat	major	25% of songs
F	major	6% of songs
C	major	19% of songs
G	major	31% of songs
D	major	1% of songs
A	major	6% of songs

l'honneur de danser cette valse avec moi, Mees Matilda?"

Miss Matilde (an accompanied waltzer): "Avec plaisir, Monsieur. Quelle est votre forme: le 'Lurch de Liverpool,'' le 'Dip de Boston,' ou le 'Kicke de Ratcliffe Highway'?"

Richardson goes on to say that the Boston version was danced in Paris, where it was known as the "Valse Boston" and regarded as a "smooth delightful dance of a skating nature."[13]

"Let Me Call You Sweetheart" is in a *Moderato* tempo, has only a handful of expressive marks, and contains the *p-f* repeated chorus of the regulation waltz song.

Thirty-two measures is the usual length of both the verse and the chorus, even when fewer or more than the normal eight lines form the stanza. So it is, for instance, with the four-line chorus of "In the Baggage Car Ahead" (1896) by Gussie L. Davis. However, the sixteen-line verse given sixty-four measures of music in "In the Baggage Car Ahead" is most unusual.

The favored melodic structure of the verse is A A B A, and of the chorus (to a different tune), A B A C. (See Table 9.8) "Let Me Call You Sweetheart" has a nonstandard verse form:

Structure:	(Verse) A B C D / (Chorus) A B A' C
No. of Measure:	8 8 8 8 8 8 8 8

Typical melodies move by small skips and stepwise motion, show a chary use of chromatics, and employ a voice range limited to the octave or ninth.

TABLE 9.8. Melodic-phrase forms

Verse	
A B A C	27% of the songs
A B A B	13% of the songs
A B C D	7% of the songs
A A B A	34% of the songs
Other	19% of the songs
Chorus (different melody)	
A B A C	31% of the songs
A B A B	13% of the songs
A B C D	13% of the songs
A A B A	13% of the songs
Other	30% of the songs

Harmonic variety, modulations, nondominant diatonic and chromatic seventh chords, and augmented-sixth chords are much less in evidence than they are in sentimental songs. When secondary dominants occur, they make the expected references to the dominant, subdominant, submediant, and mediant keys. Also significant, as it was in sentimental songs, is the new tendency to move into the key of the supertonic. This takes place in "After the Ball," "In the Baggage Coach Ahead," and George M. Cohan's "Forty-five Minutes from Broadway" (1905).

In most songs, the right hand of the piano accompaniment plays the tune while the left plays the customary "oom-pah-pah" of the waltz. In "Let Me Call You Sweetheart," the right hand not only plays the tune but also the second- and third-beat chords of the accompaniment, not a normal practice. "After the Ball" divides the accompaniment between both hands and allots the tune to the singer alone, as does most of "The Sidewalks of New York," save for six measures at the end of the verse and the chorus, in which the right hand is briefly allowed the melody.

Those waltz songs with a special vogue reveal characteristics, however derived from commonplace practices, that helped explain their popularity. For example, in "Let Me Call You Sweetheart" notice the verse melody's easy lilt of half-to-quarter note in half-phrases one and three. This is contrasted by the dotted-half note braking applied in half-phrases two and four, which relieve the otherwise jingling rhythm. The half-to-quarter tone lilt continues for the second half of the verse, making the slowing-up of the last four measures quite an effective contrast. The handling of the descending half-phrases, is masterful, ending on f', a', and f', then on a rise to d''.

The second half of the verse melody balances off the first half with a gradual descent from *e-flat''* to g', only to leave the tune up in the air by ending high on c''. The resultant melodic imbalance necessitates a continuation into the chorus. (A similar ending was mentioned for "Absence Makes the Heart Grow Fonder.")

The chorus starts on d', lower than any note of the verse, and remains in a more or less low range for sixteen measures, closing on g' and f', a nice counterpoise to the two closes on high notes of the verse. Then comes a final move from low d' to high *e-flat''* and an ending in the middle range, on *b-flat'*, which the listener senses to be absolutely right.

Although commonplace in contemporary popular songs, the harmonic coloring in the third and fourth measures of the verse (V^7 of iii to the second inversion of I) answered by measures six to eight (a diminished-seventh chord functioning as a dominant of iii to V^7) is most attractive. So also is the consequent pronounced move into the keys of the submediant and the dominant and, toward the end of the verse, the swift repetition of both these key references leading to a logical conclusion on the V^7 of the home key. The pleasantly free swing, up and down, of the chorus melody's phrases catches one's attention and boosts the tune's agreeability. As is so often the case with popular music, and particularly a waltz song, there is little else one can honestly add to justify a liking for the chorus tune. The listener just knows he fancies it, without being able to put a finger on the reason.

COON AND RAG SONGS

The quintessentially American song discussed here did not suddenly appear new-minted and full-blown in the nineties. Assuredly, the comic minstrel song born in the late 1820s was a predecessor. Although in a pseudo–African-American dialect and having a fictive African-American as protagonist, this earlier music grew mostly out of British-American traditional dance music. Often the texts were offensive and demeaning to African-Americans; nevertheless, the general public found the music attractive. Tempos were sprightly; duple time was used exclusively; tunes tended toward the angular and skipped around more than those of sentimental ballads; mild syncopations might appear. The minstrel song continued in popularity through the seventies.

Even as the minstrel song waxed strong, one American composer-pianist, Louis Moreau Gottschalk (1829–69), took an active interest in the music and dance he heard and saw in his native New Orleans, executed by its African-American and Creole-French inhabitants and by visitors from the West Indies. Several of his celebrated piano pieces, which tried to capture what he heard, anticipate the cakewalk, coon song, and rag music of the nineties—*Bamboula* (1849), *Le Bananier* (1850), *Le Banjo* (1855), and *Réponds-moi* (1861). Interestingly, *Le Banjo* quotes the tune of "Camptown Races," a Stephen Foster minstrel song from 1850. Moreover, given precedents like the well-received Gottschalk compositions, one should not be surprised to discover that several of the coon and rag songs have a perceptible Latin flavor. For example, "Under the Bamboo Tree" (1902), by Bob Cole, James Weldon Johnson, and J. Rosamond Johnson, and also "Big Brown Booloo

Eyes" (1908), by Eddie Leonard, have choruses whose melodic syncopations are supported by a *habañera-tango*–like accompaniment.

James Ford asserted that the equivalent of coon and rag music was
played by African-Americans before its surge into prominence in the
late nineties. He said that at a hotel managed by May Irwin's brother,
he got to know Charles E. Trevathan, a Southerner, and "his colored
boy Cooley." Charles Trevathan, a sportswriter,

> devoted much of his time to re-making the words and music of the
> songs that Cooley picked up in the more disreputable resorts of his
> race. Master and man worked well together and many a time I have
> heard the former say: "Ah feel awful cur'is this mawnin' "; Ah feel
> so cur'is that Ah don't want to go to work. Cooley, go get the banjos
> an' we'll rag a coupla songs."
>
> The two would play together. . . . I often listened to them with-
> out suspecting that rag-time was being created by their nimble
> fingers. It was thus that I heard the "Frog Song," the "New Bully,"
> and "Crappy Dan," long before Miss Erwin gave them their great
> vogue.[14]

The African-American vaudeville entertainer Tom Fletcher stated
that Ernest Hogan told him he first heard the tune for "All Coons Look
Alike to Me" (1896) in Chicago's red-light district, played by a pianist
who seemed "very blue." The words and tune haunted Hogan. Apparently a girlfriend had rid herself of the pianist, saying "All pimps look
alike to me." Hogan availed himself of the words and music, modifying
both in the verse but keeping the original music intact in the chorus.
Hogan said to Fletcher: "Son, we have been called every name under
the sun, so I added another. The coon is a very smart animal, so I gave
the song the title *'All Coons Look Alike to Me.'* "[15] Much to Hogan's
chagrin, when the song became extremely popular, most other African-
Americans found the title insulting.

Yet, going beyond the obvious racial aspersions and dialectical
speech patterns, and perhaps in part owing to their low-life origins,
songs like the above injected a fresh, and sometimes raunchy, spirit of
humorous satire into lyrics. One could even say that the employment
of defective sentence structures and vulgarisms reflective of these
shady origins liberated speech from the rigidities still found in the
sentimental lyrics, even as the cynical and occasionally violent protagonist, who thought and acted contrary to what society considered
proper, liberated American mores from the sometimes hypocritical
stances depicted in many serious songs. Blackface surrogates for the
American public were free to depict a world that was dingy and risky.

They pricked audiences with their nonchalant treatment of physical and mental suffering and dismissal of weighty sentiment.

Another influence on the coon and rag song was the schottische dance, which Allen Dodsworth claimed he inaugurated in the United States in 1849. After it was adapted to American tastes, it found its way back to Europe in the late eighties, where it was known as the "Military Schottische, or Barn Dance." In duple time, with a marked pulse, and more rhythmic than the polka, it is detected in the usual ragtime dances of the nineties, which Pauline Norton claims were syncopated restatements of the same tunes as those used for the Americanized schottisches.[16] Bearing her out are the many schottische versions of rag songs that Tin Pan Alley's publishers advertised as available for purchase. Interestingly, the sheet-music cover of "A Hot Time in the Old Town Tonight" describes it as both a march and a "Schottische."

A more obvious source was the two-step march, especially the kind composed by John Philip Sousa. In 1889 the American Dancing-Masters' Association launched the two-step dance, a modified galop, using Sousa's *Washington Post March* as the musical exemplar. Sylvia Dannett and Frank Rachel, in their book *Down Memory Lane*, said the "music caught on immediately. It was lively and different with a new kind of beat, and the fickle public cast aside the old quadrilles and glides and reels in favour of a new style of dancing. . . . The two-step remained the vogue for a long time because of the ninety-odd marches Sousa wrote for it in rapid succession."[17] The majority of coon and rag songs are in a moderate two-step march tempo. The sheet-music cover of "At a Georgia Camp Meeting" (1897) by Kerry Mills carries a typical legend on its cover: "A characteristic march which can be used effectively as a Two-Step, Polka, or Cake-Walk."

An important antecedent was the cakewalk, a dance that, when wedded to the two-step, constituted the essential musical character of many a coon and rag song. It arose from the prancing, backward leaning, strutting "walk" taken up and practiced by rural Southern African-Americans competing for a prize, the "cake." For years, minstrel-show entertainers had been adepts in the performance of dance steps reminiscent of the cakewalk. During the Centennial of American Independence celebration at Philadelphia in 1876, a plantation scene was featured in which African-Americans demonstrated the unadulterated cakewalk. The next year Harrigan and Hart did a stage skit entitled "Walking for Dat Cake, an Exquisite Picture of Negro Life and Customs." The First Annual Cakewalk Jubilee, of 1892, testified to the dance's growing popularity. It was a three-night contest held at Madison Square Garden for prizes. The next year, two black vaudevillians, Charlie Johnson and Dora Dean, won acclaim for their cakewalk dancing in *Creole Show*. In 1894, Billy McClain and Nate Salisbury organized an all–African-American extravaganza, put on in Brooklyn and Boston, which ended with an impressive cakewalk contest. In 1898, Will Marion Cook mounted his wildly successful musical *Clorindy, the Origin of the Cakewalk*, for which he wrote the music.[18]

By the late nineties the cakewalk had become an American social dance accepted on all levels of society. Witness Bert Williams's tongue-in-cheek letter to William K. Vanderbilt, which stated:

> In view of the fact that you have made a success as a cake-walker, having appeared in a semipublic exhibition and having posed as an expert in that capacity, we, the undersigned world-renowned cake-walkers, believing that the attention of the public has been distracted from us on account of the tremendous hit which you have made, hereby challenge you to compete with us [he and his partner, George Walker] in a cake-walking match.[19]

To give a second instance, in a letter to his son dated November 27, 1899, Ethelbert Nevin stated that he was given a birthday party during which the people present, twelve women and one man, participated in performing in costume a "surprise cake-walk for me."[20]

By this time, songs were appearing with the word "cakewalk" in their title, as in Ben Harney's "The Cakewalk in the Sky" (1896), or with music said to be characteristic of the cakewalk, as in Kerry Mills's "At a Georgia Camp Meeting" (1897). The music to the Mills song has a 2/4 time signature, "Tempo di March," and exhibits the usual melodic syncopations and "oom-pah oom-pah" accompaniment associated with the cakewalk dance and most coon and rag songs (see Figure 9.1, Some Rhythms Taken from Syncopated Melodies).

Compositions known as coon songs began making their appearance in the eighties, the two most famous being Jacob J. Sawyer's "New Coon in Town" (1883) and Sam Devere's "Whistling Coon" (1888). The latter song, however, still resembled the earlier minstrel song more than the coon songs of the nineties. Tonic and dominant chords make up the nonmodulatory harmony; chromatic alterations are absent from the melody; rhythms are mild rather than strong.

Hattie Starr's "Little Alabama Coon" came out in 1893. In 1896 two hit songs confirmed the popularity of this sort of composition—Hogan's "All Coons Look Alike to Me" and Charles E. Trevathan's "May Irwin's 'Bully' Song." Because of their laughter-provoking dialect, purporting to be that of African-Americans, and their clownish and coarse characterizations, such compositions offended many African-Americans. Witness the comment made by James Weldon

Johnson (who, with Bob Cole and his brother J. Rosamond Johnson, wrote "Under the Bamboo Tree," one of the big hits of 1902):

> The Negro songs then the rage [1899] were known as "coon songs" and were concerned with jamborees of various sorts and the play of razors, with the gastronomical delights of chicken, pork chops and watermelon, and with the experiences of red-hot "mammas" and their never too faithful "papas." These songs were for the most part crude, raucous, bawdy, often obscene. Such elements frequently are excellences in folk-songs, but rarely so in conscious imitations.[21]

Tom Fletcher disagreed with this assessment. He said Hogan's song brought the music of African-Americans into the open and made easier the careers of songwriters like Irving Jones, Chris Smith, Ted Bowman, Lawrence Deas, Jack Wilson, Al Johns, Elmer Bowman, Walter Smart, Burt Grant, Al Brown, Tom Lemonier, Williams and Walker, Bob Cole, Billy Johnson, and Will Marion Cook. In the midst of bad economic times for African-Americans, it paved the way for highly profitable "colored shows" that "blossomed like mushrooms [sic]." Soon white Americans were also writing coon songs.[22]

Coon compositions were sung by African-American performers and "great white blackface comedians," among them Lew Dockstader, Press Eldridge, and Neil Moore. Because amplifying microphones were yet to be invented, anybody who sang one of these songs had to cry it out at the top of his or her lungs; hence the sobriquet of "coon shouter." Both Fletcher and Hogan considered coon and rag song to be one and the same. Hogan, talking to Fletcher about "All Coons Look Alike to Me," said:

> That one song opened the way for a lot of colored and white songwriters. Finding the rhythm so great, they stuck to it changing the lyrics, and now you get song hits from my creations without the word "coon." *Ragtime* was the rhythm played in back rooms of cafes and other such places. The *ragtime* players were the boys who played just by ear their own creations of music which could have been lost to the world if I had not put it on paper.[23]

A large number of Americans from every walk of life were partial to coon songs, despite the contention of scandalized cultural leaders that such works were immoral, tasteless, and brutish. Note Henry Clay Barnabee's statement about Alice Nielsen, when she was a member of Barnabee's company and before she went into grand opera:

> Nearly every night, after a late supper, she would come to our [Barnabee's and his wife's] room, take a seat in a rocking chair, and sing to us Irish and "Coon" melodies. . . . She has now [1912] come into her own and is singing in Grand Opera with great and deserved success, for which I am very glad, but I shall remember the "Little Alabama Coon" long after "La Boheme," "Madama Butterfly" and the like are slumbering in unremembered silence.[24]

After 1900, the racial features abated. Dialect was left out of quite a few songs, among them "Bon Bon Buddy," words by Alex Rogers, music by Will Marion Cook, and "Down in Jungle Town" (1908), words by Edward Madden, music by Theodore Morse. The term *coon* started to signify ethnic-Americans other than blacks, as in "Bedelia" (1903), words by William Jerome, music by Jean Schwartz, which the sheet-music cover describes as an "Irish Coon Song Serenade."

From the late nineties on, coon and rag were considered different aspects of the same song style. Several writers seem to have associated the label "coon" with the text and "rag" with the music. They often assigned the identifying name "ragtime" to coon pieces. The *Etude* of October 1898 asserted that the term ragtime was "applied to the peculiar, broken rhythmic features of the popular 'coon' song." In *Metronome* of May 1899, W. H. Arnstead stated:

> Probably the majority of our readers are aware that the most popular music of the day is that known as "ragtime." . . . From New York to California and from the great lakes to the gulf, ragtime music of all styles is the rage. Look at the ballroom programmes for the past season and we find ragtime and other "coon" melodies introduced into every dance where it is practicable.[25]

Ben Harney, a black passing for white, insisted he was responsible for the first rag songs, saying he had performed rag pieces in the late eighties that he did not publish until the nineties, among them his "You've Been a Good Old Wagon But You've Done Broke Down" (1895) and "Mister Johnson" (1896).[26] Yet, he failed to make clear what distinguished these from coon songs. Indeed, the sheet-music title page of "Mister Johnson" identifies it as "A Coon Novelty."

James Weldon Johnson connected rag with the music. Johnson was also one of several African-American songwriters who consciously eliminated all offensive matter from the coon lyrics. He explained that rag was the new sound of the late nineties: "The barbaric harmonies, the audacious resolutions, often consisting of an abrupt jump from one key to another, the intricate rhythms in which the accents fell in the most unexpected places, but in which the bet was never lost, produced a most curious effect," and had "a peculiar heel-tickling, smile-provoking, joy-awakening charm."[27]

Both Johnson and William C. Handy insisted that the spiritual was an influence on rag. For example, Johnson, an educated musician, explained that when he was writing "Under the Bamboo Tree," he made free use of an inverted version of a melodic line from the spiritual "Nobody Knows de Trouble I See" and was also influenced by Cécile Chaminades' piano piece *La Lisonjora* in constructing the tunes for the chorus and verse. Handy was convinced that rag was a high-spirited version of melodies from spirituals. Referring back to his own minstrel days, he said that he felt the need then to inject more energy into spirituals like "Git on Board, Little Children" and did so along with hand-claps and gestures, thus producing something akin to ragging.[28]

By the end of the first decade of the new century, the term *coon* had mostly been replaced by *rag*. By then rag was "synonymous with syncopation," wrote E. M. Wickes. No longer was the term confined to songs on African-American subjects. "Now, everything that carries the jerky meter, or an irregular meter that possesses a pleasing lilt, is called ragtime." There was no specific formula for writing rag songs. If the music had enough snap, regular irregularities, pleasing rhythm and melody, and sudden stops and starts, it was liable to be called a rag song.[29]

Recognizing the confusion in the use of the two labels and in order to facilitate discussion, the two will be grouped together in what follows. (At the end of this book is the music for "All Coons Look Alike to Me," as an example of a coon song, and of "Hello! Ma Baby," words by Joe E. Howard, music by Ida Emerson, as an example of a rag song.)

Both songs are in dialect, have two stanzas and eight lines set to a sixteen-measure tune both in the verse and chorus. The lines in "All Coons" usually receive four prosodic stresses each. "Hello! Ma Baby," not conforming to the usual pattern, has a verse in couplets of six plus five stresses, and a chorus with four plus three stresses for the first couplet, three plus three for the second couplet, four plus four for the third couplet, and a final couplet of three plus three. A male "I" speaks in the verse and a female "I" in the chorus of the former; a male "I" speaks throughout the latter.

End rhymes in the verse of both songs are the same; *a b a b c d c d*. The chorus of the former song has the same rhyme for every line save the penultimate one; the latter's chorus rhymes *a b c c a d d d*. Lines 1 and 5 each have an inner rhyme that agrees with the end rhyme. "All Coons" interposes a four-measure "Recitative" between verse and chorus that serves as a verbal and musical lead-in to the chorus. The final verse line of "Hello! Ma Baby" acts as a lead-in to the chorus, as does the harmony accompanying it: V^7 of V to V^7. In both the title-tag, set to an attractively syncopated melodic phrase, opens the chorus. It also recurs at the end of the chorus in "All Coons."

Coon and rag songs almost unanimously confine themselves to two stanzas, the three stanzas of "Under the Bamboo Tree" being quite exceptional. The eight lines and sixteen measures for both verse and chorus prevail. However, one also finds verses in four, six, nine, ten, and twelve lines; and choruses in four, five, six, seven, and nine lines. Also, a surprising number of verses are in twenty-four measures, including the six-line "Bon Bon Buddy," the eight-line "A Hot Time in the Old Town," and the ten-line "Alexander" (1904), words by Andrew Sterling, music by Harry Von Tilzer.

End-rhyme schemes vary from song to song and within a song. What occurs the most is couplet or alternate-line rhyming. Triplet rhyme groups are sometimes seen—"Alexander's" verse appears as *a a b c c b d d e;* "Bill Bailey's" as *a a b c c d;* and "Mister Johnson's" chorus as *a a b a a b.* Prosodic stresses are normally four a line but may vary from two to six, depending on what one's interpretation of a line is. For example, the capitalization of the initial word of a line is an unreliable guide, since it is sometimes left out, or for no apparent reason a capitalization will appear that had been absent in parallel spots. Sixty-six percent of the songs lead into the chorus with a verse-close on a dominant seventh chord. (See Table 9.9.) The male "I" speaks in the chorus of 62 percent of the songs. Considering the number of professional "coon-shouters" who were women, this is surprising. (See Table 9.10) As expected, the title-tag opens the chorus of nearly all of them.

Both "All Coons" and "Hello! Ma Baby" are in 4/4 time and in the key of F major. Nevertheless, one notes the extraordinarily extensive references to the key of the relative minor in the prelude and verse of "All Coons." Neither song makes much use of marks of expression; the former lacks even a tempo indication; the latter is to move at a moderate pace. Both repeat the chorus; and the second time around, the chorus of "All Coons" is to be performed *fortissimo.*

Each song opens on a four-measure prelude sounding an indepen-

TABLE 9.9. Lead-in, verse to chorus

none	27% of songs
Verse-text plus V^7	33% of songs
V^7 only	33% of songs
Verse-text only	7% of songs

TABLE 9.10. Gender in song

Verse	Chorus	
third person	male "I"	54% of songs
third person	third person	15% of songs
third person	female "I"	8% of songs
Male "I"	male "I"	8% of songs
Female "I"	Female "I"	8% of songs
Other		7% of songs

dent harmony-oriented passage, then goes on to a two-measure vamp. Neither interlude nor postlude is heard. A dotted-eighth to sixteenth note rhythmic pattern in the verse melody is common to both, as it is to more than a few songs of the period. The melodic structure in each of the verses and choruses is A B A C. To be noted, also, are the identical two measures that close the first three phrases of "All Coons." More than in sentimental song and waltz song, the melodies repeat tones, leap about, and shift their regular metrical accents, especially in the chorus. That of "All Coons" has scarcely any chromatic alterations. More are present in "Hello! Ma Baby," but mostly in the easily sung form of a raised neighboring tone. Other than the large serving of submediant minor in "All Coons," the amount of secondary dominants introduced are not out of the ordinary for this type of composition. The wide vocal ranges are unanticipated. "All Coons" has a d' to c'' range (a seventh) in the verse, a c' to d'' range (a ninth) in the recitative, and a d' to e'' range (a ninth) in the chorus—which adds up to a total range of a tenth for the entire song, from c' to e''! "Hello! Ma Baby" has an e' to e'' range (an octave) in the verse, and a d' to e'' range (a ninth) in the chorus and for the entire song.

The typical "oom-pah oom-pah" accompaniment can be found in both songs. On the other hand, only in "Hello! Ma Baby" does the pianist's right hand play the tune along with the vocalist. Of great significance is the optional "Choice Chorus, with Negro 'Rag.' Accompaniment, Arr. by MAX HOFFMAN" that is appended to "All Coons." It demonstrates, with no room for doubt, that any coon song (and presumably any song in a two-step march tempo) could be given enhanced rag characteristics by alterations in the music of the accompaniment. Interesting in this regard is the advice given the pianist in "The Cubanola Glide" (1909), words by Vincent Bryan, music by Harry Von Tilzer; when playing the accompaniment, he is told to "rag it."

All of the other coon and rag songs are also in duple time. As with the two songs discussed, the key of F major is the most preferred, but songs can vary in key from D major to A-flat major. The bringing of the relative minor key into unusual prominence, as seen in "All Coons," occurs in a significant plurality of these pieces, among them "Mister Johnson," "Bill Bailey," and "Down in Jungle Town." A lesser number have a verse in one key and a chorus in the key a fourth above (the subdominant). "Creole Belle" and "The Cubanola Glide" furnish two examples.

Moderato is by far the most frequent speed indication. In the typical song, expression indications are meager, indeed even less than in a typical waltz song. Yet, the instruction to perform the chorus softly, then to repeat it loudly, appears in a majority of the pieces. Deciding how fast or slow a "moderate" speed may be required is left to the performer, whose decision is influenced by his or her temperament, the nature of the text, and the necessities imposed by the performance situation. If the tempo veers toward an *Andante*, the impression of a cakewalk is intensified; if toward an *Allegro*, a new-fangled ragtime piano composition is approximated.

A majority of the preludes, normally based on the tune of the verse, far fewer on the tune of the chorus, are in four or eight measures, followed by a two-measure vamp. Preludes with music of their own, as heard in "All Coons" and "Hello! Ma Baby," typify the rest of the songs. There are no postludes.

The A B A [or A'] C melodic form is found in some 60 percent of the choruses—its incidence is twice that in the waltzes. No one form predominates in the verse. Only a few songs share melodic phrases between verse and chorus—for example, in "A Hot Time in the Old Town" and "May Irwin's 'Bully' Song." As might be expected from what was already said about "All Coons" and "Hello! Ma Baby," stepwise progressions are less often seen than in sentimental and waltz songs; repeated tones, skips, and leaps are seen more often. A majority of the melodies sport no, or hardly any, chromatic alterations, however much the underlying harmony may resort to passing modulations. A few melodies, nevertheless, introduce chromatics freely—the tunes of "Creole Belle" and "The Cubanola Glide," to cite two. They are almost always heard as neighboring tones or half-step passing tones.

The vocal range needed for the tunes is amazingly extensive for popular music: 35 percent of the songs require the range of a tenth, 29 percent require the range of a ninth, and 21 percent require the range of a seventh or octave. The remaining 15 percent require the range of an eleventh or higher. As many song melodies have choruses that range wider than their verses as vice versa.

Moreover, one can expect that the tunes to these songs, especially those assigned to the chorus, will utilize one or more rhythmic patterns that contradict the meter, which continues to be strongly delineated in the persistent "oom-pah" of the accompaniment. The most commonly encountered syncopations are reproduced in Figure 9.1. Numbers 1 to 11 are syncopated formulae discovered in cakewalks, coon songs, and rag songs. None approaches the amount and variety of syncopation found in a piano-rag composition like Scott Joplin's *Maple Leaf Rag*. Only in number 12 is there a rhythmic arrangement that belongs most to rag.

Finally, one or two songs contain hardly any syncopations at all. For instance, "Any Rags?" has no syncopations whatsoever in the verse section and only a few mild displacements of the meter in the piano part of the chorus. A similar lack of syncopated rhythms will later characterize Irving Berlin's "Alexander's Ragtime Band" (1911).

Several passing modulations do sound in the average song, and transient references to the key of the supertonic minor are common. Dissonance occurs as the seventh of the home key or a secondary dominant, less often as a diminished seventh, chromatically raised augmented sixth, or a nondominant seventh chord. Out of the ordinary are the extremely chromatic inner voices of the harmony in "Bon Bon Buddy." Also unusual is the constant dissonance and the modulatory series of dominant sevenths in the chorus of "Alamo Rag" (1910), words by Ben Deeley, music by Percy Wenrich:

$$V^7 \text{ of ii / ii}^7 / V^7 \text{ of V / } V^7 /$$
$$V^7 / V^7 / I / V^7 \text{ of vi /}$$
$$V^7 \text{ of ii / ii}^7 / V^7 \text{ of V / } V^7 \text{ of V /}$$
$$V^7 / V^7 / I / I /$$

Accompaniments are more difficult than those of sentimental and waltz songs. In most songs the right hand always or almost always plays the tune. Thus, the complete denial of the melody to the pianist as seen in "All Coons" is exceptional. Assuredly, in several songs the required technical ability was not commanded by an untrained or half-trained instrumentalist. For the right hand to be able to play a syncopated melody along with some harmonic fill-in, and for the left hand to be able to accurately and constantly go back and forth between a low bass note or octave and a higher mid-piano-range chord and also to add brief eighth-note stepwise figures connecting up the melodic half-phrases or phrases, are requirements not found in the sentimental and waltz songs. A glance at "Alexander" or "Alamo Rag" will reveal difficulties beyond the abilities of many musical amateurs. The sometimes-encountered instruction to "rag it" or the option to play a more strongly ragged version of a chorus was, therefore, intended only

1. "All coons look alike to me" (1896)

2. "A hot time in the old town" (1896)

3. "At a Georgia Campmeeting" (1897)

4. "Hello! Ma baby" (1899)

5. "Bill Bailey, won't you please come home?" (1902)

6. "Bedelia" (1903)

7. "Alexander" (1904)

8. "Good-bye my lady love" (1904)

9. "Bon Bon Buddy" (1907)

10. "The cubanola glide" (1909)

11. "Beautiful eyes" (1909)

12. "Cavalier' Rustican' rag" (1910)

for skilled players. Without doubt, the usual home-parlor performer simplified any part that was beyond his or her scope.

....

MARCH SONGS AND OTHER RHYTHMIC SONGS

....

"A good snappy march ballad with an interesting story is one of the most profitable songs known to the music business," wrote E. M. Wickes. "It may deal with practically any subject suitable for song purposes—love, humor, philosophy, war, or any other of wide appeal.... Most performers prefer a march ballad for opening or closing."[30] Certainly, judging from the number of march songs composed in the nineties and first decade of the twentieth century, hundreds of American songwriters sought this profitability. Judging from those songs elevated into hits, the American public demanded, as never before, compositions running the gamut from serious to silly that went to danceable rhythms, whether the piece was typed as a waltz, coon, rag, novelty, or march song. The works dealt with here are in duple time, 2/4 or 4/4, normally performed at a moderately fast speed. They introduce varying amounts of syncopation in melody and accompaniment, thus allying them to coon and rag. Moreover, a good 40 percent of the pieces published from 1900 through 1910 are identical in musical style with rag song. If they had received a "rag song" designation in the sheet music, they would have been so classified in this study: among them, "Give My Regards to Broadway" (1904) by George M. Cohan and "Wait 'Till the Sun Shines, Nellie" (1905), words by Andrew B. Sterling, music by Harry Von Tilzer.

The sheet music of two songs of the kind now discussed are reproduced at the end of this book: "I'm Going to Do What I Please" *(1909), words by Alfred Bryan, music by Ted Snyder; and "Winter" *(1910), words again by Alfred Bryan, music by Albert Gumble. Both songs have two stanzas and eight-line verses set to sixteen measures of music.

The first song has a chorus of twelve short lines set to sixteen measures of music. Grouped together musically are lines 1 and 2 (ten stresses); lines 3 through 6 (eleven stresses); lines 7 through 9 (nine stresses); and lines 10 through 12 (nine stresses). The verse has the end rhymes *a b c b d d e d*. However, as usual in the turn-of-the-century songs, additional rhymes abound within a line. If the verse's rhyme scheme is restated in terms of the given capitalization and into shorter lines, it becomes *a a b c c b d d e e d*.

The question of whether the rather haphazard capitalization to indicate the beginning of a line, as stated in the sheet music, should be followed is, as mentioned before, one that sometimes plagues the researcher. In such instances, solutions must be pragmatic ones, choosing line lengths that seem to make the most sense, given their context. In this song, the chorus's rhyme scheme hinges mostly on the word "please"—*a b a a c a a a d a a b.* The viewpoint is that of a feminine "I." The verse, verbally and musically (V^7 of V to V), concludes with a lead into the chorus. As expected, the chorus opens with the title-tag.

The verse of "Winter" is unique in its two measures each for lines 1 and 2 and for 4 and 5, and a four-measure treatment for lines 3 and 6. Lines 7 and 8 are really not part of the verse-melodic unit but a verbal link between verse and chorus, sung in declamatory fashion above a nondominant supertonic seventh chord moving to a dominant seventh chord. The verse's end rhymes are *a a b c c b d d;* the chorus's, *a b c a a b a a.* The viewpoint is that of a male; the title-tag appears several times in the chorus.

In most ways the rhythmic songs now being discussed have quite a few prosodic characteristics similar to those of coon and rag songs.

These compositions differ from coon and rag songs in the greater incidence of verse-to-chorus linkups. Almost all of them end the verse on the dominant seventh; a majority also have a verbal linkup. They differ as well in their viewpoints. In most the verse is given over to a gender-neutral commentator and only in the chorus does the song resort to the male "I."

Examining the music next, we find that "I'm Going to Do What I Please" is in 4/4 time and the key of C major. Indications of expression are few. The tempo is *"Moderato,"* a single *f* appears in the prelude; the vamp has an *mf;* the verse a *p;* and the chorus is first performed *p* and then *f.* The four-measure prelude sounds the first and last two measures of the chorus tune. A two-measure vamp follows. No interlude or postlude is found. The verse-melody form is A A' B A'; the chorus-melody form, A B A C. The vocalist's music moves by step and also through descending minor thirds in the diatonic verse, and through an upward skip of a fourth in the more chromatic chorus.

Range is *c'* to *c"* in the verse, and *e"* to *d"* in the chorus, making a total span of a ninth. The increased height of the chorus tune is a significant feature of many rhythmic songs. The main secondary key references are to the supertonic and dominant keys. In addition, a great deal of chromatic harmony is heard as added color (nonharmonic passing and neighboring tones). The accompanist performs the tune along with the vocalist. The amount of syncopation found is extraordinary. Indeed, the rhythms are those found in the more syncopated of the rag songs; they illustrate the frequent blurring of categories in the turn-of-the-century compositions.

"Winter" is in 2/4 time and the key of E-flat major. In *"March Time,"* the work's expressive symbols are identical with those of the previous song. The eight-measure prelude utilizes the close of the chorus tune, followed by the expected two-measure vamp. The verse's melodic structure is A B C D, plus a declamatory bridge, E, to the chorus; the chorus's, A B A C. Entirely diatonic, save for one raised fourth tone in the verse melody, the tune does a great deal of skipping by thirds, in addition to its stepwise and repeated-tone motion. Temporary modulations into the key of the supertonic and of the dominant occur in the verse, and passing references to the key of the dominant and mediant occur in the chorus.

Range is *d'* to *d″* in the verse, *e-flat'* to *e-flat″* in the chorus, making a total span of a ninth. Again, one notes the increased height of the chorus. As usual, the accompaniment also contains the tune and, though clearly set up as a march, exhibits a touch or two of rag procedures.

Most of the rhythmic songs share the same musical precedents and reveal similar stylistic characteristics as those of coon and rag songs. European musical influences seem more evident in the rhythmic songs, African-American musical influences in the coon and rag songs.

Major keys from A flat to D are employed, with emphasis on the flat keys and C major. "Big Chief Battle-Axe" has a dual tonality—F minor in the verse and A-flat major in the chorus; "Don't Take Me Home" (1908), words by Vincent Bryan, music by Harry Von Tilzer, also has a dual tonality—F major in the verse and C major in the chorus. (See Table 9.11) The most favored tempos are *March Time* or *Moderato,* meaning moderately fast; the most favored dynamics are a single *f* in the prelude; a *p* in the verse; and *p-f* for the chorus and its repetition.

The preludes are evenly divided, half in eight and half in four measures. Forty percent of them are based on the chorus tune (in this

TABLE 9.11. Tonality in the songs

A-flat major	10% of the songs
E-flat major	11% of the songs
B-flat major	11% of the songs
F major	11% of the songs
C major	22% of the songs
G major	18% of the songs
Dual tonality for verse and chorus	6% of the songs

regard, rhythmic songs differ from coon and rag songs); 25 percent are based on the verse tune, and 30 percent on independent tunes. Fifty-six percent precede the verse with a two-measure vamp, and only 6 percent precede with a four-measure vamp. Thirty-eight percent of the songs have no vamp at all. The melodic structure most favored is A B A C—40 percent for the verse and 50 percent for the chorus tunes. (See Table 9.12) This is followed by A A B A (20 percent of both the verse and chorus tunes). In some songs three long-held tones acting as an anacrusis to the ensuing chorus melody are heard. The practice was evident in the mid-nineties waltz song "The Band Played On." It became more frequent after 1900. Witness its use in the duple-time "'Cheyenne" (1905), words by Harry Williams, music by Egbert Van Alstyne; "I'm Going to Do What I Please;" and "Some of These Days."

Although stepwise melodic movement is more prevalent than in coon and rag tunes, it is frequently interrupted by repeated tones and skips. Several chromatic alterations may be introduced into the melody, usually as neighboring or half-step passing tones, or in response to a passing reference to a secondary key. However, these songs make a full sweep from the extreme chromatics of "Some of These Days" (1910) by Shelton Brooks to the almost completely diatonic "Give My Regards to Broadway." In this particular, pigeonholing them is impossible.

Total range is more modest than in coon and rag, rarely more than an eighth or a ninth. The upward shift in the range of the chorus is

TABLE 9.12. Melodic-phrase forms

Verse	
A A B A	20% of the songs
A B A C	40% of the songs
A B A B	7% of the songs
A A A B	7% of the songs
A B C C	7% of the songs
A A B C	7% of the songs
A A B B	7% of the songs
Chorus (different melody)	
A A B A	20% of the songs
A B A C	53% of the songs
A B A B	7% of the songs
A A A B	7% of the songs
A B C D	7% of the songs
Other	6% of the songs

surprising. Most songs take the chorus melody to a higher level than that found in the verse tune. Possibly a heightened climactic effect was sought after. (See Table 9.13.)

Chromatic alterations in the harmony are usually of the passing and neighboring-tone variety. What secondary-key references there are, in order of greatest to least preference, touch on the dominant, submediant, supertonic, subdominant, and mediant keys. The avoidance of the home key heard in "Some of These Days" is extraordinary. Here the music of the verse modulates to the dominant, the supertonic, the dominant again, then the submediant, and finally cadences in the key of the mediant major. The chorus starts in the mediant minor, modulates to the supertonic, the dominant, the subdominant, the supertonic again, the submediant, and the dominant again. Amazingly, the music does not get back to the home key until the last two measures! On-tune accompaniments are the norm, supported most often by an "oom-pah" base. Compositions can also be found that eliminate the "oom-pah" altogether, one of them being "Coax Me" (1904), words by Andrew Sterling, music by Harry Von Tilzer.

I have already mentioned raglike syncopations as typifying about 40 percent of the pieces. Another 40 percent have some syncopation. The remainder of the compositions, while they must be executed in a vigorous march tempo, have no syncopation at all. Special mention should be made of the typical George M. Cohan two-stepping march song with a hint of rag, as heard in "The Yankee Doodle Boy" (1904) and "You're a Grand Old Flag" (1906). The popularity of Cohan songs like these was so great that a host of imitations followed. For example, Harry Von Tilzer assuredly had Cohan's music in mind when he composed "Don't Take Me Home."

TABLE 9.13. Vocal range in the songs

Verse	Chorus	
6th	8th	6% of the songs
6th	9th	6% of the songs
7th	7th	6% of the songs
7th	8th	13% of the songs
8th	8th	13% of the songs
8th	9th	19% of the songs
8th	10th	6% of the songs
9th	7th	6% of the songs
9th	9th	13% of the songs
9th	8th	6% of the songs
10th	9th	6% of the songs

IN SUMMATION: THE ROOTS OF TIN PAN ALLEY

This book has closed with an examination of rag and march compositions. These works, more than all others discussed in this study, demonstrate the vast changes that took place in popular song since the time of Stephen Foster. What follows recapitulates the most important of these changes and offers conclusions about their nature.

For the most part, songs no longer exhibit the idealism resting on rural-derived values of the older America, as depicted in the conservative songs of around 1870. The world they describe is increasingly urban, with few of the old certainties and securities. Warmth of heart gives way to cynicism; pleasure derived from concern for family and friends, to egoistic hedonism; faith in God and ultimate justice, to skepticism and self-interest. To be sure, a concerned God and selfless love continue to appear in some later songs, but scarcely to the extent that they had appeared in compositions of the seventies. Gone also are the mostly diatonic melodies, straightforward rhythms, and simple harmonies (mostly I, IV, and V) of the older songs.

In short, the transformations that took place in American songs around the turn of the century put considerable distance between them and those of around 1879—in subject, language, lyric structure, and musical styles. The transformed body of songs, which for the most part represented change induced by inescapably altered American conditions, came from songwriters sensitive to the experiences of a major portion of the American population. No intellectualization by an educated minority, no aesthetic theorizing, and no studious examination of the best artistic expressions of other countries formed a part of the shaping. Whatever the sounds of the popular compositions, they group themselves into styles that emanated from the American commonality. When people listened to the music to relax, they listened to their own inner selves.

These changes in song must first be understood as taking place within a larger American context. At some point in its existence, post–Civil War society had to confront reality and attempt to reconcile the true state of things with its dreams and wishes, however uncomfortable that confrontation might be. After 1890 the redefinition of America could no longer be avoided. Scientific doubt was infiltrating all assumptions of how humans acted and why. The Spanish-American War, nascent imperialism, corruption, monopolies, market crashes, workers' exploitation, accelerated immigration from Europe and Asia, haphazard and inhumane urbanization had forced the issue.

Federal and state governments, however reluctant to act, found it necessary to promulgate laws and regulations that introduced order into economic and social life. Observant writers like Stephen Crane, Frank Norris, Theodore Dreiser, and Jack London portrayed contemporary men and women as they actually were. The realistic Ashcan School of artists turned to painting vigorous and not always flattering depictions of the pleasures and vices of contemporary city inhabitants. Inevitably, lyricists and song composers began to respond in similar fashion. By 1900 a many-sided realism had considerably altered the simple visionary symbolism of the earlier song texts. What *is* in the actual world had in large measure displaced what *should be*. It was a change that had to happen.

Especially after 1900, the overly pathetic sentimental ballad had given way to a newer song of feeling that was more cognizant of contemporary conditions. Songwriters decreased the effect of sentimentality through lyrics of greater sophistication, often laced with satire, and music that moved at faster tempo or to the more distinct rhythms of dance. "Some of These Days" is a far cry from "Her Bright Smile Haunts Me Still" and "Over the Hill to the Poor House." Similar transformations occur in the lighter and ostensibly more humorous songs. "The Cubanola Glide" and "Alamo Rag" are quite a contrast to "The Buckskin Bag of Gold" and "Angels, Meet Me at the Cross Roads."

Grant C. Knight, among others, wrote that the nineties were critical years in the cultural history of the United States.[31] During this decade the public in a substantial way became aware of the inconsistencies inherent in its manner of life and exhibited signs of serious disunity in its beliefs. Confusion grew as men and women tried to reconcile trust in traditional doctrines with behavior dictated by what was opportune, however incompatible with ethical principles. On the one hand, Americans tried to uphold established moral standards; on the other, they acted with odious egocentrism. They were alternately swayed or repelled by leaders playing on common prejudices, who lied and promised anything to gain influence. In short, it was an era when self-reproach and a sense of inadequacy existed alongside surreptitious delight in moral transgression and in the doings of unscrupulous men and women of prominence.

Inevitably, the subject matter of the popular songs illustrated this dichotomy, often within the same song. The sometimes misshapen twists and exaggerations in the narrations and emotional content represented the conflicts and contradictions in contemporary life and led to insights about that life. Text after text elaborated themes of importance to the general public. As if seeing an image reflected in a mirror, which in turn is reflected in another mirror, then in another ad infinitum, the public recognized the reality producing the mirrored images and relished the depth of the infinite elaborations. They realized all the while that an artificial contrivance was behind it all.

In addition, everyday contemporary slang and other vernacular modes of speech now made up a large portion of song language once dominated by the pseudo-elevated and sentimental communications of the serious ballad and the concocted speech dialect of the minstrel song. Variegated harmony, chromaticisms, changeable modes and tonalities, dissonance, and syncopated rhythmic drive complicated a musical idiom in which sound had once been stripped down to the essentials of diatonic melody, clear-cut rhythms, and the three most basic triads in a tonality.

Life and the cultural expressions of that life had become far more complex, and this included music. Modes of living grew diverse; so also were the genres of song and the many compositions within each genre. A new restlessness, brashness making no attempt at restraint, and bumptious activity radiated from coon, rag, and march songs. Fewer of the new songs subscribed to the refined and gentle standards of excellence shown by so many of the older songs, and composition after composition inclined more to the low-class and vulgar, paying less obeisance to the aesthetically refined.

The captivation of up-to-date dance rhythms and "swinging" syncopation promised visceral distraction. The lilt of livelier melodies, abetted by a kaleidoscope of shifting harmonies, promised sensuous diversion from routine. More than ever, men and women now favored songs that entertained rather than edified, that addressed their senses rather than their minds.

Several further observations should be made about the songs written from 1890 through 1910 that aimed at the outset to reach a mass public. First, they constituted an individual and identifiably American cultural expression when taken as a whole, yet considerable flexibility occurred within that expression in the way words and music were set forth. At the same time that the music remained consistent with its own stylistic imperatives, it demonstrated again and again its efficacy in indicating a goodly range of human feeling. It delineated significant human situations rarely touched upon in songs originating shortly after the Civil War. (Regrettably, subtleties of expression that the public of the turn of the century could appreciate may elude us, since the distance of time directs our attention to the generalities of sound and not the particulars.) These songs also showed that the contemporary speech of Americans was undoubtedly adaptable for musical setting.

We discovered no sudden breaks with tradition, which would have bewildered the popular-music public. Modifications in sense and sound were not overnight phenomena but a matter of years. Each genre contained its own precedents, fulfilled its own expectations, and telegraphed an overall approach to understanding its musical idiom even as it also marked off the emotional boundaries that it would only cautiously transgress.

Melody was at the center of every song, even the rag song—whatever its rhythmic attractions. Indeed, the complications of instrumental ragtime when transferred to song had to be modified to make the tunes the most prominent element in a composition. Audiences had to go away humming a tune; they could not hum rhythms, however catchy.

The song composer's primary goal always remained to create as attractive a tune as possible. He was unconsciously influenced by the harmonic formulae of the day and the way "things were done," even as he tried to inject freshness into whatever composition he was composing. Compared to harmony and rhythm, melody allowed the most choices to the songwriter, when one considers the possible directions and durations of tones. Similar harmonic and rhythmic structures are seen in one work after another, yet these like structures are capable of generating distinctive melodies that distinguish song from song, elevating one to popularity and another to extinction.

Without question, a decided openness characterized the activities of popular-song composers. Their inclination was always toward becoming more inclusive, not exclusive. In line with this, they overlooked no possibilities for pleasuring the public. Whatever promised to enhance popularity entered the songs. For example, no barrier prevented American tunesmiths from quickly adapting the European waltz for domestic production and use. However much in debt to foreign precedents, the American waltz, certainly in language but also in music, can stand on its own merits. In several of its most favored examples may be found melodic-phrase structures, harmonic progressions, and rhythmic articulations that strike the ear as more American than European. For example, Europeans recognized and wrote about one distinctly American form of the waltz, known as "The Boston," whose internal rhythms and step patterns belonged to the New World.

Songwriters were also receptive to the music and cakewalking of African-Americans, translating both into the coon song. When they observed a growing acceptance of the sound, they introduced a song or two to test the market. Their speculative ventures proved to be money-makers. It follows that the reordering of professional attitudes to this novel kind of music resulted from an assessment of the public's strong support for the new sound. Although widespread prejudice against African-Americans prevailed among white men and women, the characteristic songs and dances of these people from the rural South was clearly a different matter. If they represented a direction that majority taste was taking, there was no arguing with it. Tunesmiths, some of them African-Americans, hastened to issue their own, more commercial reinterpretations. Nevertheless, it is sad to find that however vital the music sounded, the often derogatory texts reflected the prevalent racial stereotyping and bias.

Shortly, the songwriting professionals openly accepted ragtime, which itself represented to some extent the convergence of minstrel, coon, and American march music, even as some self-appointed guardians of morality railed against it (and the coon song, which preceded ragtime by a few years). Songwriters noticed that whatever was said against rag song by a vocal minority, a far larger public willingly listened to it. For the purposes of song, in addition to the previously mentioned need for melodic primacy, the more intricate rag syncopations were modified to make the compositions more accessible and usable. Much is owed to a few African-American musicians who first worked with these striking rhythms, in which the syncopated conduct of melody and harmony was opposed to a steady basic pulse in duple meter. They created a new genre commensurate with the contemporary spirit of the country and a vital influence on the twentieth-century popular music that followed.

No obstructions separated the instrumental march from the popular song. The band compositions of John Philip Sousa, Charles Barnhouse, Russell Alexander, and others had captured the public's fancy. Works intended for performance by woodwinds, brasses, and percussion—not the gentler strings—contained a zest, a lack of ponderousness, and an exuberance of utterance that captured the raw vitality and assertiveness of the nation. Inevitably, march songs containing a similar vitality came from the hands of skilled musicians like George M. Cohan and soon dominated a large segment of the entertainment market.

The slower ballad, probing people's more intimate sentiments and expressing them in smoothly flowing melodies, had always been a specialty of American songwriters going back to the productions of Oliver Shaw and Thomas Wiesenthal at the beginning of the nineteenth century. In the years that followed, others continued to produce them—John Hewitt, Marion Dix Sullivan, Stephen Foster, and George Root, to name four—because Americans continued to demand them.

Songwriters at the turn of the century could not help but be open to this musical tradition of long standing. But now the diversity of themes in the texts and the many different musical ways a song might be articulated made the ballad of 1900 far less predictable than that of 1850.

Finally, despite what was said earlier about the trend toward the musically vulgar in song, the same men and women who might sponsor "Ta-ra-ra-bom-der-e" and "May Irwin's 'Bully' Song" still had aspirations to higher planes. They continued to show a willingness to appreciate more elaborate works aiming at some elevation in thought and feeling, so long as words and music were straightforward in their manner of presentation. An agreeable tune and a nicely expressed sentiment went a long way toward resolving whatever complexities were inherent in the music. Showing a special skill in the creation of songs to fit these special requirements, Ernest Ball, Reginald De Koven, and Carrie Jacobs Bond contributed widespread hits like "Mother Macchree," "Oh, Promise Me," and "I Love You Truly," respectively.

We must conclude that, taken on its own terms, the popular music of the years 1890 to 1910 had considerable merit and satisfied a multitude of human needs. It continues to remain viable, both aesthetically and recreatively, when performed sympathetically and with understanding of the reasons that called it into existence.

What is of the greatest interest, writer after writer on twentieth-century popular music testifies that the music that took form in the years between 1890 and 1910 would continue to be a dominant force through the 1950s. Especially after 1905, and until the advent of rock and roll, it was the song world now known as Tin Pan Alley that kept popular music before the public. The hardening of the arteries that would afflict Tin Pan Alley was still half a century away. For almost fifty years the astute new breed of professionals still had the flexibility to change with the times. For example, when variety succumbed to the onslaught of more novel forms of entertainment—motion pictures, radio, and sound recordings—Tin Pan Alley quickly accommodated itself to the Broadway musical and revue, the Hollywood musical, and the dance bands, which always carried one or more vocalists. Whatever the musical need, Tin Pan Alley stood ready to supply it.

Several of the important songwriters from around 1900 bridged the time from the 1890s to the post–World War I years. Egbert Van Alstyne, who was responsible for earlier hits like "Navajo," "Cheyenne," and "In the Shade of the Old Apple Tree," would also write "Pretty Baby" (1916), "Your Eyes Have Told Me So" (1919), and "Beautiful Love" (1931). Albert Von Tilzer, already famous for "Teasing" (1904) and "Take Me out to the Ball Game" (1908), was also the writer of "I'll Be with You in Apple Blossom Time" (1920). These several compositions exhibit the same beguilingly plain tunes and modest harmonic patterns enlivened by the pulsing movement of dance. All make use of an up-to-date vernacular language that the public found natural and easy to absorb.

Harry Von Tilzer, brother to Albert, issued "A Bird in a Gilded Cage" in 1900, then "When My Baby Smiles at Me" in 1920. He also was the director of a music publishing house and hired Irving Berlin as a song plugger. Moreover, he was responsible for George Gershwin's first published song, "When You Want 'Em, You Can't Get 'Em."

George M. Cohan and Jean Schwartz are two other songwriters that immediately come to mind as continuing to write well-received songs after 1910.

James Maher and Alec Wilder claimed that during the two decades from 1890 to 1910 a tradition of musical professionalism in songwriting gained an ascendancy that would prevail until rock and roll dominated the popular market for music. They also stated that during these twenty years American songs took on and integrated certain native characteristics in lyrics and music that separate them from those of all other nations, thus confirming what has already been said about the American song's distinctiveness. They point out that Ben Harney's "You've Been a Good Old Wagon, But You've Done Broke Down" (1895) and Shelton Brooks's "Some of These Days" would never be confused with any composition emanating from London, Paris, Berlin, or Vienna. The compositions produced by the youthful Tin Pan Alley had a "vigor, novelty, and musical daring" not found in European popular music. These were qualities that would continue in song for the next five decades.[32]

Furthermore, Henry Raynor, an English writer on music, observed that this characteristically American music became an international style in the twentieth century in large part as a reaction to the "negative politeness and lack of vitality" in the European "light music" written after the era of Offenbach, Sullivan, and the Strausses. What had ensued in Europe was an overly mild, unexciting, effete, good-mannered musical speech that grew tiresome alongside the fresh, "natural way of musical speech" coming from the United States.[33]

The turn of the century also witnessed the first professional steps of songwriters who would loom large in the history of popular song after 1920. Jerome Kern had already composed "How'd You Like to Spoon with Me?" in 1905 and "I Just Couldn't Do Without You" in 1907, forerunners of the extraordinary hits he composed for the Broadway musical *Showboat* (1927) and the Hollywood musical *Swing Time* (1936). Although he spent some time in England, Kern would always value the American virtues of simple yet sophisticated melodies that seem to progress inevitably, the informal language natural to the man of the street, and the clear-cut danceable rhythms that were so much a part of the American popular music of his youth. Moreover, the American music world not only honed him as a songwriter but also as a professional man of business. He became an astute overseer of his musical interests, promoting his music where he could and extracting the profits he felt owed him.

Even more astute was Irving Berlin, who is a prime example of the songwriter molded during the earliest years of Tin Pan Alley and continuing as a dominant force in the popular-music world even into the years after World War II. The description of Berlin given by Marilyn Berger might also have fit the older Paul Dresser and several others of his generation when she states that Berlin was a shrewd transactor of business when it came to exploiting his songs and, paradoxically, "also loving, sentimental, generous, and competitive."[34]

For someone coming from a financially impoverished immigrant home, Berlin earned an astonishing $100,000 at age twenty-three, less than four years after his first song, "Marie from Sunny Italy" (1907), for which he wrote the lyrics only. Tin Pan Alley was one of the few places that would have been willing to make room for him, however deficient his background, so long as he could prove he had the necessary talent to produce a hit song.[35] An error was made on the title page of the song, where he was named "I. Berlin" instead of Israel Baline. He retained the "Berlin" and himself decided that "Irving" should replace "Israel" because it was more dignified.

In 1909 he began to write words and music for songs. Two years later, in 1911, he published an out-and-out success, "Alexander's Ragtime Band." From then on, he composed a bewildering number of extremely popular songs. For the next thirty years, whenever writers attempted to explain his success, the excellences underlined were ones necessary to any successful songwriter in Tin Pan Alley, even from its earliest days. For one, he studied the procedures of the prominent songwriters of his youth and analyzed their best songs. In particular, he admired George M. Cohan and loved musical numbers like "Mary's a Grand Old Name" and "Give My Regards to Broadway."[36]

Tony Bennett explained Berlin's genius as consisting of a complete identification with ordinary men and women and putting their dreams and emotions into musical form. Michael Feinstein said that Berlin wrote music the ordinary person wished he could write, and that all the Berlin songs have a "deceptive simplicity." Asked what made his songs popular, Berlin replied: "Popular songs are songs that become popular." He would add nothing further. To him, the public was always right and showed its instinctive sense of what was good by singing and whistling its approval.[37] Again, these comments might easily have come from the mouths of the significant figures of Tin Pan Alley from the 1890s onward.

Descriptions of the Berlin songs also could fit compositions by his songwriting peers, despite the fact that the majority of compositions he wrote equaled or exceeded the best efforts of most other tunesmiths. According to Rupert Holmes, a "whisky-dry fatalism" is found in the song "Let's Face the Music and Dance"; "unsloppy warmth" is injected into "I Got Lost in His Arms"; "absurd optimism" permeates "I Got the Sun in the Morning"; and there is a "children's hymnal feel" to the song "Counting My Blessings," which Holmes says harks back to similar works from the turn of the century. None calls attention to itself, Holmes stated, yet fertile invention is evident in every measure.[38]

Clearly, the approach to composing songs, and the attitudes of the musical professionals concerned with satisfying the larger public once established at the turn of the century, remained viable for half a century. What is even more fascinating, as the end of the twentieth century approaches, musicians and writers on music continue to promote many of the songs discussed in these chapters. In doing their best to speak eloquently to the ordinary men and women of their own time, these earlier songwriters developed modes of communication that remain intelligible to more than a few people of future generations. Ultimately, over several generations a changing public will decide whether the music is of enduring interest. In this conclusion, Tin Pan Alley would certainly have concurred.

ANTHOLOGY OF SONGS

ANTHOLOGY OF SONG

ABSENCE MAKES THE HEART GROW FONDER.

(LONGING TO BE NEAR YOUR SIDE.)

Words by *ARTHUR GILLESPIE*.

Music by *HERBERT DILLEA*.

Andante con moto.

1. Sweet-heart I have grown so lone - ly, Liv - ing thus a - way from you,
2. Has the love that once was dear - er Than all else to me grown cold?

For I love you and you on - ly; Still I won - der if you're true.
Or has ab - sence drawn us near - er, To each oth - er as of old?

209

I re-gret the harsh words spo-ken, That I know have caused you pain,
Prom-ise then you will not sev-er From the ties that bind us two.

And my heart is near-ly bro-ken, Say you love me once a-gain.....
Say you will be mine for-ev-er, Tell me that you still are true.....

ritard.

CHORUS.

Ab-sence makes the heart grow fond - - er, That is why I long for you;....

mf

Absence Makes the Heart Grow Fonder. 3 p.—2nd page. M. W. & Sons. 2290

210

Lone-ly thro' the nights I pon - der, Wond'ring dar-ling if you're true. . . . .

Dis-tance on - ly lends en - chant - ment. Tho' the o - cean waves di - vide, . . .

Ab-sence makes the heart grow fond - er, Long-ing to be near your side. . . . .

ritard.

Absence Makes the Heart Grow Fonder. 3 p.—3rd page. M. W. & Sons. 2296

All Coons Look Alike To Me.

Words and Music by ERNEST HOGAN.

1. Talk a-bout a coon a hav-ing trou-ble, I
2. Nev-er said a word to hurt her feel-ings, I

(vamp till ready)

think I have e-nough of ma own, Its all a-bout ma Lu-cy Jane-y Stubbles, And
always bou't her presents by the score, And now my brain with sorrow am a reel-ing, Cause

she has caused my heart to mourn, Thar's an-oth-er coon bar-ber from Vir-gin-ia, In so-
she won't accept them any more, If I treat-ed her wrong she may have loved me, Like

ci-'ty he's the leader of the day, And now ma hon-ey gal is gwine to quit me, Yes she
all the rest she's gone and let me down, If I'm luck-y I'm a gwine to catch my pol-i-cy, And

Recite.

gone and drove this coon a-way, . . She'd no ex-cuse, . . To turn me loose, I've been a-
win my sweet thing way from town, For I'm wor-ried, . . Yes, I'm des-p'rate, I've been Jo-

-bused, . . I'm all con-fused, . . Cause these words she did say. . . .
-nahed, . . And I'll get dang'rous, If these words she says to me. . . .

All coons look alike to me. 4—3. M. W. & Sons.

213

All coons look alike to me. 4.—4.

Choice Chorus, with Negro "Rag," Accompaniment, Arr. by MAX HOFFMANN.

All coons look a-like to me, I've got an-oth-er beau, you see,

And he's just as good to me as you, nig! ev-er tried to be,

He spends his mon-ey free, I know we cant a-gree, So

I don't like you no how, All coons look a-like to me. me. *8va.*

All coons look alike to me. 4—5.   *8va.*

215

Amber Tresses Tied in Blue.

SONG AND CHORUS.

Words by SAMUEL M. MITCHELL.

Music by H. P. DANKS.

1. Far a-way in sun-ny mead — ows, Where the mer-ry sunbeams
2. Ere the sum-mer days de - part — ed, We had made a sol-emn
3. 'Twas de-creed that fate should part us, Ere the leaves of Autumn

play'd, Oft I lin-ger'd 'mid the clo — ver,
vow, And I nev - er, nev - er wea — ried
fell, And two lov - ing hearts were sev — er'd,

4

Sing - ing to a vil - lage maid;
Kiss - ing her sweet cheek and brow;
That had loved each oth - er well;

She was fair - er than the
She was dear - er than the
She was all I had to

fair - est, Ev - er faith - ful, fond, and true,
dear - est, Pure as drops of morn - ing dew,
cher - ish, She has bade a last a - dieu,

And she wore beneath a bon - net,
And adown her neck was hang - ing
And I see in ev'ry vis - ion,

Am - ber tresses tied in blue.
Am - ber tresses tied in blue.
Am - ber tresses tied in blue.

Interlude after Chorus.

Amber Tresses Tied in Blue.

CHORUS.

Sop.

She was fair-er than the fair - est, Ev - er faithful, fond and true;

Alto.

Tenor.

She was fair-er than the fair - est, Ev - er faithful, fond and true;

Bass.

Piano.

And she wore be-neath a bon - net, Am - ber tress - es tied in blue.

And she wore be - neath a bon - net, Am - ber tress - es tied in blue.

"ANGELS, MEET ME AT THE CROSS ROADS."

SONG AND CHORUS.

By WILL S. HAYS.

INTRODUCTION.
MODERATO.

mf

1.   Come down, Ga - bri - el,
2. I'se libed for months, an I'se
3.   Plant my foot on de
4.   Stand back, sin - ners,
5. Dem an - gels an't got

1 blow	your	horn,	Call	me	home	in	de	ear - ly	morn;
2 libed	for	years,	Can't	get	used	to	my	weep - in'	tears;
3 gold	en	rocks,	Put	my	mon - ey	in	de	mis - sion	box; When
4 let	me	pass;	I	see	de	lane	to	de	house at last;
5 long	to	wait; Dey's	stand -	ing	now	at	de	gold - en	gate, When

Entered, according to Act of Congress, in the year 1875, by J. L. PETERS, in the Office of the Librarian of Congress, at Washington.
9,347—3.

4

1 Send de char - i - ot down dis way, Come and haul me home to stay. O!
2 Lost my way on de road in sin, Wake up, an - gels, pass me in. O!
3 I git dar, an you hear me call, Come on, den, for dar's room for all. O!
4 Come an' jine wid de 'an - gel band, We'll all git home to de hap - py land. O!
5 we git dar, on de tod - er shore, Dey'll go in - side, an dey'll shut de door. O!

CHORUS.

Soprano.

An - gels meet me at de Cross roads, meet me, An - gels, meet me at de Cross roads, meet me,

Alto.

meet me, meet me,

Tenor.

meet me, meet me,

Bass.

Accomp.

Angels Meet Me at de Cross Roads 9,347—3.

An - gels, meet me at de Cross - roads, meet me, Don't charge a sin-ner an - y toll.

Meet me, meet me, meet me, meet me, Don't charge a sin-ner an - y toll.

Meet me, meet me, meet me, meet me, Don't charge a sin-ner an - y toll.

DANCE.

Angels Meet Me at de Cross Roads, 9,647.—3.

HELLO! MA BABY.

By HOWARD and EMERSON.

Moderato.

(Hel - lo! Hel - lo! Hel - lo!

1. I'se got a lit - tle ba - by, but she's
2. This morn - ing, thro' the 'phone, she said her

out of sight, I talk to her a - cross the tel - e - phone;...... I'se
name was Bess, And now I kind of know where I am at;........ I'se

never seen my hon - ey but she's mine, all right; So
sat - is - fied be - cause I'se got my babe's ad - dress,' Here

take my tip, an' leave this gal a - lone............
past - ed in the lin - ing of my hat............

Ev - 'ry sin - gle morn - ing, you will hear me yell, "Hey
I am might - y scared, 'cause if the wires get crossed, 'Twill

Cen - tral! fix me up a - long the line.".......... He con -
sep - a - rate me from ma ba - by mine,. .... Then some

-nects me with ma hon-ey, then I rings the bell, And
oth-er coon will win her, and my game is lost, And

this is what I say to ba-by mine,..........
so each day I shout a-long the line, ...

CHORUS.

"Hel-lo! ma ba-by, Hel-lo! ma hon-ey,

Hel-lo! ma rag-time gal.......... Send me a kiss by

wire,............ Ba - by my heart's on fire!............

If you re - fuse me, Hon - ey, you'll lose me, Then you'll be left a-

- lone; oh, ba - by, Tel - e - phone and tell me I'se your

own. Hel - lo! hel - lo! hel - lo! there own.........................

I had $15 in my inside Pocket.

Words and Music by HARRY KENNEDY.

1. I'm an I - rish - man now don't mind that, For you can't play tag with Pad - dy
2. Oh, the gang they hung a - round the bar, Like a swarm of ed - u - ca - ted

Flynn, In the four - teenth ward I claim my how'ld, But the
mice, Oh they made me drink a "clari - nette" punch And a

gang they play'd me for a skin, They said that they'd make me Al - der - man, Then they
whis - key "San ga - ree" on ice, They stood me on my head, when my wealth gave out, Then they

took me 'round to see Red Bill, We were drink - ing rye - and - rock, till
hung me on a fence to dry, In the ear - ly morn - ing light, for -

four o - 'clock, And they made me po - ny up for all the swill.....
'ninst Judge White, These.. words to him I plain - tive - ly did cry.....

I had 15 dollars in my inside pocket.—2.

CHORUS.

I had fif-teen dol-lars in my in-side pock-et, Don't you see, to me it is a warn-ing, Saturday night I made a call on a friend of Tam-'ny Hall And the div-il a cent I had on Sun-day morn-ing.

I had 15 dollars in my inside pocket.—3

I'm Going To Do What I Please

Words by ALFRED BRYAN

Music by TED SNYDER

Not long a-go......
Folks thought it fun - - ny

I had a beau,........ Folks told me he'd.... nev - er do!......
I kept my mon - - ey Right down where I...... wore my shoes;........

"Get some one nice!"......... Was their ad - vice;............. So I got num - ber
Folks crit - i - cised me, And all ad - vised me Bank it or you...... will

two.................. Short - ly aft - er I cast num - ber one a - side,......
lose!................. When I put the mon - ey in the bank next day,......

He was left a mil - lion, when his un - cle died. Wish that I took...... him,
Cash - ier grabbed the bun - dle and he ran a - way. Now I am bust - ed,

Sor - ry I shook him, That is just why...... I sigh:.............
Sor - ry I trust - ed, That is just why...... I say:.............

Do What I Please

CHORUS

I'm going to do what I please And I don't care who I please just so long

as I please my - - self; I'm going to

go where I please...... I'm going to come when I please, I'm going to

do what I want....... That's me, if you please,...... I'm going to

Do What I Please

Do What I Please

232

Let Me Call You Sweetheart

(I'm in Love with You.)

Music by
LEO FRIEDMAN
and Words by
BETH SLATER WHITSON

Writers of
"Meet Me To-Night in Dreamland",
"My! But I'm Longing for Love", etc.

I am dream - ing Dear of you
Long - ing for you all the while

Day by day_____ Dream - ing when the
More and more_____ Long - ing for the

Copyright MCMX by Leo Friedman, Chicago,— British Copyright Secured.
Copyright Assigned Dec. 13, 1910 to Harold Rossiter Music Co., Chicago.

skies are blue When they're gray; _____ When the
sun - ny smile, I a - dore; _____ Birds are

sil - v'ry moon - light gleams Still I wan - der on in dreams
sing - ing far and near Ros - es bloom - ing ev - 'ry - where

rall

In a land of love, it seems Just with you. _____
You, a - lone, my heart can cheer You just you. _____

rall

CHORUS

Let me call you "Sweetheart" I'm in love with you ___

Let me hear you whisper that you love me too ___

Keep the love - light glowing In your eyes so true ___ Let me

call you "Sweetheart" I'm in love with you. you. ___

235

Respectfully Dedicated to Miss. Sue Smith.

Love Me, and the World is Mine.

3362

Words by DAVE·REED Jr.

In C.

Music by ERNEST R. BALL.

I wan - der on as in a dream, My
My soul soars on to realms a - bove Thro'

goal a par - a - dise must be,____ For there an an - gel waits'twould
mys - tic lands it seems to go,____ As if 'twere borne on wings of

seem, Yet lo, dear heart,'tis on - ly thee. Suns may
love, The love that on - ly an gels know. Your bright

M.W.&SONS 7517-3

4

shine to light my way dear, Wealth be mine for aye dear,
eyes like bea-cons guide me, Thro' the clouds that hide me,

Queens may pledge their rich-es too;_____ Yet the world would still be lone-ly,
Would that they were mine to woo;_____ All the joys the world may hold dear,

With such vir-tues on-ly, Life to me dear, means just
Lands and wealth un-told dear, Seem as naught com-pared to

Maestoso.

you._____ I care_____ not for the stars that
you._____

shine, _____ I dare ____ not hope to e'er be

thine, _____ I on - ly know I

love you, Love me, ___ and the world ___ is mine. ___

Love me, ___ and the world ___ is mine. ___

Over the Hill to the Poor House.

SONG AND CHORUS.

Words by GEO. L. CATLIN.

Music by DAVID BRAHAM.

1. What?
2. Ah
3. It's

no! it can't be that they've driv-en   Their   fa - ther, so help - less and
me! on that old door-step yon - der,   I've   sat with my babes on my
long years since my Mary was tak - en,   My   faith - ful, af - fec - tion - ate

Entered according to Act of Congress. A. D. 1874, by WM. A. POND & CO., in the Office of the Librarian of Congress at Washington.

239

5

CHORUS.

drea-ry,...... And my heart for re - lief vain - ly seeks...... For I'm
loved them,...... But they've driv - en him out in the street.......
born in !...... And now I'm turned out from its door.....

old, and I'm help-less and fee - ble, The days of my youth have gone by;........ Then

o - ver the hill to the poor house, I wan-der a-lone there to die.......

4 Oh, children ! loved children ! yet hear me,
   I have journeyed along on life's stage ;
With the hope that you all would be near me,
   To comfort and cheer my old age :
My life-blood I'd gladly have given,
   To shield and protect you ! but hark !
Though my heart breaks, I'll say it's you've driven
   Me out here to die in the dark.—Cho.

5 But, perhaps, they'll live happier without me ;
   Farewell, dear old home, ah ! farewell,
Each pathway and tree here about me,
   Some memory precious can tell :
Well ! the flowers will bloom bright as ever,
   And the birds sing as sweet to the morn ;
Then over the hill from the poor house,
   Next Spring the old man shall be borne.—Cho.

241

Performing rights reserved

Winter

Words by
ALFRED BRYAN

Music by
ALBERT GUMBLE

March Allegro

Win - ter time is freez-ing time, Teas-ing time and squeez-ing time. That's the
Don't be bash-ful, it's no use; Win-ter time's a good ex-cuse. When you

time to love___ With your la - dy love you go,
want to spoon___ Cud - dle close and hold her tight,

Skim-ming o'er the ice and snow, Sil - ver moon a - bove.
Make her think it's June to - night, Talk of hon - ey moon.

Hear the sleigh bells ring! Hear them ding - a - ling!
Wed - ding bells will ring Some - time in the Spring.

L.H.

CHORUS

Win - ter, Win - ter, When the snow is soft - ly

fall - ing, That's the time to squeeze, when it starts to freeze.

Winter 4

In Oc - to - ber and No - vem - ber and De - cem - ber, just re - mem - ber

Win ter, Win - ter, When your sweet-heart comes a -

call - ing, By the fire - side so bright you'll sit and tease her,

That's the time to squeeze her, when it's win - - ter. ter.

D.C.

Winter
Quartet for Male or Mixed Voices

CHORUS
(Melody in 2d. Tenor or Soprano)

arr. by **RIBE DANMARK**

ΝΟΤΕS

Chapter 1. THE PUBLIC FOR POPULAR SONG

1. For a thorough discussion of American popular song before the Civil War, see Nicholas E. Taws, *Sweet Songs for Gentle Americans: The Parlor Song in America, 1790–1860* (Bowling Green, Ohio: Bowling Green Popular Press, 1980) and *A Music for the Millions: Antebellum Democratic Attitudes and the Birth of American Popular Music* (New York: Pendragon, 1984); also see Hans Nathan, *Dan Emmett and the Rise of Early Negro Minstrelsy* (Norman, Oklahoma: University of Oklahoma, 1962); and Grace D. Yerbury *Song in America: from Early Times to About 1850* (Metuchen, New Jersey: Scarecrow, 1971).

2. *Mark Twain's Letters*, vol. 2, arranged with comment by Albert Bigelow Paine (New York: Harper & Brothers, 1917), 525–28.

3. The first quotation is contained in Stuart Chase, *The Proper Study of Mankind* (New York: Harper & Brothers, 1948), p. 85; the second, in Patrick Maynard, "Depiction, Vision, and Convention," in *Philosophy Looks at the Arts*, revised edition, edited by Joseph Margolis (Philadelphia: Temple University Press, 1978), p. 284. See also John Shepherd, "Introduction," in *Whose Music?*, edited by John Shepherd et al. (New Brunswick, N.J.: Transaction Books, 1977), p. 1.

4. Russel Nye, *The Unembarrassed Muse* (New York: Dial, 1970), p. 2; Daniel J. Boorstin, *The Americans: The Democratic Experience* (New York: Random House, 1973), pp. 104–105.

5. Nicholas E. Tawa, *Serenading the Reluctant Eagle* (New York: Schirmer, 1984), pp. 5–19, 128–32.

6. George Boas, "Vox Populi," in *The Dictionary of the History of Ideas*, volume 4, edited by Philip P. Wiener (New York: Scribner's Sons, 1973), 496–500.

7. Brander Matthews, *The American of the Future and Other Essays* (New York: Scribner's Sons, 1909), p. 243.

8. William Dean Howells, *Imaginary Interviews* (New York: Harper & Brothers, 1910), p. 38.

9. Eugene Field, *The Poems of Eugene Field* (New York: Scribner's Sons, 1916), pp. 8–9.

10. James T. Powers, *Twinkle Little Star* (New York: Putnam, 1939), p. 251.

11. Henry James, *The American* (New York: Scribner's Songs, 1907), pp. 1–2. For a contemporary recognition of the widening chasm between high and popular culture, see Charles Dudley Warner, "What Is Your Culture to Me?," *Scribner's Monthly* 4 (1872), 470–78.

12. Finley Peter Dunne, *Mr. Dooley in the Hearts of His Countrymen* (Boston: Small, Maynard, 1899), pp. 127–28.

13. Matthew Arnold, *Civilization in the United States* (1888; reprint, Freeport, N.Y.: Books for Libraries Press, 1972), pp. 22, 91–92, 172–73, 176–77; James Fullerton Muirhead, *A Land of Contrasts*, 2nd ed. (London: Lane, 1900), pp. 26, 84–85.

14. Henry T. Finck, *My Adventures in the Golden Age of Music* (New York: Funk & Wagnalls, 1926), pp. 86, 252.

15. Alan Trachtenberg, ed., *Democratic Vistas: 1860–1880* (New York: Braziller, 1970), p. 335; James Bryce, *The American Commonwealth*, vol. 1 (New York: Macmillan, 1910), p. 349. See also Max Lerner, *America as a Civilization*, vol. 2 (New York: Simon & Schuster, 1957), 780–82, 785.

16. Herbert Quick, *One Man's Life* (Indianapolis: Bobbs-Merrill, 1925), p. 340.

17. For further information on this aspect of American urban culture, see Nicholas E. Tawa, *A Sound of Strangers: Musical Culture, Acculturation, and the Post–Civil War Ethnic American* (Metuchen, N.J.: Scarecrow, 1982).

18. W. C. Handy, *Father of the Blues: An Autobiography*, edited by Arna Bontemps (New York: Macmillan, 1955), pp. 22–23, 60; John E. DiMeglio, *Vaudeville, U.S.A.* (Bowling Green, Ohio: Bowling Green University Popular Press, 1973), p. 116.

19. E. J. Kahn, Jr., *The Merry Partners: The Age and Stage of Harrigan and Hart* (New York: Random House, 1955), p. 160.

20. Isaac Goldberg, *Tin Pan Alley* (New York: Day, 1930), p. 89; William Moulton Marston and John Henry Feller, *F. F. Proctor, Vaudeville Pioneer* (New York: Smith, 1943), p. 48.

21. Arthur Meier Schlesinger, *The Rise of the City, 1878–1898* (New York: Macmillan, 1933), p. 141; the nature of rural society is described in Pitrim A. Sorokin and Carle C. Zimmerman, *Principles of Rural-Urban Sociology* (New York: Holt, 1929), pp. 115–18, 20, 23, 28, 49, 54, 56–57.

22. Hamlin Garland, *Main-Travelled Roads* (New York: Harper & Row, 1922), pp. 75, 77. The book was first issued in 1891.

23. Hamlin Garland, *Boy Life on the Prairie* (New York: Macmillan, 1899), pp. 161–62.

24. The quotations in the first sentence are from Daniel Frohman, *Daniel Frohman Presents, An Autobiography* (New York: Kendall & Sharp, 1935),

pp. 30–31; in the next two sentences, from Theodore Dreiser, *Dawn* (London: Constable, 1931), pp. 373–74.

25. Kahn, *The Merry Partners*, pp. 3–5.
26. Charles W. Stein, ed., "Preface" to *American Vaudeville as Seen by Its Contemporaries* (New York: Knopf, 1984), p. xi.
27. Winston Churchill, *Mr. Crewe's Career* (New York: Macmillan, 1908), p. 493.
28. Goldberg, *Tin Pan Alley*, p. 81.
29. Arthur Loesser, *Men, Women, and Pianos* (New York: Simon & Schuster, 1954), pp. 20–21, 521, 547–48; see also Michael R. Turner, *The Parlour Song Book* (New York: Viking, 1973), pp. 2–3, 4; Bryce, *The American Commonwealth*, vol. 2, p. 870; Schlesinger, *The Rise of the City*, pp. 304–05.
30. Isidore Witmark and Isaac Goldberg, *The Story of the House of Witmark: From Ragtime to Swingtime* (New York: Furman, 1939), p. 124.
31. Goldberg, *Tin Pan Alley*, p. 95. On the earlier demand of popular songs, see Nicholas E. Tawa, *Sweet Songs for Gentle Americans* (Bowling Green, Ohio: Bowling Green University Popular Press, 1980), p. 24.
32. Dreiser, *Dawn*, p. 48.
33. Theodore Dreiser, *Sister Carrie* (New York: Norton, 1970), p. 87; the book was first published in 1900.
34. George W. Cable, *Bonaventure* (New York: Scribner's Sons, 1893), p. 227.
35. E. M. Wickes, *Writing the Popular Song* (Springfield, Mass.: The Home Correspondence School, 1916), p. 4.
36. Charles Hamm, *Yesterdays* (New York: Norton, 1979), p. 274; Theodore Dreiser, *Twelve Men* (London: Constable, 1930); *Mark Twain's Letters*, vol. 1, 367.
37. Muirhead, *A Land of Contrasts*, p. 22.
38. Goldberg, *Tin Pan Alley*, p. 7.
39. Peter Gay, *Education of the Senses* (New York: Oxford University Press, 1984), p. 12.
40. Daniel Goleman, *Vital Lies, Simple Truths* (New York: Touchstone, 1986), p. 163.
41. Dreiser, *Sister Carrie*, p. 356.
42. Howells, *Imaginary Interviews*, p. 43.
43. The quotations respectively are from *The Autobiography of Mark Twain*, arr. and ed. Charles Neider (New York: Harper & Row, 1959), p. 191; Goldberg, *Tin Pan Alley*, p. 2; John A Sloboda, *The Musical Mind* (Oxford, England: Clarendon Press, 1985), p. 1.
44. Stein, *American Vaudeville*, pp. 68–77.
45. Field, *The Poems of Eugene Field*, p. 59.
46. Charles Edward Gaus, "Empathy," *Dictionary of the History of Ideas*, volume 2, edited by Philip P. Wiener (New York: Scribner's Sons, 1973), pp. 85–87.
47. Vance Thompson, *The Life of Ethelbert Nevin* (Boston: Boston Music, 1913), p. 198.

48. The depiction of these characteristics in pre–Civil War song is the main object of my book *A Music for the Millions*.

49. Lerner, *America as a Civilization*, volume 2, 624.

50. Sorokin and Zimmerman, *Principles of Rural-Urban Sociology*, pp. 336–37, 344; Jorge Millas, *The Intellectual and Moral Challenge of Mass Society*, translated by David J. Parent (Ann Arbor: Applied Literature Press, 1977), pp. 9–10.

51. George M. Beard, *American Nervousness* (New York: Putnam's Sons, 1881), pp. 7, 82–83.

Chapter 2. THE COMPOSER OF POPULAR SONGS

1. Nicholas E. Tawa, *Sweet Songs for Gentle Americans: The Parlor Song in America, 1790–1860* (Bowling Green, Ohio: Bowling Green University Popular Press, 1980), pp. 6–7; Charles Hamm, *Yesterdays* (New York: Norton, 1979), p. 283.

2. Russel Nye, *The Unembarrassed Muse* (New York: Dial, 1970), pp. 6–7.

3. Theodore Dreiser, *The Color of a Great City* (New York: Liveright, 1923), pp. 154–55; Theodore Dreiser, *Twelve Men*, London: Constable, 1930), p. 92.

4. E. M. Wickes, *Writing the Popular Song* (Springfield, Mass.: The Home Correspondence School, 1916), p. 2.

5. Dean L. Root, *American Popular Stage Music, 1860–1880* (Ann Arbor, Michigan: UMI Research Press, 1981), pp. 60–61.

6. Tom Fletcher, *100 Years of the Negro in Show Business* (1954; reprint New York: Da Capo, 1984), pp. 74, 79.

7. David Ewen, *Popular American Composers* (New York: Wilson, 1962), pp. 55–56.

8. Ibid., pp. 153–54.

9. Ibid., pp. 20–21, 122–23, 153–54.

10. Theodore Dreiser, *Twelve Men*, p. 72.

11. Isaac Goldberg, *Tin Pan Alley* (New York: Day, 1930), pp. 132–33; Isidore Witmark and Isaac Goldberg, *The Story of the House of Witmark* (New York: Furman, 1939), p. 232; Ewen, *Popular American Composers*, pp. 172–73.

12. This information on Nevin is scattered among the pages of Vance Thompson, *The Life of Ethelbert Nevin* (Boston: Boston Music, 1913).

13. Hazel Meyer, *The Gold in Tin Pan Alley* (Philadelphia: Lippincott, 1958), pp. 30–31.

14. Rita Olcott, *Song in His Heart* (New York: House of Field, 1936), pp. 176–78.

15. F. O. Jones, ed. *A Handbook of American Music and Musicians* (Canaseraga, N.Y.: Jones, 1886), *see under* "Hays, William Shakespeare," pp. 73–74.

16. Ibid., *see under* "Danks, Hart P.," p. 47.

17. Charles K. Harris, *After the Ball* (New York: Frank-Maurice, 1926), p. 15.

18. *The Poems and Prose Sketches of James Whitcomb Riley*, volume 6 (New York: Scribner's Sons, 1910), pp. 147–48.
19. Witmark and Goldberg, *The Story of the House of Witmark*, pp. 340–41.
20. Goldberg, *Tin Pan Alley*, p. 99; also see David Ewen, *American Popular Song* (New York: Random House, 1966), pp. 226, 358.
21. Witmark and Goldberg, *The Story of the House of Witmark*, pp. 333–34.
22. Vera Dreiser, with Brett Howard, *My Uncle Theodore* (New York: Nash, 1976), pp. 75, 78.
23. Root, *American Popular Stage Music, 1860–1880*, p. 61.
24. George Gershwin, "Introduction," to Goldberg, *Tin Pan Alley*, pp. vii–viii.
25. Dreiser, *Twelve Men*, p. 90.
26. Harry Von Tilzer, "Introduction," to Wickes, *Writing the Popular Song*, p. xvi.
27. *Mark Twain's Letters*, volume 2, 483–84.
28. Witmark and Goldberg, *The Story of the House of Witmark*, pp. 333–34.
29. Dreiser, *The Color of a Great City*, pp. 151–52.
30. Mabel Rowland, ed. *Bert Williams, Son of Laughter* (New York: English Crafters, 1923), p. 38.
31. Von Tilzer, "Introduction," to Wickes, *Writing the Popular Song*, pp. xv–xvi.
32. John McCabe, *George M. Cohan: The Man Who Owned Broadway* (New York: Doubleday, 1973), p. 80.
33. James Weldon Johnson, *Along the Way* (New York: Viking, 1969), p. 150.
34. Ibid., p. 194; see also Dreiser, *The Color of a Great City*, p. 138.
35. Brooks Atkinson, *Broadway* (New York: Macmillan, 1970), p. 112.
36. William Dean Howells, *Imaginary Interviews* (New York: Harper & Brothers, 1910), p. 48.
37. Ian Whitcomb, *After the Ball* (New York: Simon & Schuster, 1972), p. 7.
38. Sigmund Spaeth, *A History of Popular Music* (New York: Random House, 1948), p. 276.
39. Dreiser, *Twelve Men*, pp. 91–92.
40. Ibid., p. 72.
41. Rowland, "Preface," *Bert Williams*, p. xi.

Chapter 3.   THE PUBLISHERS OF POPULAR SONGS

1. Ian Whitcomb, *After the Ball* (New York: Simon & Schuster, 1972), p. 6.
2. E. M. Wickes, *Writing the Popular Song* (Springfield, Mass.: The Home Correspondence School, 1916), pp. 6–7.
3. Gertrude Atherton, *Adventures of a Novelist* (New York: Blue Ribbon, 1932), p. 139.
4. Isaac Goldberg, *Tin Pan Alley* (New York: Day, 1930), pp. 108–09.
5. Isidore Witmark and Isaac Goldberg, *The Story of the House of Witmark: From Ragtime to Swingtime* (New York: Furman, 1939), p. 114.
6. Charles Hamm, *Yesterdays* (New York: Norton, 1979), p. 290.
7. Goldberg, *Tin Pan Alley*, p. 216.

8. Witmark and Goldberg, *The Story of the House of Witmark*, pp. 283–84.
9. David Ewen, *American Popular Song* (New York: Random House, 1966), p. 74.
10. Ibid., p. 49.
11. Charles Newman, *The Post-Modern Aura* (Evanston: Northwestern University Press, 1985), pp. 47–48.
12. Joseph Wood Krutch, *The Measure of Man* (New York: Grosset & Dunlap, 1954), pp. 43–44, 52.
13. Witmark and Goldberg, *The Story of the House of Witmark*, p. 68; Goldberg, *Tin Pan Alley*, p. 63.
14. Hazel Meyer, *The Gold in Tin Pan Alley* (Philadelphia: Lippincott, 1958), p. 27.
15. Witmark and Goldberg, *The Story of the House of Witmark*, p. 442; Ellen Moers, *Two Dreisers* (New York: Viking, 1969), p. 90; Goldberg, *Tin Pan Alley*, p. 219. The sales figures at the end of the paragraph come from the last book.
16. See, for example, the directory of American music publishers, from 1768 through 1889, in Harry Dichter and Elliott Shapiro, *Handbook of Early American Sheet Music, 1768–1889* (New York: Dover, 1977), pp. 165–248.
17. Witmark and Goldberg, *The Story of the House of Witmark*, pp. 64–65; Ewen, *American Popular Songs*, p. 237.
18. Sigmund Spaeth, *A History of Popular Music* (New York: Random House, 1948), p. 229; Ewen, *American Popular Songs*, p. 183.
19. Witmark and Goldberg, *The Story of the House of Witmark*, pp. 79–80.
20. Wickes, *Writing the Popular Song*, p. x; Goldberg, *Tin Pan Alley*, p. 217.
21. Ibid., p. 44; Hamm, *Yesterdays*, p. 264; Ewen, *American Popular Songs*, p. 275.
22. Hamm, *Yesterdays*, p. 264.
23. Ibid., p. 285; Ewen, *American Popular Songs*, pp. 24, 253.
24. David Ewen, *All the Years of American Popular Song* (Englewood Cliffs: Prentic-Hall, 1977), p. 101; Spaeth, *A History of Popular Song*, pp. 260, 266; Jean Geil, in *The New Grove Dictionary of American Music*, vol. 4, *see under* "Rossiter, Will," 97.
25. The history of the controversy and its resolution may be found in Witmark and Goldberg, *The Story of the House of Witmark*, pp. 294–311.
26. Ibid., pp. 286–93.
27. E. J. Kahn, Jr., *The Merry Partners: The Age and Stage of Harrigan and Hart* (New York: Random House, 1955), pp. 178–79.
28. H. Wiley Htichcock, in *The New Grove Dictionary of American Music*, volume 4, *see under* "Tin Pan Alley," 396.
29. The quotation is from the article "Whence the Song," which was published in *Harper's Weekly* on December 8, 1900; it may be found reproduced in Theodore Dreiser, *The Color of a Great City* (New York: Liveright, 1923), pp. 140–41.

30. Charles K. Harris, *After the Ball* (New York: Frank-Maurice, 1926), pp. 65–66; Wickes, *Writing the Popular Song*, p. 7.

31. The process described here is given in greater detail in Goldberg, *Tin Pan Alley*, pp. 106–107, 198–200.

32. Wickes, *Writing the Popular Song*, p. 55.

33. Daniel J. Boorstin, *The Americans: The Democratic Experience* (New York: Random House, 1973), pp. 137–38.

34. H. Wiley Hitchcock, "Introduction," Henry Clay Work, *Songs* (New York: Da Capo, 1974), n.p.

35. Ewen, *American Popular Songs*, pp. 30–31, 380; Goldberg, *Tin Pan Alley*, p. 97.

36. See Nicholas E. Tawa, *Sweet Songs for Gentle Americans* (Bowling Green, Ohio: Bowling Green University Popular Press, 1980), pp. 101–19, for an examination of earlier publicity practices.

37. Edward B. Marks, *They All Had Glamour: From the Swedish Nightingale to the Naked Lady* (New York: Messner, 1944), p. 5.

38. Ibid., pp. 3–4.

39. Goldberg, *Tin Pan Alley*, p. 206.

40. Ibid., pp. 111–12, 119; Witmark and Goldberg, *The Story of the House of Witmark*, pp. 64, 70; David Ewen, *All the Years of American Popular Music* (Englewood Cliffs: Prentice-Hall, 1977), p. 107.

41. Harris, *After the Ball*, p. 40.

42. John E. DiMeglio, *Vaudeville, U.S.A.* (Bowling Green, Ohio: Bowling Green University Popular Press, 1973), p. 85.

43. See Dreiser, *The Color of a Great City*, pp. 146–49.

44. David Ewen, *The Life and Death of Tin Pan Alley* (New York: Funk & Wagnalls, 1964), p. 29.

45. Ewen, *American Popular Songs*, pp. 93, 313–14.

46. Ibid., pp. 55–56, 259, 267, 352; Witmark and Goldberg, *The Story of Tin Pan Alley*, p. 219, 222–24.

47. Witmark and Goldberg, *The Story of Tin Pan Alley*, p. 116–17; Goldberg, *Tin Pan Alley*, pp. 128–29.

48. For more on the claque, see Abel Green and Joe Laurie, Jr., *Show Biz from Vaude to Video* (New York: Holt, 1951), p. 99.

Chapter 4. THE PUBLIC PERFORMANCES OF POPULAR SONGS

1. Channing Pollock, *The Footlights Fore and Aft* (Boston: Badger, 1911), pp. 181–82; Oliver Logan, "Women and Theatres," reprinted in *Democratic Vistas: 1860–1880*, edited by Alan Trachtenberg (New York: Braziller, 1970), pp. 303–4.

2. DeWolf Hopper, *Reminiscences of DeWolf Hopper: Once a Clown, Always a Clown* (Garden City, N.Y.: Garden City, 1927), p. 3.

3. Henry Clay Barnabee, *Reminiscences*, edited by George Leon Varney (Boston: Chapple, 1913), p. 252; Mabel Rowland, ed., *Bert Williams, Son of Laughter* (New York: English Crafters, 1923), pp. 11–12; Rita

Olcott, *Song in His Heart* (New York: House of Field, 1936), pp. 54, 62.

4. Barnabee, *Reminiscences*, pp. 246–47.

5. Felix Isman, *Weber and Fields: Their Tribulations, Triumphs, and Their Associates* (New York: Boni & Liveright, 1924), pp. 240–41.

6. Isidore Witmark and Isaac Goldberg, *The Story of the House of Witmark: From Ragtime to Swingtime* (New York: Furman, 1939), p. 91.

7. E.M. Wickes, *Writing the Popular Song* (Springfield, Mass.: The Home Correspondence School, 1916), pp. 28–29; Joe Laurie, Jr., *Vaudeville: From the Honky-Tonks to the Palace* (New York: Holt, 1953), p. 55.

8. Sophie Tucker, *Some of These Days* (Garden City: Doubleday Doran, 1945), pp. 30–31.

9. David Ewen, *American Popular Songs* (New York: Random House, 1966), p. 48.

10. Hopper, *Reminiscences*, pp. 56–57.

11. Constance Rourke, *Troupers of the Gold Coast* (New York: Harcourt, Brace, 1928), pp. 233–34.

12. "Whence the Song," reprinted in Theodore Dreiser, *The Color of a Great City* (New York: Liveright, 1923), p. 152.

13. Allen Churchill, *The Great White Way* (New York: Dutton, 1962), p. 208; see also Witmark and Goldberg, *The Story of the House of Witmark*, pp. 106–07.

14. Tucker, *Some of These Days*, pp. 74–76.

15. Pollock, *The Footlights Fore and Aft*, p. 202.

16. Barnabee, *Reminiscences*, p. 449.

17. Francis Wilson, *Francis Wilson's Life of Himself* (Boston: Houghton Mifflin, 1924), p. 45; Witmark and Goldberg, *The Story of the House of Witmark*, p. 128–30; Isaac Goldberg, *Tin Pan Alley* (New York: Day, 1930), p. 50.

18. See the article by Stanley Lebergott, on "Wage Trends, 1800–1900," in *Trends in the American Economy in the Nineteenth Century*, Studies in Income and Wealth, XXIV (Princeton: Princeton University Press, 1960), 462–82.

19. Olcott, *Song in His Heart*, p. 99; Tucker, *Some of These Days*, p. 29.

20. Ludwig Lewisohn, "The Golden Age of Vaudeville," which first appeared in *Current Life*, in June 1907, is reproduced in *American Vaudeville as Seen by Its Contemporaries*, edited by Charles W. Stein (New York: Knopf, 1984): see p. 113.

21. James L. Ford, *Forty Odd Years in the Literary Shop* (New York: Dutton, 1921), p. 90.

22. Rourke, *Troupers of the Gold Coast*, pp. 155, 195.

23. Caroline Caffin, *Vaudeville* (New York: Kennerley, 1914), pp. 25–26.

24. Ibid., pp. 28–29.

25. Ibid., pp. 35–38.

26. Parker Morell, *Lillian Russell: The Era of Plush* (New York: Random House, 1940), pp. 13, 166.

27. Caffin, *Vaudeville*, pp. 61, 67–68.

28. John McCabe, *George M. Cohan: The Man Who Owned Broadway* (New York: Doubleday, 1973), pp. 62–64.
29. Ann Charters, *Nobody: The Story of Bert Williams* (New York: Macmillan, 1970), pp. 10–11, 66–67.
30. Joe Laurie, Jr., *Vaudeville*, pp. 202–03.
31. Vera Dreiser, *My Uncle Theodore*, p. 87; Laurie, *Vaudeville*, p. 56.
32. Gerald Bordman, "Cahill, Marie," in *The New Grove Dictionary of American Music*, I, 341; David Ewen, *The Life and Death of Tin Pan Alley* (New York: Funk & Wagnalls, 1964), pp. 85–86; Ewen, *American Popular Songs*, pp. 386, 390–91.
33. For descriptions of the qualities necessary to the antebellum singer, and the manner of his or her delivery, see Nicholas Tawa, *Sweet Songs for Gentle Americans: The Parlor Song in America, 1790–1860* (Bowling Green, Ohio: Bowling Green University Popular Press, 1980), pp. 64–85.
34. Barnabee, *Reminiscences*, pp. 239–41.
35. Quoted in McCabe, *George M. Cohan*, pp. 69–70.
36. Ewen, *The Life and Death of Tin Pan Alley*, pp. 34–35.
37. Tucker, *Some of These Days*, pp. 21–22.
38. Isman, *Weber and Fields*, p. 86.
39. Laurie, *Vaudeville*, p. 12.
40. Shirley Staples, *Male-Female Comedy Teams in American Vaudeville, 1865–1932* (Ann Arbor: UMI Research Press, 1984), p. 3.
41. Reprinted in *Democratic Vistas: 1860–1880*, edited by Alan Trachtenberg, p. 172.
42. Ibid., pp. 173–74.
43. Ibid., p. 175.
44. Ibid., p. 176.
45. James T. Powers, *Twinkle Little Star* (New York: Putnam, 1939), p. 54.
46. Charters, *Nobody*, pp. 18, 24–25.
47. Olcott, *Song in His Heart*, pp. 61–62.
48. Isman, *Weber and Fields*, pp. 141–42.
49. Eugene Clinton Elliott, *A History of Variety-Vaudeville in Seattle, from the Beginning to 1914* (Seattle: University of Washington Press, 1944), pp. 9–11, 15, 19.
50. M. B. Leavitt, *Fifty Years in Theatrical Management* (New York: Broadway, 1912), p. 16.
51. Douglas Gilbert, *American Vaudeville: Its Life and Times* (New York: Whittlesey House, 1940), pp. 22–23.
52. William Dean Howells, *Impressions and Experiences* (New York: Harper & Brothers, 1896), pp. 195–97.
53. Caffin, *Vaudeville*, p. 20.
54. John E. DiMeglio, *Vaudeville, U.S.A.* (Bowling Green, Ohio: Bowling Green University Popular Press, 1973), pp. 64–68.
55. Churchill, *The Great White Way*, p. 207; Tucker, *Some of These Days*, pp. 33–35.
56. Leavitt, *Fifty Years in Theatrical Management*, pp. 183, 186–87.

57. Charles K. Harris, *After the Ball* (New York: Frank-Maurice, 1926), pp. 4–5.
58. Elliott, *A History of Variety-Vaudeville in Seattle*, p. 10.
59. Otis Skinner, *Footlights and Spotlights* (New York: Blue Ribbon, 1924), pp. 119–20.
60. Gilbert, *American Vaudeville*, p. 39.
61. William Moulton Marston and John Henry Feller, *F. F. Proctor, Vaudeville Pioneer* (New York: Smith, 1943), p. 46.
62. Arthur Meier Schlesinger, *The Rise of the City, 1878–1898, A History of American Life*, vol. 10 (New York: Macmillan, 1933), pp. 100–02.
63. Root, *American Popular Stage Music, 1860–1880*, p. 47; David Ewen, *All the Years of American Popular Music* (Englewood Cliffs; Prentice-Hall, 1977), pp. 87–89; Goldberg, *Tin Pan Alley*, p. 65.
64. Gilbert, *American Vaudeville*, p. 32; Laurie, *Vaudeville*, p. 59.
65. Theodore Dreiser, *Dawn* (London: Constable, 1931), p. 372.
66. See, respectively, Gilbert, *American Vaudeville*, p. 4; Stein, *American Vaudeville*, p. 4; Dayton Stoddart, *Lord Broadway, Variety's Sime* (New York: Funk, 1941), p. 27; Schlesinger, *The Rise of the City, 1878–1898*, p. 301.
67. Staples, *Male-Female Comedy Teams in American Vaudeville, 1865–1932*, pp. 78–79.
68. DiMeglio, *Vaudeville, U.S.A.*, p. 11; Philip C. Lewis, *Trouping* (New York: Harper & Row, 1973), pp. 9, 11, 15, 18.
69. Reprinted in *American Vaudeville*, ed. Stein, pp. 22–31.
70. Ibid., p. 62; also see Pollock, *The Footlights Fore and Aft*, pp. 321–22.
71. Marston, *F. F. Proctor, Vaudeville Pioneer*, p. 70; Staples, *Male-Female Teams in American Vaudeville, 1865–1932*, pp. 126–27.
72. Tom Fletcher, *100 Years of the Negro in Show Business* (1954; reprint, New York: Da Capo, 1984), p. 207.
73. Robert Edmund Sherwood, *Here We Are Again* (Indianapolis: Bobbs-Merrill, 1926), pp. 256–60.
74. Howells, *Impressions and Expressions*, pp. 160–61.
75. Dreiser, *The Color of a Great City*, pp. 174–83.
76. Olcott, *Song in His Heart*, pp. 69–71.
77. Eugene Field, *The Poems of Eugene Field* (New York: Scribner's Sons, 1916), p. 106.
78. Ned Pedigo, *With a Bum Show Out West* (Preston, Kansas: Pedigo, 1905), pp. 10–11.
79. Gertrude Andrews, *The Story of Corse Payton* (Brooklyn: Andrews, 1901), pp. 51–52, 61; Leavitt, *Fifty Years in Theatrical Management*, p. 230.
80. Charles Leroy Whittier, *Dear Dad: Our Life in the Theater Around the Turn of the Century* (Freeport, Maine: Bond Wheelwright, 1972), pp. 22–23.
81. Thomas Ryan, *Recollections of an Old Musician* (New York: Dutton, 1899), pp. 175–77.
82. George M. Cohan, *Twenty Years on Broadway* (New York: Harper & Brothers, 1925), pp. 19–20.

83. Gilbert, *American Vaudeville*, p. 79; Tucker, *Some of These Days*, p. 40.
84. William Dean Howells, *Imaginary Interviews* (New York: Harper & Brothers, 1910), pp. 36–37. The quotation originally appeared in the article "On Vaudeville," published in *Harper's Magazine* 106 (April 1903): 811–15.
85. Whittier, *Dear Dad*, pp. 78–79.
86. Laurie, *Vaudeville*, pp. 74–75; Harris, *After the Ball*, p. 110.

Chapter 5. UNDERSTANDING AMERICAN POPULAR SONGS

1. Nicholas E. Tawa, *A Music for the Millions* (New York: Pendragon, 1984), pp. 1–62.
2. Douglas Gilbert, *Lost Chords, the Diverting Story of American Popular Songs* (Garden City: Doubleday, Doran, 1942), p. 3: Max Morath, "Introduction," *Favorite Songs of the Nineties* (New York: Dover, 1973), p. vii.
3. *Mark Twain's Letters*, volume 2, edited with comment by Albert Bigelow Paine (New York: Harper & Brothers, 1917), 515, 528.
4. First published by Century, in New York, in 1916; quoted in Isidore Witmark and Isaac Goldberg, *The Story of the House of Witmark: From Ragtrime to Swingtime* (New York: Furman, 1939), p. 231.
5. Michael R. Turner, *The Parlour Song Book* (New York: Viking, 1973), p. 7.
6. *The New Columbia Encyclopedia*, edited by William H. Harris and Judith S. Levey (New York: Columbia University Press, 1975), *see under* "World's Columbian Exposition," p. 3007.
7. Stuart Chase, *The Proper Study of Mankind* (New York: Harper & Brothers, 1948), p. 62.
8. Monroe C. Beardsley, "The Aesthetic Point of View," *Philosophy Looks at the Arts*, revised edition, edited by Joseph Margolis (Philadelphia: Temple University Press, 1978), p. 20.
9. Stephen Crane, "There Was a Man with a Tongue of Wood," in *A Little Treasury of American Poetry*, revised edition, edited by Oscar Williams (New York: Scribner's Sons, 1952), p. 276.
10. Bertram G. Work, in the "Preface" to Henry Clay Works, *Songs* (New York: Da Capo, 1974); Charles K. Harris, *After the Ball* (New York: Frank-Maurice, 1926), p. 57; Theodore Reik, *The Need to Be Loved* (New York: Farrar, Straus, 1963), p. 177; Vance Thompson, *The Life of Ethelbert Nevin* (Boston: Boston Music, 1913), pp. 206–07; Phineas T. Barnum, *The Life of P. T. Barnum* (Buffalo: Courier, 1888), p. 187.
11. One song may become instantly popular; another may have to wait until matched with a specific vocalist; still another may fail one year and become a hit one or more decades later.
12. Isabel Parker Semler, in collaboration with Pierson Underwood, *Horatio Parker* (New York: Putnam's Sons, 1942), pp. 73–74.
13. Harris, *After the Ball*, p. 19.
14. Maurice Willson Disher, *Victorian Song, from Dive to Drawing Room* (London: Phoenix House, 1955), p. 9.
15. Dickinson to Mrs. Jonathan L. Jenkins, late May 1877, *The Letters of Emily*

Dickinson, volume 2, edited by Thomas H. Johnson (Cambridge: Bell-knap, 1958), p. 581.

16. Harris, *After the Ball*, pp. 62–63; see also Brett Page, *Writing for Vaudeville* (Springfield, Mass.: Home Correspondence School, 1915), pp. 348–50.

17. What is stated here is confirmed in E. M. Wickes, *Writing the Popular Song* (Springfield, Mass.: Home Correspondence School, 1916), pp. 36, 38–39, 41, 58–60.

18. F. O. Jones, *A Handbook of American Music and Musicians* (Canaseraga, N. Y.: Jones, 1886) *see under* "Hayes, William Shakespeare," pp. 73–74.

19. For a discussion of the influence of Jewish music, see Nicholas Tawa, *A Sound of Strangers* (Metuchen, N. J.: Scarecrow, 1982), pp. 66, 71–72, 152–56, 162–76.

20. John McCabe, *George M. Cohan: The Man Who Owned Broadway* (New York: Doubleday, 1973), p. 35.

21. Finley Peter Dunne, *Mr. Dooley in the Hearts of His Countrymen* (Boston: Small, Maynard, 1899), p. 68.

22. Wickes, *Writing the Popular Song*, pp. 100–01; Henry Clay Barnabee, *Reminiscences*, edited George Leon Varney (Boston: Chapple, 1913), pp. 209–10.

23. Theodore Dreiser, *Twelve Men* (London: Constable, 1930), p. 90.

Chapter 6. CONSERVATIVE SONGS

1. Walt Whitman, "Thoughts," *Leaves of Grass* (New York: Book's, Inc. n.d.), p. 357.

2. Robert H. Wiebe, *The Search for Order, 1877–1920* (London: Macmillan, 1967), pp. 2–3.

3. Charles Hamm, *Yesterdays* (New York: Norton, 1979), p. 254.

4. Tom Fletcher, *1000 Years of the Negro in Show Business* (1954; reprint, New York: Da Capo, 1984), pp. 83, 89.

5. David Ewen, *American Popular Songs* (New York: Random House, 1966), p. 172; Sigmund Spaeth, *A History of Popular Music* (New York: Random House, 1948), p. 198.

6. Ewen, *American Popular Songs*, pp. 182–83.

7. E. M. Wickes, *Writing the Popular Song* (Springfield, Mass.: Home Correspondence School, 1916), pp. 1–2.

8. Ernest Tuveson, "Alienation in Christian Theology," *Dictionary of the History of Ideas*, edited by Philip P. Wiener (New York: Scribner's Sons, 1973), pp. 34–36.

9. Sarah Orne Jewett, *A Marsh Island* (Boston: Houghton, Mifflin, 1885), pp. 180–81.

10. Richard Sennett, *The Fall of Public Man* (New York: Vintage, 1978), p. 11.

11. F. O. Jones, ed. *A Handbook of American Music and Musicians* (Canaseraga, New York: Jones, 1886), *see under* "Sweet Bye and Bye," p. 164.

12. The changes that took place are discussed in Nicholas E. Tawa, "Minstrel Songs and Parlor Melodies," *Sweet Songs for Gentle Americans: The Parlor*

Song in America, 1790–1860 (Bowling Green, Ohio: Bowling Green University Popular Press, 1980), pp. 89–100.

13. Clayton W. Henderson, "Minstrelsy," *The New Grove Dictionary of American Music*, III, 245–47.

14. Nicholas E. Tawa, *A Music for the Millions* (New York: Pendragon, 1984), pp. 63–100.

15. Jones, *A Handbook of American Music and Musicians, see under* "Fisk Jubilee Singers," p. 57; Charles Hamm, *Yesterdays* (New York: Norton, 1979), p. 272.

16. James L. Ford, *Forty Odd Years in the Literary Shop* (New York: Dutton, 1921), p. 52.

17. Isaac Goldberg, *Tin Pan Alley* (New York: Day, 1930), pp. 85–86.

18. Hamm, *Yesterdays*, p. 276.

Chapter 7. SONGS FOR A CHANGING SOCIETY

1. Robert N. Bellah, et al., *Habits of the Heart: Individualism and Commitment in American Life* (Berkeley: University of California Press, 1985), pp. 42, 148; Arthur Meier Schlesinger, *The Rise of the City, 1878–1898* (New York: Macmillan, 1933), p. 63.

2. William A. Madden, "Sense and Sentiment, Victorian," *Dictionary of the History of Ideas*, volume 4, edited by Philip P. Wiener (New York: Scribner's Sons, 1973), pp. 221–22.

3. Walt Whitman, "Democratic Vistas," *Complete Poetry and Select Prose*, edited by James E. Miller, Jr. (Boston: Houghton Mifflin, 1959), p. 461; *The Letters of Emily Dickinson*, edited by Thomas H. Johnson, volume 2 (Cambridge: Belknap, 1958), p. 511.

4. *Mark Twain's Letters*, volume 1, arranged with comment by Albert Bigelow Paine (New York: Harper & Brothers, 1917), p. 323; Theodore Dreiser, *A Book About Myself* (New York: Boni & Liveright, 1922), pp. 425–26.

5. *A Little Treasury of American Poetry*, revised edition, edited by Oscar Williams (New York: Scribner's Sons, 1952), pp. 250–53.

6. Thomas Ryan, *Recollections of an Old Musician* (New York: Dutton, 1899), p. 273.

7. Stuart Chase, *The Proper Study of Mankind* (New York: Harper & Brothers, 1948), pp. 64, 66; William James, *Pragmatism* (1907; reprint New York: Longman, Green, 1948), pp. 168–69.

8. Sigmund Spaeth, *A History of Popular Music* (New York: Random House, 1948), p. 220.

9. Nicholas E. Tawa, *A Music for the Millions: Antebellum Democratic Attitudes and the Birth of American Popular Music* (New York: Pendragon, 1984), pp. 122, 149–50.

10. Spaeth, *A History of Popular Music*, p. 241.

11. Bellah, *Habits of the Heart*, p. 6.

12. *The Letters of Emily Dickinson*, volume 2, p. 582.

13. Ann Douglas, *The Feminization of American Culture* (New York: Avon, 1978), pp. 5–6.

14. Gertrude Atherton, *Adventures of a Novelist* (New York: Blue Ribbon, 1932), pp. 38–39.

15. Robert C. Toll, *Blacking Up: The Minstrel Show in Nineteenth-Century America* (New York: Oxford University Press, 1974), p. 139.

16. *The Notebooks of Henry James*, edited by F. O. Matthiessen and Kenneth B. Murdock (New York: Oxford University Press, 1947), p. 47.

17. Sarah Orne Jewett, *A Country Doctor* (Boston: Houghton Mifflin, 1887), pp. 119–20, 142.

18. Martin Cyril D'Arcy, *The Mind and Heart of Love* (New York: Holt, 1947), pp. 9, 21.

19. *The Autobiography of Mark Twain*, arranged and edited by Charles Neider (New York: Harper & Row, 1959), p. 61.

20. Edward Marks, as told to Abbott J. Liebling, *They All Sang: From Tony Pastor to Rudy Vallee* (New York: Viking, 1955), pp. 59–60, 69–70; Brander Matthews, *A Book About the Theater* (New York: Scribner's Sons, 1916), p. 232; George M. Cohan, *Twenty Years on Broadway* (New York: Harper & Row, 1925), p. 215.

21. Spaeth, *A History of Popular Music*, p. 242.

Chapter 8. ACKNOWLEDGING THE INCONSTANT HUMAN CREATURE

1. Carl N. Degler, *Out of Our Past* (New York: Harper & Row, 1970), pp. v–vi.

2. Henry Steele Commager, *The American Mind* (New Haven: Yale University Press, 1950), p. 46.

3. Theodore Dreiser, *The Color of a Great City* (New York: Liveright, 1923), pp. v–vii; Edward Marks, as told to Abbott J. Liebling, *They All Sing: From Tony Pastor to Rudy Vallee* (New York: Viking, 1935), pp. 127–29.

4. Finley Peter Dunne, *Mr. Dooley in Peace and in War* (New York: Small, Maynard, 1898), p. 9.

5. Dreiser, *The Color of a Great City*, p. 170.

6. William James, *Pragmatism* (New York: Longman, Green, 1948), pp. 16, 244. The book was first published in 1907.

7. Commager, *The American Mind*, p. 55.

8. Respectively, Arthur Meier Schlesinger, *A Critical Period in American Religion, 1875–1900*, from The Proceedings of the Massachusetts Historical Society, volume 64, June 1932 (Boston: Mass. Historical Society, 1932), p. 13; William James, *The Varieties of Religious Experience* (New York: Modern Library, n.d.), pp. 90–92. The book was first published in 1902.

9. Isaac Goldberg, *Tin Pan Alley* (New York: Day, 1930), pp. 130–31; James T. Mahar, "Introduction," to Alec Wilder, *American Popular Song* (New York: Oxford University Press, 1972), pp. xxiv–xxv.

10. Max Morath, "Introduction" to *Favorite Songs of the Nineties*, edited by Robert A. Fremont (New York: Dover, 1973), p. viii.

11. *Mark Twain–Howell Letters*, volume 2, edited by Henry Nash Smith and William M. Gibson (Cambridge: Belknap, 1960), p. 669.

12. Finley Peter Dunne, *Mr. Dooley's Philosophy* (New York: Harper, 1900), p. 227.
13. Robert H. Wiebe, *The Search for Order, 1877–1920* (London: Macmillan, 1967), pp. 37–38.
14. Winston Churchill, *Mr. Crewe's Career* (New York: Macmillan, 1908), p. 57.
15. Theodore Dreiser, *A Book About Myself* (New York: Boni & Liveright, 1922), p. 108.
16. George W. Cable, *Bonaventure* (New York: Putnam's Sons, 1893), p. 249.
17. Ellen Moers, *Two Dreisers* (New York: Viking, 1969), pp. 98–99.
18. Joseph Wood Krutch, *The Measure of Man* (New York: Grosset & Dunlap, 1954), pp. 38–39; *A Little Treasury of American Poetry*, revised edition edited by Oscar Williams (New York: Scribner's Sons, 1952), p. 275.
19. How Italian-Americans and other immigrants really felt about their urban situation and the music depicting them is discussed fully in Nicholas Tawa, *A Sound of Strangers* (Metuchen, N.J.: Scarecrow, 1982), pp. 3–35.
20. Richard Sennett, *The Fall of Public Man* (New York: Vintage, 1978), pp. 187–88; Goldberg, *Tin Pan Alley*, p. 67.
21. Vera Dreiser, with Brett Howard, *My Uncle Theodore* (New York: Nash, 1976), p. 39.
22. See, respectively, David Ewen, *All the Years of American Popular Songs* (Englewood Cliffs: Prentice-Hall, 1977), p. 118; David Ewen, *American Popular Songs* (New York: Random House, 1966), pp. 386, 53–54, 151–52.
23. Stuart Chase, *The Proper Study of Mankind* (New York: Harper & Row, 1948), p. 95.
24. Alexis de Tocqueville, *Democracy in America* (New York: Knopf, 1951), p. 99.
25. Commager, *The American Mind*, p. 407.
26. Richard Sennett, *The Fall of Public Man* (New York: Vintage, 1978), p. 9.
27. Dunne, *Mr. Dooley in Peace and War*, pp. 136–37.
28. E. M. Wickes, *Writing the Popular Song* (Springfield, Mass.: The Home Correspondence School, 1916), pp. 48–52.
29. Daniel J. Boorstin, *The Americans: The Democratic Experience* (New York: Random House, 1973), pp. 230–32.

Chapter 9. TEXT AND MUSIC IN THE NEW SONGS

1. E. M. Wickes, *Writing the Popular Song* (Springfield, Mass.: The Home Correspondence School, 1916), pp. 6, 13.
2. Ibid., pp. 13, 15.
3. Charles Hamm, *Yesterdays* (New York: Norton, 1979). pp. 291–92.
4. Edward Marks, as told to Abbott J. Liebling, *They All Sang: From Tony Pastor to Rudy Vallee* (New York: Viking, 1935), p. 8.
5. Theodore Dreiser, *Twelve Men* (London: Constable, 1930), p. 188.
6. Brett Page, *Writing for Vaudeville* (Springfield, Mass.: Home Correspondence School, 1915), pp. 327, 330, 359.

7. E. M. Wickes, *Writing the Popular Song* (Springfield, Mass.: Home Correspondence School, 1916), pp. 43–45.

8. Vance Thompson, *The Life of Ethelbert Nevin* (Boston: Boston Music, 1913), p. 197.

9. Wickes, *Writing the Popular Song*, pp. 8–9.

10. Hans Fantl, *The Waltz Kings* (New York: Morrow, 1972), p. 31.

11. Thomas Ryan witnessed the conquests of Strauss; see his *Recollections of an Old Musician* (New York: Dutton, 1899), pp. 198–201.

12. David Ewen, *American Popular Songs* (New York: Random House, 1966), pp. 30–31.

13. Philip J. S. Richardson, *The Social Dances of the 19th Century* (London: Jenkins, 1960), pp. 98–99, 115.

14. James L. Ford, *Forty Odd Years in the Literary Shop* (New York: Dutton, 1921), pp. 276–77.

15. Tom Fletcher, *100 Years of the Negro in Show Business* (1954; reprint, New York: Da Capo, 1984), p. 138.

16. Richardson, *The Social Dances of the 19th Century*, p. 118; Pauline Norton, "Schottische," in *The New Grove Dictionary of American Music*, volume 4, p. 162.

17. The quotation is reproduced in Richardson, *The Social Dances of the 19th Century*, p. 119.

18. Ann Charters, *Nobody: The Story of Bert Williams* (New York: Macmillan, 1970), p. 35; Eileen Southern, *The Music of Black Americans* (New York: Norton, 1971), pp. 273–74, 295.

19. Quoted in Charters, *Nobody*, p. 36.

20. Thompson, *The Life of Ethelbert Nevin*, p. 209.

21. James Weldon Johnson, *Along This Way* (New York: Viking, 1969), pp. 152–53.

22. Fletcher, *100 Years of the Negro in Show Business*, pp. 50, 137.

23. Ibid., pp. 137, 141–42.

24. Henry Clay Barnabee, *Reminiscences*, edited by George Leon Varney (Boston: Chapple, 1913), p. 215.

25. Both quotations may be found reprinted in Edward A. Berlin, *Ragtime* (Berkeley: University of California Press, 1980), pp. 7–8.

26. Ibid., p. 24.

27. James Weldon Johnson, "Autobiography of an Ex-Colored Man," in *Three Negro Classics*, edited by J.H. Franklin (New York: Avon, 1965), pp. 447–48.

28. Marks, *They All Sang*, p. 97; Isaac Goldberg, *Tin Pan Alley* (New York: Day, 1930), pp. 141–42.

29. Wickes, *Writing the Popular Song*, pp. 32–33.

30. Ibid., pp. 10–11.

31. Grant C. Knight, *The Critical Period in American Literature* (Chapel Hill: University of North Carolina Press, 1951), pp. 29–30.

32. See the "Introduction" by James T. Maher, pp. xxiv–xxvi, and p. 3 of Alec

Wilder's *American Popular Song,* edited by James T. Maher (New York: Oxford University Press, 1972).

33. Henry Raynor, *Music and Society Since 1815* (New York: Taplinger, 1978), p. 157.

34. Marilyn Berger, "Berlin at 100," *New York Times* (May 8, 1988), section 2, p. 1.

35. Michael Freedland, *Irving Berlin* (New York: Stein & Day, 1974), p. 39.

36. Ibid., p. 20.

37. Ernie Santosuosso, "Irving Berlin: An American Original," *Boston Globe* (May 8, 1988), pp. 87, 93.

38. Rupert Holmes, "His Songs Are the Scale That Measures All Others," *New York Times* (May 8, 1988), sec. 2, p. 14.

BIBLIOGRAPHY

America and the Americans, from a French Point of View. 9th ed. New York: Scribner's Sons. 1897

Ammer, Christine. *Unsung: A History of Women in American Music.* Westport, Conn: Greenwood, 1980.

Andrews, Gertrude. *The Story of Corse Payton.* Brooklyn: Andrews, 1901.

Appelbaum, Stanley, ed. *Show Songs from the Black Crook to the Red Mill.* New York: Dover, 1974.

Arnold, Matthew. *Civilization in the United States.* 1888. Reprint. Freeport, N.Y.: Books for Libraries, 1972.

Aronson, Rudolph. *Theatrical and Musical Memoirs.* New York: McBride, Nast, 1913.

Atherton, Brooks. *Broadway.* New York: Macmillan, 1970.

Atherton, Gertrude. *Adventures of a Novelist.* New York: Blue Ribbon, 1932.

Austin, William. *"Susanna," "Jeanie," and "The Old Folks at Home."* New York: Macmillan, 1975.

Barnabee, Henry Clay. *Reminiscences.* Edited by George Leon Varney. Boston: Chapple, 1913.

Barnum, Phineas T. *The Life of P. T. Barnum.* Buffalo: Courier, 1888.

Beard, George M. *American Nervousness.* New York: Putnam's Sons, 1881.

Beer, Thomas. *The Mauve Decade: American Life at the End of the Nineteenth Century.* New York: Knopf, 1926.

Bellah, Robert N.; Madsen Richard; Sullivan, William M.; Swindler, Ann; and Tipton, Steven M. *Habits of the Heart: Individualsim and Commitment in American Life.* Berkeley: University of California, 1985.

Bergler, Edmund. *Laughter and the Sense of Humor.* New York: Intercontinental Medical Book, 1956.

Berlin, Edward A. *Ragtime.* Berkeley: University of California, 1980.

Bigsby, C. W. E., ed. *Approaches to Popular Culture.* London: Arnold, 1976.

Bikle, Lucy Leffingwell Cable. *George W. Cable: His Life and Letters*. New York: Scribner's Sons, 1928.

Blesh, Rudi, and Janis, Harriet. *They All Played Ragtime*. 4th ed. New York: Oak, 1971.

Boardman, W. H. ("Billy"). *Vaudville Days*. London: Jarrolds, 1935.

Boorstin, Daniel J. *The Americans: The Democratic Experience*. New York: Random House, 1973.

Booth, Mark W. *The Experience of Songs*. New Haven: Yale University Press, 1981.

Bordman, Gerald. *Jerome Kern*. New York: Oxford University Press, 1980.

Brooks, Van Wyck. *The Confident Years: 1885–1915*. New York: Dutton, 1952.

Bryce, James. *The American Commonwealth*. 2 vols. New York: Macmillan, 1910.

Butcher, Margaret Just. *The Negro in American Culture*. New York: Knopf, 1969.

Caffin, Caroline. *Vaudeville*. New York: Kennerley, 1914.

Charles, Norman. "Social Values in American Popular Songs (1890–1950)." Ph.D. dissertation, University of Pennsylvania, 1958.

Charters, Ann. *Nobody: The Story of Bert Williams*. New York: Macmillan, 1970.

Chase, Stuart. *The Proper Study of Mankind*. New York: Harper & Brothers, 1948.

Churchill, Allen. *The Great White Way*. New York: Dutton, 1962.

Claghorn, Charles Eugene. *The Mocking Bird: The Life and Diary of Its Author, Septimus Winner*. Philadelphia: Magee, 1937.

Clemens, Samuel. [Mark Twain]. *The Autobiography of Mark Twain*. Arranged and edited by Charles Neider. New York: Harper & Row, 1959.

———. *Mark Twain's Letters*. 2 vols. Arranged with comment by Albert Bigelow Paine. New York: Harper & Brothers, 1917.

Cohan, George M. *Twenty Years on Broadway*. New York: Harper & Brothers, 1925.

Commager, Henry Steele, ed. *America in Perspective*. New York: Random House, 1947.

———. *The American Mind*. New Haven: Yale University Press, 1950.

Cooke, George Willis. *John Sullivan Dwight*. 1898. Reprint. New York: Da Capo, 1969.

Curti, Merle. *Probing Our Past*. New York: Harper & Brothers, 1955.

D'Arcy, Martin Cyril. *The Mind and Heart of Love*. New York: Holt, 1947.

Degler, Carl N. *Out of Our Past*. Rev. ed. New York: Harper & Row, 1970.

De Koven, Mrs. Reginald. *A Musician and His Wife*. New York: Harper & Brothers, 1926.

Dennison, Sam. *Scandalize My Name*. New York: Garland, 1982.

De Voto, Bernard. *Mark Twain's America*. Boston: Little, Brown, 1932.

[Dickinson, Emily]. *The Letters of Emily Dickinson*. Vols. 2 and 3, edited by Thomas H. Johnson. Cambridge: Belknap, 1958.

Diehl, Anna Randall. *The Story of Jennie O'Neil Potter.* New York: Blanchard, 1901.

Di Meglio, John E. *Vaudeville, U.S.A.* Bowling Green, Ohio: Bowling Green University Popular Press, 1973.

Disher, Maurice Willson. *Victorian Song, from Dive to Drawing Room.* London: Phoenix House, 1955.

Douglas, Ann. *The Feminization of American Culture.* New York: Avon, 1978.

Dreiser, Theodore. *A Book About Myself.* New York: Boni & Liveright, 1922.

———. *The Color of a Great City.* New York: Liveright, 1923.

———. *Dawn.* London: Constable, 1931.

———. *Letters of Theodore Dreiser.* Vol. 1, edited by Robert H. Elias. Philadelphia: University of Pennsylvania Press, 1959.

———. *Sister Carrie.* 1900. Reprint. New York: Norton, 1970.

———. *Twelve Men.* 1919. Reprint. London: Constable, 1930.

Dreiser, Vera, with Brett Howard. *My Uncle Theodore.* New York: Nash, 1976.

Dunne, Finley Peter. *Mr. Dooley in Peace and in War.* Boston: Small, Maynard, 1898.

———. *Mr. Dooley in the Hearts of His Countrymen.* Boston: Small, Maynard, 1899.

———. *Mr. Dooley's Philosophy.* New York: Harper, 1900.

Elliott, Eugene Clinton. *A History of Variety-Vaudeville in Seattle, from the Beginning to 1914.* Seattle: University of Washington Press, 1944.

Elson, Louis C. *The National Music of America and Its Sources.* Boston: Page, 1899.

Engel, Lehman. *The American Musical Theater.* Rev. ed. New York: Collier, 1975.

———. *Words with Music.* New York: Macmillan, 1972.

Ewen, David. *All the Years of American Popular Music.* Englewood Cliffs, N.J.: Prentice Hall, 1977.

———. *American Popular Songs.* New York: Random House, 1966.

———. *The Life and Death of Tin Pan Alley.* New York: Funk & Wagnalls, 1964.

———. *Popular American Composers from Revolutionary Times to the Present.* New York: Wilson, 1962.

Fantel, Hans. *The Waltz Kings.* New York: Morrow, 1972.

Faulkner, E. J., ed. *Man's Quest for Security.* Lincoln: University of Nebraska Press, 1966.

Field, Eugene. *The Poems of Eugene Field.* New York: Scribner's Sons, 1916.

Finck, Henry T. *My Adventures in the Golden Age of Music.* New York: Funk & Wagnalls, 1926.

Fitz-gerald, S. J. Adair. *Stories of Famous Songs.* 2 vols. Philadelphia: Lippincott, 1910.

Fletcher, Tom. *100 Years of the Negro in Show Business.* 1954. Reprint. New York: Da Capo, 1984.

Ford, James L. *Forty Odd Years in the Literary Shop.* New York: Dutton, 1921.

Fremont, Robert A., ed. *Favorite Songs of the Nineties.* New York: Dover, 1973.

Frohman, Daniel. *Daniel Frohman Presents, An Autobiography.* New York: Kendall & Sharp, 1935.

Gagey, Edmond M. *The San Francisco Stage.* New York: Columbia University Press, 1950.

Gallegly, Joseph. *Footlights on the Border: The Galveston and Houston Stage Before 1900.* Gravenhage, Netherlands: Mouton, 1962.

Garland, Hamlin. *Boy Life on the Prairie.* New York: Macmillan, 1899.

———. *Main-Travelled Roads.* New York: Harper & Row, 1922.

Gay, Peter. *Education of the Senses.* The Bourgeois Experience: Victoria to Freud, I. New York: Oxford University, 1984.

Gilbert, Douglas. *Lost Chords, The Diverting Story of American Popular Songs.* Garden City, N.Y.: Doubleday, 1942.

———. *American Vaudeville: Its Life and Times.* New York: Whittlesey House, 1940.

Ginger, Ray. *Age of Excess: The United States from 1877 to 1914.* New York: Macmillan, 1965.

Goldberg, Isaac. *Tin Pan Alley.* New York: Day, 1930.

Gorsline, Douglas. *What People Wore.* New York: Bonanza, 1942.

Green, Abel, and Laurie, Joe, Jr. *Show Biz from Vaude to Video.* New York: Holt, 1950.

Green, Stanley. *The World of Musical Comedy.* New York: A. J. Barnes, 1968.

Hamm, Charles. *Yesterdays.* New York: Norton, 1979.

Handy, W. C. *Father of the Blues.* Edited by Arna Bontamps. New York: Macmillan, 1955.

Harris. Charles K. *After the Ball.* New York: Frank-Maurice, 1926.

Hopper, De Wolf. *Once a Clown, Always a Clown: Reminiscences of De Wolf Hopper.* Garden City, N.Y.: Garden City Publishing, 1927.

Howells, William Dean. *Criticism and Fiction, and Other Essays.* New York: New York University Press, 1959.

———. *Imaginary Interviews.* New York: Harper & Brothers, 1910.

———. *Impressions and Experiences.* New York: Harper & Brothers, 1896.

Isman, Felix. *Weber and Fields: Their Tribulations, Triumphs, and Their Associates.* New York: Boni & Liveright, 1924.

Jacks, L. P. *My American Friends.* London: Constable, 1933.

James, William. *Pragmatism . . . Together with Four Related Essays Selected from the Meaning of Truth.* New York: Longman, Green, 1948.

———. *The Varieties of Religious Experience.* 1902. Reprint. New York: Modern Library, n.d.

Jasen, David A., and Tichenor, Trebor Jay. *Rags and Ragtime.* New York: Seabury, 1978.

Johnson, James Weldon. *Along This Way.* New York: Viking, 1969.

———. *Black Manhattan.* 1930. Reprint. New York: Arno Press and the New York Times, 1968.

———. "Autobiography of an Ex-Colored Man" In *Three Negro Classics,* edited by J. H. Franklin. New York: Avon, 1965.

Jones, F. O., ed. *A Handbook of American Music and Musicians.* Canaseraga, N.Y.: Jones, 1886.

Jones, Howard Mumford. *The Pursuit of Happiness.* Ithaca, N.Y.: Cornell University Press, 1966.

Kahn, E. J., Jr. *The Merry Partners: The Age of Harrigan and Hart.* New York: Random House, 1955.

Kaye, Joseph. *Victor Herbert.* New York: Watt, 1931.

Key, V. O., Jr. *Public Opinion and American Democracy.* New York: Knopf, 1961.

Krutch, Joseph Wood. *The Measure of Men.* New York: Grosset & Dunlap, 1954.

Krutch, Joseph Wood, et al. *Is the Common Man Too Common?* Norman: University of Oklahoma Press, 1954.

Langtry, Lillian. *The Days I Knew.* London: Hutchinson, 1925.

Laurie, Joe, Jr. *Vaudeville: From the Honky-Tonks to the Palace.* New York: Holt, 1953.

Lears, T. J. Jackson. *No Place of Grace: Antimodernism and the Transformation of American Culture, 1880–1920.* New York: Pantheon, 1981.

Leavitt, M. B. *Fifty Years in Theatrical Management.* New York: Broadway, 1912.

Lee, Edward. *Music of the People.* London: Barrie & Jenkins, 1970.

Lerner, Max. *America as a Civilization.* 2 vols. New York: Simon & Schuster, 1957.

Lewis, Lloyd, and Smith, Henry Justin. *Oscar Wild Discovers America (1882).* New York: Harcourt, Brace, 1936.

Lewis, Philip C. *Trouping.* New York: Harper & Row, 1973.

Loesser, Arthur. *Humor in American Song.* New York: Soskin, 1942.

———. *Men, Women and Pianos.* New York: Simon & Schuster, 1954.

McCabe, John. *George M. Cohan: The Man Who Owned Broadway.* New York: Doubleday, 1973.

Marcosson, Isaac, and Frohman, Daniel. *Charles Frohman: Manager and Man.* New York: Harper & Brothers, 1916.

Marcuse, Maxwell F. *Tin Pan Alley in Gaslight.* Watkins Glen, N.Y.: Century House, 1959.

Mark Twain-Howells Letters. 2 vols, edited by Henry Nash Smith and William M. Gibson. Cambridge: Belknap, 1960.

Marks, Edward B. *They All Had Glamour: From the Swedish Nightingale to the Naked Lady.* New York: Messner, 1944.

Marks, Edward, as told to Abbott J. Liebling. *They All Sang: From Tony Pastor to Rudy Vallee.* New York: Viking, 1935.

Marston, William Moulton, and John Henry Feller. *F. F. Proctor, Vaudeville Pioneer.* New York: Smith, 1943.

Mattfeld, Julius. *Variety Music Cavalcade, 1620–1969*. 3rd ed. Englewood Cliffs, N.J.: Prentice-Hall, 1971.

Matthews, Brander. *The American of the Future, and Other Essays*. New York: Scribner's Sons, 1909.

———. *A Book about the Theater*. New York: Scribner's Sons, 1916.

———. *Pen and Ink*, 3rd ed. New York: Scribner's Sons, 1902.

———. *These Many Years*. New York: Scribner's Sons, 1919.

Meyer, Hazel. *The Gold in Tin Pan Alley*. Philadelphia: Lippincott, 1958.

Millas, Jorge. *The Intellectual and Moral Challenge of Mass Society*. Translated by David J. Parent. Ann Arbor: Applied Literature, 1977.

Moers, Ellen. *Two Dreisers*. New York: Viking, 1969.

Morehouse, Ward. *George M. Cohan: Prince of the American Theater*. 1943. Reprint. Westport, Conn.: Greenwood, 1972.

Morell, Parker. *Lillian Russell: The Era of Plush*. New York: Random House, 1940.

Muirhead, James Fullerton. *A Land of Contrasts*. 2nd ed. London: Lane, 1900.

Mussulman, Joseph A. *Music in the Cultured Generation*. Evanston: Northwestern University Press, 1971.

Nye, Russell. *The Unembarrassed Muse*. New York: Dial, 1970.

Odell, George C. D. *Annals of the New York Stage*. Vol. 2. New York: Columbia University, 1939.

[Offenbach, Jacques]. *Orpheus in America*. Translated by Lander McClintock. Bloomington: Indiana University Press, 1957.

Olcott, Rita. *Song in His Heart*. New York: House of Field, 1936.

O'Neill, M. J. *How He Does It! Sam T. Jack*. Chicago: American Advertising and Bill Posting Company, 1895.

Orton, William Aylott. *America in Search of Culture*. Boston: Little, Brown, 1933.

Page, Brett. *Writing for Vaudeville*. Springfield, Mass.: Home Correspondence School, 1915.

Paskman, Dailey. *"Gentlemen, Be Seated,"* Rev. ed. New York: Potter, 1976.

Pearsall, Ronald. *Victorian Popular Music*. Detroit: Gale Research, 1973.

Pedigo, Ned. *With a Bum Show out West*. Preston, Kan.: Pedigo, 1905.

Pollock, Channing. *The Footlights Fore and Aft*. Boston: Badger, 1911.

Power, James T. *Twinkle Little Star*. New York: Putnam, 1939.

Quick, Herbert. *One Man's Life*. Indianapolis: Bobbs-Merrill, 1925.

Rather, Lois. *Two Lillies in America*. Oakland, Calif.: Rather, 1973.

Reik, Theodore. *The Need to Be Loved*. New York: Farrar, Straus, 1963.

Richardson, Philip J. S. *The Social Dances of the 19th Century*. London: Jenkins, 1960.

Root, Dean L. *American Popular Stage Music, 1860–1880*. Ann Arbor: UMI Research, 1981.

Rourke, Constance. *American Humor*. 1931. Reprint. Garden City: Doubleday, 1953.

———. *Troupers of the Gold Coast*. New York: Harcourt, Brace, 1928.

Rowland, Mabel, ed. *Bert Williams, Son of Laughter*. New York: English Crofters, 1923.

Ryan, Thomas. *Reflections of an Old Musician*. New York: Dutton, 1899.

Schlesinger, Arthur Meier. *A Critical Period in American Religion, 1875–1900*. From the Proceedings of the Massachusetts Historical Society, vol. 64. Boston: Massachusetts Historical Society, 1932.

———. *The Rise of the City, 1878–1898*. A History of American Life, vol. 10. New York: Macmillan, 1933.

Seldes, Gilbert. *The Stammering Century*. 1928. Reprint. Gloucester, Mass.: Smith, 1972.

Semler, Isabel Parker, in collaboration with Pierson Underwood. *Horatio Parker*. New York: Putnam's Sons, 1942.

Sennett, Richard. *The Fall of Public Man*. New York: Vintage, 1978.

Shepherd, John; Verden, Phil; Vulliamy, Graham; and Wishard, Trevor. *Whose Music?* New Brunswick, N.J.: Transition Books, 1977.

Sherwood, Robert Edmund. *Here We Are Again*. Indianapolis: Bobbs-Merrill, 1926.

Skinner, Otis. *Footlights and Spotlights*. New York: Blue Ribbon, 1924.

Sloboda, John A. *The Musical Mind*. Oxford: Clarendon Press, 1985.

Smart, George Thomas. *The Temper of the American People*. Boston: Pilgrim, 1912.

Smith, Cecil Michener. *Musical Comedy in America*. New York: Theatre Arts, 1950.

Smith, Henry Nash, ed. *Popular Culture and Industrialism, 1865–1890*. New York: New York University Press, 1967.

Sobel, Bernard. *A Pictorial History of Vaudeville*. New York: Bonanza, 1961.

Sorokin, Pitrim A., and Zimmerman Carle C. *Principles of Rural-Urban Sociology*. New York: Holt, 1929.

Southern, Eileen. *The Music of Black Americans*. New York: Norton, 1971.

Spaeth, Sigmund. *A History of Popular Music*. New York: Random House, 1948.

———. *Read 'Em and Weep*. Rev. ed. New York: Arco, 1945.

Spell, Lota M. *Music in Texas*. Austin: n.p., 1936.

Staples, Shirley. *Male-Female Comedy Teams in American Vaudeville, 1865–1932*. Ann Arbor: UMI Research Press, 1984.

Stein, Charles W., ed. *American Vaudeville as Seen by Its Contemporaries*. New York: Knopf, 1984.

Stoddart, Dayton. *Lord Broadway, Variety's Sime*. New York: Funk, 1941.

Strang, Lewis C. *Celebrated Comedians of Light Opera and Musical Comedy in America*. Boston: Page, 1901.

———. *Famous Actors of the Day in America*. Boston: Page, 1900.

———. *Famous Actresses of the Day in America*. Boston: Page, 1899.

———. *Famous Actresses of the Day in America, Second Series.* Boston: Page, 1902.

Swan, Howard. *Music in the Southwest, 1825–1950.* San Marino, Cal.: Huntington Library, 1952.

Tawa, Nicholas E. *A Music for the Millions: Antebellum Democratic Attitudes and the Birth of American Popular Music.* New York: Pendragon, 1984.

———. *A Sound of Strangers: Musical Culture, Acculturation, and the Post–Civil War Ethnic American.* Metuchen, N.J.: Scarecrow, 1982.

———. *Sweet Songs for Gentle Americans: The Parlor Song in America, 1790–1860.* Bowling Green, Ohio: Bowling Green University Popular Press, 1980.

Taylor, Joseph H. *Joe Taylor, Barnstormer.* New York: Jenkins, 1913.

Thompson, Vance. *The Life of Ethelbert Nevin.* Boston: Boston Music, 1913.

Toll, Robert C. *Blacking Up: The Minstrel Show in Nineteenth-Century America.* New York: Oxford University, 1974.

Trachtenberg, Alan, and Neill, Peter. *The City.* New York: Oxford University, 1971.

Trachtenberg, Alan, ed. *Democratic Vistas: 1860–1880.* New York: Braziller, 1970.

Tucker, Sophie. *Some of These Days.* Garden City: Doubleday, Doran, 1945.

Turner, Michael R. *The Parlour Song Book.* New York: Viking, 1973.

Wagner, Charles. *My Impressions of America.* Translated by Mary Louise Hendee. New York: McLure, Phillips, 1906.

Warde, Frederick. *Fifty Years of Make Believe.* New York: International, 1920.

Waters, Edward N. *Victor Herbert.* New York: Macmillan, 1955.

Whitcomb, Ian. *After the Ball.* New York: Simon & Schuster, 1972.

Wickes, E. M. *Writing the Popular Song.* Springfield, Mass.: Home Correspondence School, 1916.

Whittier, Charles Leroy. *Dear Dad: Our Life in the Theater Around the Turn of the Century.* Freeport, Me.: Bond Wheelwright, 1972.

Wiebe, Robert H. *The Search for Order, 1877–1920.* London: Macmillan, 1967.

———. *The Segmented Society: An Historical Preface to the Meaning of America.* New York: Oxford University, 1975.

Wilder, Alex. *American Popular Song.* New York: Oxford University, 1972.

Wilson, Francis. *Francis Wilson's Life of Himself.* Boston: Houghton Mifflin, 1924.

Winter, William. *The Life of David Belasco.* 2 vols. New York: Moffat, Yard, 1918.

Witmark, Isidore, and Goldberg, Isaac. *The Story of the House of Witmark: From Ragtime to Swingtime.* New York: Furman, 1939.

Work, Henry Clay. *Songs* New York: Da Capo, 1974.

Zeidman, Irving. *The American Burlesque Show.* New York: Hawthorn, 1967.

Ziff, Larzer. *The American 1890s.* New York: Viking, 1966.

SELECTIVE BIBLIOGRAPHY OF SONGS

The year of copyright is cited.

"Absence Makes the Heart Grow Fonder," w. Arthur Gillespie, m. Herbert Dillea. New York: Witmark, 1900.

"After the Ball," w. and m. Charles K. Harris, arr. Joseph Clauder. Chicago: Harris, 1892.

"Agnes by the River," w. Mary J. McDermit, m. Henry C. Work. Cleveland: Brainard's Sons, 1866.

"Ah, Love, But a Day!" w. Robert Browning, m. Mrs. H. H. A. Beach. Boston: Schmidt, 1900.

"Ain't You Glad You've Found Me," w. Harry Williams, m. Egbert Van Alstyne. New York: Remick, 1907.

"The Alabama Blossoms," w. amd m. Frank Dumont, arr. James E. Stewart. New York: Peters, 1874.

"Alamo Rag," w. Ben Deely, m. Percy Wenrich. New York: Remick, 1910.

"Alexander," w. Andrew Sterling, m. Harry Von Tilzer. New York: Von Tilzer, 1904.

"Alice, Where Art Thou Going," w. William A. Heelan, m. Albert Grumble. New York: Remick, 1906.

"All Coons Look Alike to Me," w. and m. Ernest Hogan. New York: Witmark, 1896.

"All That I Ask of You Is Love," w. Edgar Selden, m. Herbert Ingraham. New York: Shapiro, 1910.

"Always Take Mother's Advice," w. and m. Jennie Lindsay. New York: Woodward, 1884.

"Amber Tresses Tied in Blue," w. Samuel M. Mitchell, m. Hart P. Danks. Buffalo: Cottier & Denton, 1874.

"Angel Gabriel," m. James E. Stewart. New York: Peters, 1875.

"Angels, Meet Me at the Cross Roads," w. and m. Will S. Hays. New York: Peters, 1875.

"Anona," by Vivian Grey [Miss Mabel McKinley]. New York: Feist, 1903.

"Any Little Girl, That's a Nice Little Girl, Is the Right Little Girl for Me," w. Thomas J. Gray, m. Fred Fischer. New York: Shapiro, 1910.

"Any Rags?" w. and m. Thomas S. Allen. New York: Krey, 1902.

"Arab Love Songs," w. George V. Hobart, m. Silvio Hein. New York: Cahill, 1908.

"Are You Sincere?" w. Alfred Bryan, m. Albert Grumble. New York: Remick, 1908.

"Arrah Wanna," w. Jack Drislane, m. Theodore Morse. New York: Haviland, 1906.

"Asleep in the Deep," w. Arthur J. Lamb, m Henry W. Petrie. New York: Mills, 1897.

"At a Georgia Campmeeting," by Kerry Mills. New York: Mills, 1897.

"At Dawning," w. Nelle Richmond Eberhart, m. Charles Wakefield Cadman. Boston: Ditson, 1906.

"The Babies on Our Block," w. Edward Harrigan, m. David Braham. New York: Pond, 1879.

"Baby Mine," w. Charles Mackay, m. Archibald Johnston. New York: Spear & Dehnhoff, 1875.

"The Band Played On," w. John F. Palmer, m. Charles B. Ward. New York: New York Music, 1895.

"Beautiful Eyes," w. George Whiting and Carter DeHaven, m. Ted Snyder. New York: Snyder, 1909.

"Beautiful Isle of Somewhere," w. Mrs. Jessie Brown Pounds, m. John S. Fearis. Chicago: Excell, 1897.

"Bedelia," w. William Jerome, m. Jean Schwartz. New York: Shapiro, Bernstein, 1903.

"Betsy's the Belle of the Bathers," w. and m. Richard Carle. New York: Witmark, 1907.

"Big Brown Booloo Eyes," w. amd m. Eddie Leonard. New York: Cohan & Harris, 1908.

"Big Chief Battle-Axe," w. amd m. Thomas S. Allen. Boston: Jacobs, 1907.

"The Big Sun Flower," sung by Billy Emerson [w. amd m. Bobby Newcomb]. Cincinnati: Church, Jr., 1867.

"Bill Bailey, Won't You Please Come Home?" w. and m. Hughie Cannon. New York: Howley, Haviland & Dresser, 1902.

"A Bird from o'er the Sea." by C. A. White. Boston: White, Smith, 1880.

"The Bird on Nellie's Hat," w. Arthur J. Lamb, m. Alfred Solman. New York: Stern, 1906.

"Bring Back My Bonnie to Me," w. and m. H. J. Fulmer [Charles E. Pratt]. New York: Harms, 1882.

"Bon Bon Buddy," w. Alex Rogers, m. Will Marion Cook. New York: Gotham-Attucks, 1907.

"The Bowery," w. Charles H. Hoyt, m. Percy Gaunt. New York: Harms, 1892.

"The Buckskin Bag of Gold," w. and m. Henry C. Work. Cleveland: Brainard's Sons, 1869.

"Budweiser's a Friend of Mine," w. Vincent Bryan, m. Seymour Furth. New York: Shapiro, 1907.

"The Bull-frog and the Coon," w. Felix F. Feist, m. Joseph S. Nathan. New York: Feist, 1906.

"By the Light of the Silvery Moon," w. Edward Madden, m. Gus Edwards. New York: Edwards, 1909.

"Bye, Bye, Dearie," w. Andrew B. Sterling, m. Harry Von Tilzer. New York: Von Tilzer, 1907.

"Call Me up Some Rainy Afternoon," w. and m. Irving Berlin. New York: Snyder, 1910.

"Can't You See I'm Lonely," w. Felix F. Feist, m. Harry Armstrong. New York: Feist, 1905.

"Carrie," w. Junie McCree, m. Albert Von Tilzer. New York: York, 1909.

"Carry Me Back to Old Virginny," w. and m. James A. Bland. Boston: Perry, 1878.

"Cavalier' Rustican' Rag," w. Harry Williams, m. Egbert Van Alstyne. New York: Remick, 1910.

"Cheyenne," w. Harry Williams, m. Egbert Van Alstyne. New York: Remick, 1905.

"Chinatown, My Chinatown," w. William Jerome, m. Jean Schwartz. New York: Remick, 1910.

"Coax Me," w. Andrew Sterling, m. Harry Von Tilzer. New York: Von Tilzer, 1904.

"Come back to the Farm!" w. amd m. Henry C. Work. Cleveland: Brainard's Sons, 1867.

"Come, Josephine, in My Flying Machine," w. Alfred Bryan, m. Fred Fisher. New York: Shapiro, 1910.

"The Convict and the Bird," w. and m. Paul Dresser. New York: Woodward, 1888.

"Cradle's Empty, Baby's Gone," w. amd m. Harry Kennedy. Boston: Ditson, 1880.

"Creole Belle," w. George Sidney, m. J. Bodewalt Lampe. Detroit: Whitney-Warner, 1900.

"Croquet," w. C. H. Webb, m. John Rogers Thomas. New York: Pond, 1867.

"The Cubanola Glide," w. Vincent Bryan, m. Harry Von Tilzer. New York: Von Tilzer, 1909.

"Daddy Wouldn't Buy Me a Bow-wow," w. and m. Joseph Tabrar. New York: Harms, 1892.

"Dad's a Millionaire," w. and m. Henry C. Work. Cleveland: Brainard's Sons, 1867.

"Daisies Won't Tell," w. and m. Anita Owens. New York: Remick, 1908.

"Dearie," by Clare Kummer. New York: Stern, 1905.

"Dear Old Girl," w. Richard Henry Buck, m. Theodore M. Morse. New York: Howley, Haviland & Dresser, 1903.

"Dear Sing Sing," w. William Jerome, m. Jean Schwartz. New York: Shapiro, Remick, 1903.

"De Golden Wedding," w. and m. James A. Bland. Boston: Perry, 1880.

"Dixie Dan," w. Will D. Cobb, m. Seymour Furth. New York: Shapiro, 1907.

"Don't Be Angry with Me, Darling," w. W. L. Gardner, m. Hart Pease Danks. Brooklyn: Wheeler, 1870.

"Don't Be Cross with Me," w. Will M. Hough and Frank R. Adams, m. Joseph E. Howard. New York: Harris, 1908.

"Don't Take Me Home," w. Vincent Bryan, m. Harry Von Tilzer. New York: Von Tilzer, 1908.

"Don't You Think It's Time to Marry?" w. Addison Burkhardt, m. Gus Edwards. New York: Edwards, 1906.

"Don't You Want a Paper, Dearie?" w. Paul West, m. Jerome D. Kern. New York: Harms, 1906.

"Down at the Huskin' Bee," w. Monroe H. Rosenfeld, m. S. R. Henry. New York: Stern, 1909.

"Down by the Old Mill Stream," w. and m. Tell Taylor. Chicago: Taylor, 1910.

"Down in the Jungle Town," w. Edward Madden, m. Theodore Morse. New York: Haviland, 1908.

"Down in the Old Cherry Orchard," w. Alfred Bryan, m. S. R. Henry. New York: Stern, 1908.

"Down Where the Wurzburger Flows," w. Vincent P. Bryan, m. Harry Von Tilzer. New York: Von Tilzer, 1902.

"Do Your Duty, Doctor!" w. Irving Berlin, m. Ted Snyder, New York: Snyder, 1909.

"A Dream," w. Charles B. Cory, m. J. C. Bartlett. Boston: Ditson, 1895.

"Driven from Home," w. and m. Will S. Hays. New York: Peters, 1868.

"Drummer Song," w. William Jerome, m. Jean Schwartz. New York: Remick, 1905.

"Eileen Allanna," w. E. S. Marble, m. John Rogers Thomas. New York: Pond, 1873.

"Everybody Works But Father," w. and m. Jean Havez. New York: Helf & Hagere, 1905.

"The Five-cent Shave," w. and m. Thomas Cannon. New York: Harding, 1880.

"A Flower from Mother's Grave," w. and m. Harry Kennedy. Boston: Ditson, 1878.

"Forty-five Minutes from Broadway," by George M. Cohan. New York: Mills, 1905.

"The Fountain in the Park," by Ed. Haley [Robert A. Keiser?]. New York: Woodward, 1884.

"The Full Moon Union," w. Edward Harrigan, m. David Braham. New York: Pond, 1880.

"Gee But It's Great to Meet a Friend from Your Home Town," w. William Tracy, m. James McGavisk. New York: Helf, 1910.

"Give My Regards to Broadway," by George M. Cohan. New York: Mills, 1904.

"Good Sweet Ham," w. and m. Henry Hart, arr. James E. Stewart. New York: Peters, 1873.

"Goodbye, Becky Cohen," w. and m. Irving Berlin. New York: Snyder, 1910.

"Good-bye, Liza Jane," arr. Eddie Fox. Philadelphia: Lee & Walker, 1871.

"Good-bye, My Lady Love," w. and m. Joseph E. Howard, arr. A. La Rue. New York: Harris, 1904.

"Grandfather's Clock," w. and m. Henry C. Work. New York: Cady, 1876.

"A Handful of Earth from My Dear Mother's Grave," w. and m. Joseph Murphy. Detroit: Whitney, 1885.

"Happy Birds," w. C. T. Steele, m. Edward Holst. Boston: Ditson, 1887.

"Hear Dem Bells," by D. S. McCosh. Cincinnati: Willis, 1880.

"Hello, Central, Give Me Heaven," w. and m. Charles K. Harris. Milwaukee: Harris, 1901.

"Hello! Ma Baby," w. and m. Joseph E. Howard and Ida Emerson. New York: Harms, 1899.

"Her Bright Smile Haunts Me Still," w. J. E. Carpenter, m. W. T. Wrighton. Boston: Ditson, 1868.

"Honey Boy," w. Jack Norworth, m. Albert Von Tilzer. New York: York, 1907.

"Hoo-oo! (Ain't You Coming out Tonight?)," w. and m. Herbert Ingraham. New York: Shapiro, 1908.

"A Hot Time in the Old Town," w. Joe Hayden, m. Theodore A. Metz. New York: Willis, Woodward, 1896.

"I Don't Care," w. Jean Lenox, m. Harry O. Sutton. New York: Shapiro, Remick, 1905.

"I Don't Want to Play in Your Yard," w. Philip Wingate, m. H. W. Petrie. Chicago: Petrie, 1894.

"I Had $15 in My Inside Pocket," w. and m. Harry Kennedy. Boston: Ditson, 1885.

"I Hope I Don't Intrude," w. and m. William H. Delehanty. Boston: Goullaud, 1877.

"I Love My Steady, But I'm Crazy for My 'Once-in-a while,' " w. Irving Hinkley, m. Allan W. S. Macduff. Boston: Daly, 1909.

"I Love My Wife, But Oh, You Kid!" w. and m. Harry Armstrong and Billy Clark. Chicago: Rossiter, 1909.

"I Love You Truly," w. and m. Carrie Jacobs-Bond. Chicago: Jacobs-Bond & Son, 1906.

"I Owe $10 to O'Grady," w. and m. Harry Kennedy. Boston: Ditson, 1887.

"If the Waters Could Speak as They Flow," w. and m. Charles Graham. New York: Woodward, 1887.

"I'll Take You Home Again, Kathleen," w. and m. Thomas P. Westendorf. Cincinnati: Church, 1876.

"I'm Going to Do What I Please," w. Alfred Bryan, m. Ted Snyder. New York: Snyder, 1909.

"In My Merry Oldsmobile," w. Vincent Bryan, m. Gus Edwards. New York: Witmark, 1905.

"In the Baggage Coach Ahead," w. and m. Gussie L. Davis. New York: Howley, Haviland, 1896.

"In the Good Old Summer Time," w. Ren Shields, m. George Evans. New York: Howley, Haviland & Dresser, 1902.

"In the Evening by the Moonlight," w. and m. James A. Bland. Boston: Perry, 1879.

"In the Morning by the Bright Light," w. and m. James A. Bland. Boston: Perry, 1879.

"In the Shade of the Old Apple Tree," w. Harry H. Williams, m. Egbert Van Alstyne. New York: Shapiro, Remick, 1905.

"The Irish Jubilee," w. James Thornton, m. Charles Lawler. New York: Witmark, 1890.

"Jennie, the Flower of Kildare," w. Frank Dumont, m. James E. Stewart. New York: Peters, 1873.

"Johnny, Get Your Gun," by Monroe H. Rosenfeld. New York: Harms, 1886.

"Just A-wearyin' for You," w. Frank L. Stanton, m. Carrie Jacobs-Bond. Chicago: Jacobs-Bond & Son, 1901.

"Just Tell Them That You Saw Me," w. and m. Paul Dresser. New York: Howley, Haviland, 1895.

"Kentucky Babe," w. Richard Henry Buck, m. Adam Geibel. Boston: White-Smith, 1896.

"Let Me Call You Sweetheart," w. Beth Slater Whitson, m. Leo Friedman. Chicago: Rossiter, 1910.

"The Letter That Never Came," w. Paul Dresser, m. Max Sturm [Paul Dresser]. New York: Harms, 1886.

"Life's a Funny Proposition After All," by George M. Cohan. New York: Mills, 1904.

"Lillie of the Snow-storm," w. and m. Henry C. Work. Cleveland: Brainard's Sons, 1866.

"The Little Brown Jug," w. and m. R. A. Eastburn [Joseph E. Winner]. Philadelphia: Winner, 1869.

"Little Footsteps," w. Michael Bennett Leavitt, m. James A. Barney. Boston: White, Smith & Perry, 1868.

"The Little Lost Child," w. Edward B. Marks, m. Joseph W. Stern. New York: Stern, 1894.

"The Little Old Log Cabin in the Lane," w. and m. Will S. Hays. New York: Peters, 1871.

"A Lock of My Mother's Hair," w. Frank Dumont, m. Eddie Fox. c. 1877 by Chas. F. Escher, Jr.

"Love Among the Roses," w. William H. Delehanty, m. E. N. Catlin. Boston: Russell, 1869.

"Love Me, and the World Is Mine," w. Dave Reed, Jr., m. Ernest R. Ball. New York: Witmark, 1906.

"Lullaby," w. and m. Joseph K. Emmet. Cincinnati: Helmick, 1876.

"Maggie Murphy's Home," w. Edward Harrigan, m. David Braham. New York: Pond, 1890.

"Maggie, the Cows Are in the Clover," w. and m. Al. W. Filson, New York: Harms, 1886.

"Marguerite," w. and m. C. A. White. Boston: White-Smith, 1883.

"Mariutch (Make-a the Hootch-a Ma Kootch) Down at Coney Isle," w. Andrew B. Sterling, m. Harry Von Tilzer. New York: Von Tilzer, 1908.

"Mary's a Grand Old Name," by George M. Cohan. New York: Mills, 1905.

"May Irwin's 'Bully' Song," w. and m. Charles E. Trevathan. Boston: White-Smith, 1896.

"Meet Me in St. Louis, Louis," w. Andrew B. Sterling, m. Kerry Mills. New York: Mills, 1904.

"Meet Me To-night in Dreamland," w. Beth Slater Whitson, m. Leo Friedman. Chicago: Rossiter, 1909.

"Mighty Lak' a Rose," w. Frank L. Stanton, m. Ethelbert Nevin. Cincinnati: Church, 1901.

"Mister Johnson," w. and m. Ben R. Harney. New York: Witmark, 1896.

"Molly and I and the Baby," w. and m. Harry Kennedy. New York: Harding, 1892.

"Mollie Darling," w. and m. Will S. Hays. New York: Peters, 1871.

"Molly O! (Mavourneen)," w. and m. William J. Scanlan. New York: Harms, 1891.

"The Moth and the Flame," w. George Taggart, m. Max S. Witt. New York: Stern, 1899.

"Mother Machree," w. Rida Johnson Young, m. Chauncey Olcott and Ernest R. Ball. New York: Witmark, 1910.

"Mother Was a Lady," w. Edward B. Marks, m. Joseph W. Stern. New York: Stern, 1896.

"The Mottoes That Are Framed upon the Wall," w. William Devere, m. W. S. Mullaly. New York: Woodward, 1888.

"The Mulligan Guard," w. Edward Harrigan, m. David Braham. New York: Pond, 1873.

"My Dad's Dinner Pail," w. Edward Harrigan, m. David Braham. New York: Pond, 1883.

"My Gal Is a High Born Lady," w. and m. Barney Fagan, arr. Gustave Luders. New York: Witmark, 1896.

"My Gal Sal," w. and m. Paul Dresser. New York: Dresser, 1905.

"My Love's a Rover," by C. A. White. Boston: White, Smith, 1881.

"My Mariuccia Take a Steamboat," w. George Ronklyn, m. Al Piantadosi. New York: Shapiro, Bernstein, 1906.

"My Pretty Red Rose," w. and m. Joseph P. Skelly. New York: Blume, 1877.

"My Wild Irish Rose," w. and m. Chauncey Olcott. New York: Witmark, 1899.

"The Mystic Veil," w. and m. Henry C. Work. New York: Cady, 1875.

"Navajo," w. Harry H. Williams, m. Egbert Van Alstyne. New York: Shapiro, Bernstein, 1903.

"Never Take No for an Answer," w. and m. J. F. Mitchell. New York: Woodward, 1886.

"Nobody," w. Alex Rogers, m. Bert A. Williams. New York: Gotham-Attucks, 1905.

"Nobody's Darling," w. and m. Will S. Hays. New York: Peters, 1870.

"Oh Dem Golden Slippers!" w. and m. James A. Bland. Boston: Perry, 1879.

"Oh, Promise Me!" w. Clement Scott, m. Reginald De Koven. New York: Schirmer, 1889.

"Oh! Sam," w. and m. Will S. Hays. New York: Peters, 1872.

"Oh! That We Two Were Maying," w. Charles Kingsley, m. Ethelbert Nevin. Boston: Boston Music, 1888.

"The Old Wooden Rocker," by Florence Harper. New York: Spear & Dehnhoff, 1878.

"On the Banks of the Wabash, Far Away," w. and m. Paul Dresser. New York: Howley, Haviland, 1897.

"The Outcast Unknown," w. and m. Paul Dresser. New York: Woodward, 1887.

"Over the Hill to the Poor House," w. George L. Catlin, m. David Braham. New York: Pond, 1874.

"Paddy Duffy's Cart," w. Edward Harrigan, m. David Braham. New York: Pond, 1881.

"Peek-a-boo!" w. and m. William J. Scanlan. New York: Harms, 1881.

"A Perfect Day," w. and m. Carrie Jacobs-Bond. Chicago: Bond, 1910.

"Poverty's Tears Ebb and Flow," w. Edward Harrigan, m. David Braham. New York: Pond, 1885.

"The Red Rose Rag," w. Edward Madden, m. Percy Wenrich. New York: Remick, 1909.

"Red Wing," w. Thurland Chattaway, m. Kerry Mills. New York: Mills, 1907.

"Remember Boy, You're Irish," w. and m. William J. Scanlan. New York: Harms, 1886.

"Reuben and Rachel," w. Harry Birch, m. William Gooch. Boston: White, Smith & Perry, 1871.

"Rock-a-bye Baby," w. and m. Effie I. Canning. Boston: Blake, 1886.

"Roll Out! Heave Dat Cotton," w. and m. William Shakespeare Hays. Boston: Ditson, 1877.

"The Rosary," w. Robert Cameron Rogers, m. Ethelbert Nevin. Boston: Boston Music, 1898.

"Sadie Salome, Go Home," w. Edgar Leslie, m. Irving Berlin. New York: Snyder, 1909.

"Say Au Revoir But Not Goodbye," w. and m. Harry Kennedy. Brooklyn: Kennedy, 1893.

"She Is More to Be Pitied Than Censured," w. and m. William B. Gray. New York: Gray, 1898.

"She Was Bred in Old Kentucky," w. Harry Braisted, m. Stanley Carter. New York: Stern, 1898.

"Shew! Fly, Don't Bother Me," w. Billy Reeves, m. Frank Campbell, arr. Rollin Howard. Boston: White, Smith & Perry, 1869.

"Shine On, Harvest Moon," w. Jack Norworth, m. Nora Bayes and Jack Norworth. New York: Remick, 1908.

"Shivering and Shaking out in the Cold," by Sam Lucas. Boston: White, Smith, 1875.

"The Sidewalks of New York," w. and m. Charles B. Lawlor and James W. Blake, arr. Charles Miller. New York: Howley, Haviland, 1894.

"Silver Threads Among the Gold," w. Eben E. Rexford, m. Hart Pease Danks. New York: Harris, 1873.

"The Skidmore Fancy Ball," w. Edward Harrigan, m. David Braham. New York: Pond, 1878.

"Sleep, Baby, Sleep (Irene's Lullaby)," w. and m. John J. Handley. Chicago: National, 1885.

"Some of These Days," w. and m. Shelton Brooks. Chicago: Rossiter, 1910.

"Somebody's Grandpa," m. C. F. Wood. New York: Saalfield, 1880.

"Somebody's Waiting for You," w. Vincent Bryan, m. Al Grumble. New York: Remick, 1906.

"The Song of the Red Man," w. and m. Henry C. Work. Cleveland: Brainard's Sons, 1868.

"Stay in Your Own Back Yard," w. Karl Kennett, m. Lyn Udall. New York: Witmark, 1899.

"The Sunshine of Paradise Alley," w. Walter H. Ford, m. John W. Bratton. New York: Witmark, 1895.

"Susan Jane," w. and m. Will S. Hays. New York: Peters, 1871.

"Sweet By and By," w. S. Fillmore, m. Joseph P. Webster. Chicago: Lyon & Healy, 1868.

"Sweet Echo Dell," w. and m. Henry C. Work. New York: Cady, 1876.

"Sweet Genevieve," w. George Cooper, m. Henry Tucker. New York: Pond, 1869.

"Sweet Mary Ann," w. Edward Harrigan, m. David Braham. New York: Pond, 1878.

"Take Me out to the Ball Game," w. Jack Norwoth, m. Albert Von Tilzer. New York: York, 1908.

"Ta-ra-ra-bom-der-e," w. and m. Henry J. Sayers. New York: Woodward, 1891.

"Teasing," w. Cecil Mack, m. Albert Von Tilzer. New York: York, 1904.

"There's a Light in the Window," w. and m. Bobby Newcomb. New York: Harms, 1885.

"Thinking Love, of Thee," w. J. Cheever Goodman, m. Edward E. Rice. Boston: Goullaud, 1878.

"Thy Beaming Eyes," w. William Henry Gardner, m. Edward MacDowell, Boston: Schmidt, 1890.

"Trabling back to Georgia," w. Arthur W. French, m. Charles D. Blake. Boston: Russell, 1874.

"Twelve Months Ago To-night," w. John F. Mitchell, m. William H. Fox. New York: Harding, 1889.

"Wait 'Till the Clouds Roll By," w. J. T. Wood, m. H. T. Fulmer [Charles E. Pratt?]. New York: Harms, 1881.

"Wait 'Till the Sun Shines, Nellie," w. Andrew B. Sterling, m. Harry Von Tilzer. New York: Von Tilzer, 1905.

"Waiting!" w. E. H. Flagg, m. Harrison Millard. New York: Pond, 1867.

"Waltz Me Around Again, Willie," w. William D. Cobb, m. Ren. Shields. New York: Mills, 1906.

"We Parted by the River Side," w. and m. Will S. Hays. St. Louis: Peters, 1866.

"When the 'Evening Star' Went Down," w. and m. Henry C. Work. Cleveland: Brainard's Sons, 1866.

"When the Mists Have Cleared Away," [w. Annie Herbert], m. Arthur Henshaw. Boston: Russell, 1880.

"When the Robins Nest Again," w. and m. Frank Howard. New York: Harms, 1883.

"When You Were Sweet Sixteen," w. and m. James Thornton. New York: Witmark, 1898.

"Where Did You Get That Hat?" w. and m. Joseph J. Sullivan. New York: Harding, 1888.

"Where Is My Wand' ring Boy Tonight?" w. and m. Robert Lowry. New York: Biglow & Main, 1877.

"Whispering Hope," w. and m. Alice Hawthorne [Septimus Winner]. Boston: Ditson, 1868.

"The Whistling Coon," w. and m. Sam Devere. New York: Pond, 1888.

"White Wings," w. and m. Banks Winter. New York: Woodward, 1884.

"Why Did They Dig Ma's Grave So Deep?" w. and m. Joseph P. Skelly. New York: Saalfield, 1880.

"The Widow Nolan's Goat," w. Edward Harrigan, m. David Braham. New York: Pond, 1881.

"Will You Love Me in December as You Do in May?" w. J. J. Walker, m. Ernest R. Ball. New York: Witmark, 1905.

"Winter," w. Alfred Bryan, m. Albert Grumble. New York: Remick, 1910.

"With All Her Faults I Love Her Still," w. and m. Monroe H. Rosenfeld. New York: Hitchcock, 1888.

"Under the Bamboo Tree," by Bob Cole and the Johnson brothers [James Weldon and J. Rosamond Johnson]. New York: Stern, 1902.

"The Yankee Doodle Boy," by George M. Cohan. New York: Mills, 1904.

"You Naughty, Naughty Men," w. T. Kennick, m. G. Bicknell. New York: Dodworth & Son, 1866.

"You're a Grand Old Flag," by George M. Cohan. New York: Mills, 1906.

"You're the Flower of My Heart, Sweet Adeline," w. Richard H. Gerard [Richard Gerard Husch], m. Harry Armstrong. New York: Witmark, 1903.

"You've Been a Good Old Wagon, But You've Done Broke Down," by Ben R. Harney. New York: Witmark, 1895.

¶NDEX

Abbey, The (New York), 66
"Absence Makes the Heart Grow
    Fonder," 90, 154, 166–68, 170–72,
    180
Academies of music, 72
Accompaniment, 111, 116, 164, 175,
    177, 180, 184, 189, 191, 197
Adams, Frank R., 157
Adelphi Theater (Boston), 72
Adventures of Huckleberry Finn, 121
Adventures of Tom Sawyer, 121
Advertising, 48–49, 90
Aesthetic distance, 98
African Americans, 9–10, 25, 28–29,
    64–65, 68, 181–83, 185
"After the Ball," 26, 44, 45, 50, 86, 94,
    138, 154, 176, 178, 180
"Agnes by the River," 111
"Ah, Love, But a Day!," 173
"Alamo Rag," 191
Albee, Edward F., 75
"Alexander," 147, 155–56, 188, 191
"Alexander's Ragtime Band," 191,
    205
"All Coons Look Alike to Me," 151,
    155, 182, 184–85, 187–91
"All That I Ask of You Is Love," 171
Allen, Thomas S., 147
Alstyne, Egbert Van, 141, 159, 167,
    196, 203
"Always Take Mother's Advice," 101,
    104

Amateur performers, 8–9, 71–72, 191,
    193
Amateur songwriters, 42–43, 45–46, 51
Amateur-night shows, 71–72
"Amber Tresses Tied in Blue," 97, 103,
    106, 109–111
American civilization, 7–8, 17, 19, 87
American composers. *See* Songwriters
American Dancing-Master's Associa-
    tion, 183
American influence on foreign song,
    85–86, 204
American Nervousness, 143
"And Her Golden Hair Was Hanging
    Down Her Back," 33
Andrews Opera Company, 8–9
"Angels, Meet Me at the Cross Roads,"
    113, 115–17
"Anona," 90, 156–57
Antebellum song, 17–18, 22, 29, 67,
    86–87, 101, 121, 164, 198
Anthony, Susan B., 29
"Any Little Girl, That's a Nice Little
    Girl, Is the Right Little Girl For
    Me," 152
"Any Rags," 147, 191
"Arab Love Song," 149
"Are You Sincere?," 157, 178
Armstrong, Harry, 154, 165
Arnold, Matthew, 7
"Arrah Wanna," 158
Arrangers, 28, 47, 50

285

"Asleep in the Deep," 105
"At a Georgia Campmeeting," 24, 44, 59, 183–84
"At Dawning," 173
Atherton, Gertrude, 38, 126
Attitudes of the public, 5–8
Audience, cultivated, 2–3, 122
Audience, popular, 2–4, 6, 8–12, 15, 75, 85, 86, 122

Babe Connor's, 151
"Babies on Our Block, The," 133
"Babylon Falling," 48
Baker, Belle, 51
Bal Mobile (New York), 66
Ball, Ernest, 24, 25, 28, 40, 42, 141, 172
Ballads, 106
"Band Played On, The," 49, 176, 196
Bands and orchestras. See Orchestras and bands
Barnabee, Henry Clay, 57, 65–66, 97, 185
"Barney, Take Me Home Again," 102
Barnstorming, 79
Barnum, P. T., 10
Bayes, Nora, 52, 60, 62–63, 71–72
Beach, Amy, 25, 172, 173
Beard, George M., 19, 143
"Beautiful Eyes," 156
"Beautiful Love," 203
"Bedilia," 25, 186
Beer halls, 66
"Ben Bolt," 113
Berlin, Irving, 25, 28, 152, 159, 191, 205–206
Bernstein, Louis, 39
Bertram, Helen, 60
"Betsey's the Belle of the Bathers," 151
Bicknell, G., 129
"Big Brown Booloo Eyes," 182
"Big Chief Battle-Axe," 195
"Big Sunflower, The," 133
Bijou Theater (Seattle), 70
"Bill Bailey, Won't You Please Come Home?," 146–47, 155–56, 188, 190
Billy Kersand Minstrel Troupe, 25
"Bird in the Gilded Cage, The," 31, 86, 204
"Bird on Nellie's Hat, The," 156

Black Crook, The, 129
Blackface performers, 5, 26, 65, 72–73, 80, 131, 182–83, 185
Blake, James W., 149
Bland, James, 23, 25, 101–102, 113–14
Blind Sol, 25
Böhme, Franz, 26
"Bon Bon Buddy," 147, 186, 188
Bonehill, Bessie, 50
Boston, 57, 74–75
Boston Music (publisher), 172
Boston Peace Jubilee, 176
Boston waltz, 178–79, 201
Bostonians, The, 128
"Bottle's Empty, Whiskey's Gone," 124
"Bowery, The," 25, 58, 92–93, 139
Bowman, Elmer, 185
Bowman, Ted, 185
Box houses, 69–70, 73
Braham, David, 23, 30, 132, 134, 139
Bratton, John W., 145, 176
"Break the News to Mother," 40, 66
Brice, Fanny, 51, 71
British composers, 22
British singers, 67
Brooks, Shelton, 45, 143, 196, 204
Brown, George W., 102
Browne, Augusta, 29
Bruce's Modern Minstrels, 77
Bryan, Alfred, 139, 157–58, 178, 193
Bryan, Vincent, 145, 150, 158, 189, 195
Buck, Richard Henry, 154, 168
"Buckskin, Bag of Gold, The," 133
"Budweiser's a Friend of Mine," 93–94, 150
"Bully Song, The," 65, 151, 184, 190
Bullyragging, 65
Bunnell's Museum, 70
Buoyant songs. See Lively songs
Business practices, 44–53
Busking, 77
"By the Light of the Silvery Moon," 25

Cable, George, 13, 148
Cadences, 97, 106, 110–11, 164, 167
Cadman, Charles Wakefield, 173
Cahill, Marie, 65
Cakewalk, 76, 96, 181, 183–84, 190
"Cakewalk in the Sky, The," 184
Call of the Wild, The, 146
Campbell, Frank, 116

Canning, Effie I., 104
Cannon, Hughie, 146
"Can't You See I'm Lonely," 154
Cantor, Eddie, 71
Careers on the stage, 57–61
Carle, Richard, 151
Carpenter, J. E., 103
"Carrie," 154
"Carry Me Back to Old Virginny," 25, 101
Catlin, E. N., 113, 127
"Cavalier' Rustican' Rag," 159
Cavendish, Millie, 129, 152
Centennial of American Independence (Philadelphia), 183
Chaminades, Cécile, 187
Charity hotels, 78
Chattanooga, Tennessee, 81
Chattaway, Thurland, 169
"Cheyenne," 196, 203
Chicago, 27, 45, 151, 182
Child performers, 65, 81
Children as song subjects, 159
"Chinatown, My Chinatown," 159
Chinese, 9
"Coax Me," 152
Chorus of a song, 91, 94–97, 111, 129–30, 134, 163–64, 169–70, 193
Christy's Minstrels, 48
Chromaticism, 96, 117, 164, 171, 175, 177, 190–91, 194, 196–97
Church, John (publisher), 43
Churchill, Winston, 146
Claques, 52
Cleveland Conservatory of Music, 24, 28
Cline, Maggie, 58, 74
Clorindy, The Origin of the Cakewalk, 184
"Coax Me," 197
Cohan, George M., 26, 32–34, 64, 66, 74, 79–80, 96, 131, 139, 149, 167, 193, 197, 204
Cohan and Harris Minstrels, 131
Cohan Mirth Makers, The, 79–80
Cohen, Meyer, 50
Cole, Bob, 65, 181, 185
Collins, Lottie, 65
Collyer, Danny, 50
"Come Back to the Farm," 108, 126
"Come Home, Father!," 48

"Come, Josephine, in My Flying Machine," 139, 158
Comer, Imogene, 65
Comic opera, 76
Comic songs. *See* Lively songs
Comic-and-straight performers, 80
Competition, 40–41, 46
Coney Island, 25
Conservative songs, 100–117, 198
Contents of Children's Minds, The, 159
Cook, Will Marion, 147, 184–86
Coon shouters, 65, 185
Coon song, 9, 40, 87, 96, 181–93
Cooper, George, 103
Copyright, 45–46
Cordelia's Aspirations, 132
"Counting My Blessings," 206
Country Doctor, A, 128
Crabtree, Lotta, 59, 62
"Cradle's Empty, Baby's Gone," 40, 123–24
Crane, Stephen, 121, 148
"Creole Belle," 190
Creole Show, 184
"Croquet," 133
"Cubanola Glide, The," 76, 189–90
Currier, Frank D., 46

Dacre, Henry, 176
"Daddy Wouldn't Buy Me a Bow-wow," 159
"Dad's a Millionaire," 132
"Daisy Bell," 66, 86, 176
Dance and song, 96, 115–16, 193
Danks, Hart Pease, 24, 27, 43, 97, 170
"Darktown Strutters' Ball, The," 45
Darwin, Charles, 120, 145
Davis, Gussie, 24, 179
"De Golden Wedding," 115
Dean, Dora, 183
"Dear Old Girl," 25, 154, 168
"Dearie," 29
Deas, Lawrence, 185
DeHaven, Carter, 156
DeKoven, Reginald, 26, 33, 76, 172
Delaney, William, 124
Delehanty, William H., 113, 131
Deming, Arthur, 52
Department stores, 46
"Der Deitcher's Dog," 175
Descent of Man, The, 145

Devere, Sam, 184
Devere, William, 124
Dickinson, Emily, 93–94, 121, 126
Dillea, Herbert, 154
Dime museums, 10, 70
Ditson, Charles H. (publisher), 38
"Dixie," 113
"Do Your Duty, Doctor!," 152–53
Dockstader, Lew, 185
Dodsworth, Allan, 178, 183
"Don't Be Angry with Me, Darling,"
    24, 43
"Don't Be Cross with Me," 157
"Don't Take Me Home," 145, 195, 197
"Down by the Old Mill Stream," 145,
    167
"Down in Jungle Town," 145–46, 186,
    190
"Down Went McGinty," 10
"Down Where the Wurzburger Flows,"
    52, 60
Dreiser, Theodore, 13, 30, 59, 78, 121,
    139, 151
Dresser, Louise, 51, 65, 98
Dresser, Paul, 14, 22, 25, 28, 30, 31, 34,
    65, 124, 129, 147–48, 151
Drislane, Jack, 158
"Driven from Home," 27, 105–107
Dufferin Trio, 81
Dumont, Frank, 104
Dunne, Finley Peter, 6–7
Dutch-character performers, 73, 80
Dwight, John Sullivan, 84
Dwight's Journal of Music, 84
Dynamic and Expression Indications,
    108, 116, 168, 175, 177, 188, 194–
    95

Eberhart, Nelle Richmond, 173
Edison, Thomas, 14
Edwards, Gus (songwriter and pub-
    lisher), 25, 51, 158
Eldridge, Press, 185
Emerson, Billy, 78
Emerson, Ida, 158
Emerson, Ralph Waldo, 153
Emery, Stephen, 26
Emmett, Dan, 113
Emotion and mood, 89, 164
"Empty Is the Bottle, Father's Tight,"
    124

Enchantment, 5–6
"End of a Perfect Day, The," 29
English, Thomas Dunn, 113
Entertainment, 11, 59
Entertainment, Places of, 66–72, 131
European composers, 22
European singers, 67
Evans, George, 42
"Everybody Works But Father," 158
Expression and Dynamics. See
    Dynamic and Expression Indica-
    tions

Family audience, 10
Family performers, 80–81
Fearis, John S., 105
Feist, Felix, F, 154
Feist, Leo, 39
Field, Eugene, 6, 16, 75, 78
Fillmore, S., 105
Finck, Henry, 7
Fisher, Fred, 139, 152, 158
Flagg, E. H., 174
Fletcher, Tom, 182, 185
Ford, Walter H., 145, 176
Foreign influence on popular song, 85–
    86, 116, 122
Forty-Five Minutes from Broadway, 66,
    76
"Forty-Five Minutes from Broadway,"
    139, 148, 180
Foster, Stephen, 43, 101, 113, 121,
    132
Fountain, The (San Francisco), 69
Fox, Eddie, 112
Fox, Robert, 72
Foy, Eddie, 74
Free and easies, 66–69
French, Arthur, 102
Friedman, Leo, 44, 177
Furth, Seymour, 150

Gapped scales, 165
Gardner, William Henry, 173
Garland, Hamlin, 11
Gaunt, Percy, 58, 139
Gender in song lyrics, 105–106, 114,
    134, 167, 177, 187–89, 194
Gerard, Richard H. (Richard Gerard
    Hausch), 165
German immigrants, 176

German Village Restaurant (New York), 58, 61
Gershwin, George, 31, 204
Gilbert and Sullivan, 76, 122, 176
Gilded Age, The, 121
Gillespie, Arthur, 154
Gilson, Lottie, 50, 74, 152
"Git on Board, Little Children," 187
"Give My Regards to Broadway," 64, 148, 193, 196
Gooch, William, 134
"Goodbye, Becky Cohen," 159
"Good-bye, Liza Jane," 112, 115
Gottschalk, Louis Moreau, 181
Graham, Charles, 43
"Grandfather's Clock," 88, 125
Gray, Thomas J., 152
Gray, William B., 148
Grey, Vivian (Miss Mabel McKinley), 156
Gumble, Albert, 157, 178, 193
Gumble, Mose, 50
Guttersniping, 77

Hall, G. Stanley, 159
Hammerstein II, Oscar, 34
"Handful of Earth from My Dear Mother's Grave, A," 125, 130
Handley, John J., 125
Handy, William C., 10, 187
Happiness, 17
Harmony, 90, 97–98, 106, 108, 110–11, 114–15, 131, 164, 168, 175, 177, 180, 184, 186, 189, 191, 197
Harms, Thomas B. (publisher), 38–39
Harney, Benjamin, 26, 143, 184, 186, 204
Harper, Florence, 104
Harrigan, Edward, 30, 112, 132, 139, 151
Harrigan and Hart, 12, 23, 46, 132, 183
Harris, Charles K., 24, 26, 28, 34, 39–40, 43–45, 50, 88–89, 154, 158, 176
Hart, Joe, 50
Hart, Katie, 50
Hart, Tony, 6, 30, 50
Haverly Minstrels, 78
Havez, Jean, 158
Hayden, Joe, 152
Hays, William Shakespeare, 27, 41, 95, 104–106, 113, 134, 175

Headliners, 51, 58
Hein, Silvio, 149
"Hello, Central, Give Me Heaven," 158
"Hello! Ma Baby," 26, 158, 187–90
"Her Bright Smile Haunts Me Still," 103, 106, 111
"Her Golden Hair Was Hanging Down Her Back," 14
Herbert, Victor, 76
Hinkley, Irving, 139
Hobart, George V., 149
Hogan, Ernest, 151, 182, 184–85
Home, music in the, 12–14, 129–30
"Honey Boy," 141, 166
"Hoo-oo! (Ain't You Coming Out To-night?)," 159
Hopper, De Wolf, 56, 58
"Hot Time in the Old Town, A," 151–52, 183, 188, 190
Hough, Will M., 157
Howard, Joseph E., 26, 157–58
Howard Athenaeum (Boston), 72
"How'd You Like to Spoon with Me?," 204
Howells, William Dean, 5, 15, 16, 34, 70–71, 75, 77, 121, 144
Howley, Haviland, and Dresser (publisher), 42
Hoyt, Charles H., 58, 139
Huber's Prospect Gardens, 66

"I Believe It for My Mother Told Me So," 13
"I Don't Care," 157
"I Don't Care If You Never Come Back," 143
"I Don't Want to Play in Your Yard," 159, 178
"I Got Lost in His Arms," 206
"I Got the Sun in the Morning," 206
"I Had $15 in My Inside Pocket," 133–34
"I Hope I Don't Intrude," 131
"I Just Couldn't Do Without You," 204
"I'll Be with You in Apple Blossom Time," 204
"I'll Take You Home Again, Kathleen," 14, 43, 102, 105, 107, 109
"I Love My Steady, But I'm Crazy for My Once-in-awhile," 139

"I Love My Wife, But Oh, You Kid!," 152

"I Love You Truly," 24, 172

"I Owe $10 to O'Grady," 133

"I'm Going to Do What I Please," 191–92, 194, 196

Immigrants, 9, 120, 176

"In My Merry Oldsmobile," 158

"In the Baggage Car Ahead," 179–80

"In the Evening by the Moonlight," 102

"In the Good Old Summer Time," 42

"In the Morning by the Bright Light," 113

"In the Shade of the Old Apple Tree," 42, 141, 167, 203

Ingraham, Herbert, 159, 171

"Irish Jubilee, The," 158

Irish-character performers, 27, 80

Irwin, May, 65, 74, 151

Isolation. See Loneliness

Italians, 9, 150–51

Jack Halahan's Cramorne Theater (San Francisco), 69

Jacobs-Bond, Carrie, 24, 29, 91, 172

James, Henry, 128

Jerome, William, 159, 186

Jewett, Sarah Orne, 104, 128

Jews in music, 9, 39, 96

"Johnny, Get Your Gun," 113

Johns, Al, 185

Johnson, Billy, 185

Johnson, Charlie, 183

Johnson, J. Rosamond, 25, 33, 65, 181, 185

Johnson, James Weldon, 33–34, 181, 185–87

Jones, Irving, 185

Joplin, Scott, 191

Jubilee Singers of Fisk University, 113

Jungle, The, 145

"Just A-wearyin' for You," 24, 91, 172

"Just Tell Them That You Saw Me," 34, 147–48, 157

Kenny's Theater (Brooklyn), 71

Keith, Benjamin Franklin, 10, 74–75

Keith and Proctor Management, 138

Keith Theater (Boston), 74

Keith's Union Square Theater (New York), 74

Kelly, John W., 58

Kennedy, Harry, 40, 123, 133, 141, 165

Kennett, Karl, 158

Kennick, T., 129

Kern, Jerome, 204–205

Kersand, Billy. See Billy Kersand Minstrel Troupe

Key transposition, 90

Keys, 96, 107–108, 114–16, 134, 168–69, 174, 178, 189–90, 194–95

"Kingdom Coming," 48

Kingsley, Charles, 174

Klaw and Erlanger Management, 138

Klindworth, Karl, 26

Kneass, Nelson, 113

Kummer, Clare, 29

Lamb, Arthur J., 105, 156

Lanner, Joseph, 176

Latin-American influence, 181–82

Lawlor, Charles, B., 149, 158

Lead sheets, 30

Lead-ins, 167, 177, 187–88, 194

Leadville, Colorado, 73

Leavitt, Michael Bennett, 79, 104

Leavitt's Gigantean Minstrels, 112

Lenox, Jean, 157

Leonard, Eddie, 182

Leslie, Edgar, 159

"Let Me Call You Sweetheart," 44, 177–80

"Let's Face the Music and Dance," 206

"Letter That Never Came, The," 124, 130

Libbey, J. Aldrich, 50

"Life's a Funny Proposition," 64, 96

Lighting, gas and electric, 73

"Lillie of the Snow-storm," 127

Lindsay, Jessie, 66, 101, 104

"Little Alabama Coon," 29, 184, 186

"Little Annie Rooney," 14

"Little Brown Jug," 132

"Little Footsteps," 104–105, 107

Little Johnny Jones, 64, 76

"Little Lost Child, The," 24, 52, 158

"Little Old Log Cabin in the Lane, The," 113

Lively songs, 111–17, 131–35

Lloyd, Marie, 50

Lobbying, 45–46
"Lock of My Mother's Hair, A," 104, 110
Loew, Marcus, 75
Logan, Oliver, 56
London, Jack, 145
Loneliness, 18, 153–55
Louis the Whistler, 50
Louisiana, 13
Louisiana Purchase Exposition, 143
Love, 18, 129, 133, 141–42, 154–55, 173–74
"Love Among the Roses," 113, 115
"Love Me and the World Is Mine," 40, 42, 93, 141, 172, 174–75
Lucas, Sam, 23
Lyon and Healy, 50
Lyricists, 29–30, 91–95, 103–104
Lyrics, 30, 40, 84, 87, 129, 144–47, 158, 164, 182

McClain, Billy, 184
McCree, Junie, 154
MacDowell, Edward, 25, 172–73
Macduff, Allan W. S., 139
McGlennon, Felix, 33
McTeague, 146
Macy's Department Store, 46
Madden, Edward, 145, 186
Maggie: A Girl of the Streets, 121
"Maggie Murphy's Home," 138–39
"Man Who Broke the Bank at Monte Carlo, The," 14
Man's Woman, A, 146
Maple Leaf Rag, 191
March, 183–84, 202
March Songs and Rhythmic Songs, 193–97
"Marguerite," 129
"Marie from Sunny Italy," 205
"Mariutch (Mak-a the Hootch-a Ma Kootch) Down at Coney Isle," 139
Marketplace for songs, 32, 34, 40, 47–48
Marks, Edward B. (songwriter and publisher), 24, 39, 49–50, 156, 158, 169
Marks and Stern (publisher), 52
"Mary's a Grand Old Name," 167
Mason City, Iowa, 8–9
Masonic Roof Garden, 65

"May Irwin's 'Bully Song'." *See* "Bully Song, The"
"Meet Me in St. Louis, Louis," 24, 152
"Meet Me Tonight in Dreamland," 44
Melody, 87–92, 96–98, 108–109, 116, 134, 163, 169–71, 173, 179–80, 189–90, 196, 201
Metcalfe, James, 32
Meter, musical, 95, 108, 134, 168, 174–75, 177, 184, 189, 193–95
Meter, poetic, 92, 94–95, 107–108, 114, 116, 130, 167–68, 187, 193
Metz, Theodore, 33, 151–52
Midway Plaisance (San Francisco), 69
"Mighty Lak'a Rose," 26, 91, 141, 173, 175
Mill, John Stuart, 120
Millard, Harrison, 174
Mills, Kerry, 24, 39, 44, 152, 169, 183–84
Minor's Bowery Theater (New York), 71
Minstrel Songs, 111–17, 131
Minstrelsy, 25–26, 72, 77–79, 112, 131
Mr. Crewe's Career, 146
"Mister Johnson," 143, 186, 188, 190
Mitchell, John F., 125
Mitchell, Samuel, 103
Modern Instance, A, 121
Modified songs, 120–35, 198
Modulation, 111, 114–15, 134, 164, 171, 181, 186, 188, 191, 194, 197
"Molly and I and the Baby," 141
"Molly O! (Mavourneen)," 158
Monroe and Rice, 50
Moore, Neil, 185
Moore, Raymond, 49
Morris, George, 132
Morse, Theodore M., 25, 145, 154, 158, 168, 186
"Moth and the Flame, The," 156
"Mother Machree," 104, 158
Mother songs, 68, 81
"Mother Was a Lady," 156, 169
Motion pictures, 76
"Mottoes That Are Framed upon the Wall, The," 124
Mozart Hall (New York), 72
Mullaly, W. S., 124
"Mulligan Guard, The," 134
Museums. *See* Dime museums

Music halls, 67
Musical instruction, 12–13
Musical stage, 26, 76, 81
"My Best Girl's a Corker," 143
"My Dad's Dinner Pail," 132
"My Gal Sal," 151
"My Mariuccia Take a Steamboat," 159
"My Old New Hampshire Home," 26, 43, 163
"My Pretty Red Rose," 106
"My Wild Irish Rose," 27, 158

"Navajo," 203
Neurasthenia, 19
Nevin, Ethelbert, 16, 22, 26, 89, 91, 141, 172, 174, 184
"New Coon in Town," 184
New England Conservatory of Music, 25
New Songs of the Turn of the Century, 161–97, 199–200
New York City, 24, 38, 40, 43, 47, 68, 77–78, 138
New York Clipper, 45
New York Sun, 49
New York Tribune, 124
New York World, 49
Newcomb, Bobby, 124, 133
Nielsen, Alice, 185–86
"Nobody," 25, 64
"Nobody Knows de Trouble I See," 187
"Nobody's Darling," 104–105, 175
Norris, Frank, 146
Norworth, Jack, 141, 158, 167
Nugent, Maude, 29, 66

Offenbach, Jacques, 122, 176
"Oh Dear, What Can the Matter Be," 16
"Oh, Dem Golden Slippers," 113
"Oh! Promise Me," 26, 76, 172, 175
"Oh! That We Two Were Maying," 174
Olcott, Chauncey, 27, 57, 61, 69, 78, 158–59
"Old Dog Tray," 113, 132
Old Homstead, The, 78
"Old Oaken Bucket," 132
"Old Wooden Rocker, The," 104
Olympic Theater (New York), 71
"On the Banks of the Wabash," 14, 30, 34, 163

"On the Road to Mandalay," 173
Opera house, 8, 10
Opera House (Warsaw, Indiana), 74
Operetta, 76, 176
Opposition to popular music, 9–10
Orchestras and bands, 47, 57, 65, 66, 71, 74, 78, 80
Origin of Species, 145
Originality, Lack of, 84, 86–87
Orpheum Theater (San Francisco), 69
Orpheum Vaudeville Circuit, 65
"Outcast Unknown, The," 129
"Over the Hill to the Poor House," 127, 130
Owney Geoghegan's Free and Easy, 68

"Paddy Duffy's Cart," 133
Palma, Frank, 50
Palmer, John F., 49, 176
Parker, Horatio, 90–91
Pastor, Tony, 10, 25, 50, 72
Pastor's Opera House (Paterson, New Jersey, then New York City), 74
Payments to songwriters for songs, 43
Payola, 50–51
Payton, Corse, 79
Pedigo, Ned, 79
"Peek-a-boo," 104
Pelham's Café, 25
Pepita, 61
"Perfect Day, A," 172
Performance of songs, 56–81
Performer and audience. *See* Singer and audience
Performers, 11, 56–81
Peters, J. L., 41
Petrie, Henry W., 105, 159, 178
Phonograph, 76
Phrases, musical, 91, 94–95, 97, 110, 116
Pianos and pianists, 12, 13, 74
Piantadosi, Al, 159
Pickaninnies, 65
"Picture That Is Turned Toward the Wall, The," 43
Piracy, 33, 45–46, 169
"Please Go 'Way and Let Me Sleep," 51
Pleasure-pain principle, 17
Pluggers and the plugging of songs, 25, 49–50
Polka, 115, 183

Pollock, Channing, 56, 60
Pond, William (publisher), 38
Portsmouth, New Hampshire, 57
Pound, Jessie Brown, 105
Preludes, postludes, and interludes, 110, 115–17, 169, 175, 178, 188–90, 194–96
"Pretty Baby," 203
Proctor, F. F., 10, 75
Professional copies of songs, 47–48
Public for entertainment, 5, 8–12
Publisher and songwriter, 41–44
Publishers, 9, 13, 23, 24, 25, 27, 38–53, 138
Punch, 107, 165–66, 168, 174

Quartets, 81
Quickstep, 115

Radio, 76
Rag song, 4, 95–96, 143, 181–93
Reality, 14, 144–53
Reconstruction period, 100–101
"Red Wing," 169
Reed, Dave, Jr., 141, 172
Religious opposition, 9
Remick, Jerome (publisher), 39, 50
Restaurants, 66–67
"Reuben and Rachel," 134
Rhymes, 94, 107, 114, 130, 134, 167, 177, 187–88, 193–94
Riley, James Whitcomb, 28
Rise and Fall of Silas Lapham, The, 121
Rivers, Frank, 72
Robin Hood, 76
Robinson, Edwin Arlington, 121–22
"Rock-a-bye Baby," 104
Rogers, Alex, 147, 186
Rogers, Robert Cameron, 173
Ronklyn, George, 159
Root, George, 43, 101
Root and Cady (publisher), 48
"Rosary, The," 16, 22, 26, 172–73
Rosenfeld, Monroe, H., 33, 46, 114, 129, 143
Rossiter, Harold (publisher), 44
Rossiter, William (publisher), 44–45
Royalties, 43–44
Rural audience, 8–9, 11, 13
Russell, Henry, 132
Russell, Lillian, 51, 61, 62–63, 74

"Sadie Salome, Go Home," 159
St. Louis, 151
Salisbury, Nate, 184
Saloons, 11, 26, 57, 66, 67, 73
San Francisco, 57, 60, 68–69
Savo, Jimmy, 71
Sawyer, Jacob J., 184
"Say 'Au Revoir' But Not 'Good-bye',", 141, 165
Sayers, Henry J., 151
Scanlon, William J., 104, 158
Schirmer, G. (publisher), 38, 172
Schmidt, Arthur P. (publisher), 172
Schottische, 183
Schulte, Minnie, 66
Schumann, Robert, 169
Schumann-Heink, Ernestine, 16–17, 173
Schwartz, Jean, 25, 159, 186, 204
Selden, Edgar, 171
Self-interest, 18
Sentimental songs, 25, 34, 40, 68, 81, 87–89, 93, 101–111, 123–31, 166–72
Sex and Sexuality, 150–52
Shapiro, Maurice, 39
Shapiro-Bernstein (publisher), 25, 43, 50
Sharpley, Sam, 72
Shaw, Oliver, 202
"She Is More to Be Pitied Than Censured," 148, 157
"She Was Bred in Old Kentucky," 163
Sheet music, 4, 41–42, 49, 183, 186, 194
Sheet-music demonstrators, 25
Sheet-music salesmen, 25
Sherman, Clay and Co., 50
Sherwood, Robert Edmund, 77
"Shew! Fly, Don't Bother Me," 116
Shields, Ren, 42
"Sidewalks of New York, The," 149–50, 180
Siegel, Cooper, and Company, 46
"Silver Threads Among the Gold," 6, 24, 43, 86–88, 170
Simplicity, 108–109, 175
Sinclair, Upton, 145
Singer and audience, 15–16, 61–66
Singing in character, 65–66
Single performers, 80

Sister Carrie, 121
Skelly, Joseph P., 24, 105–106
"Skidmore, Fancy Ball, The," 134
Slang, 200
"Sleep, Baby, Sleep," 125
Smart, Walter, 185
Smith, Chris, 185
Smith, Harry B., 33
Smith's Variety Theater (Saginaw, Michigan), 72
Snyder, Ted, 152, 156, 193
Societal change, 17, 87, 100–101, 120–23, 138, 153, 155, 199
Solman, Alfred, 156
"Some of These Days," 45, 143, 152, 196–97, 204
"Somebody Loves Me," 29
"Somebody's Grandpa," 124
Song, artistic and semi-artistic, 2–3, 5, 26, 91, 172–75
   definition, 2
   standards for criticism, 2–3
Song, popular, 2–3, 10, 18, 32–33, 84
   definition, 2
   function, 86–90
   genres, 90, 96, 162–63
   standards for criticism, 2–3, 10, 32–33, 84, 95
   structure, 97, 110–11, 117, 170–71, 175, 179, 189–90, 194–96
   urban orientation, 18
Song and Chorus, 105
"Song of the Red Man, The," 127
Song-and-dance performers, 26, 78, 80
Songbooks, 45
Song-slides, 52
Songwriters, 22–35, 201–202
   Backgrounds, 23–29
   Songwriter and public, 31–35
   Songwriter and publisher. *See* Publisher and songwriter
Sousa, John Philip, 139, 183
Speaks, Oley, 173
Spirituals, 113, 187
Squatters Sovereignty, 12
Standard Theater (Seattle), 70
Stanton, Elizabeth C., 29
Stanton, Frank L., 141
Stanzas, 107, 114, 129–30, 134, 166–67, 176–77, 188
Starr, Hattie, 29, 30, 184

"Stay in Your Own Back Yard," 158
Sterling, Andrew B., 139, 147, 150, 152, 188, 193, 197
Stern, Joseph W. (songwriter and publisher), 24, 39, 50, 156, 158, 169
Stooges, 51–52
Strains, musical, 91, 97
Strauss, Johann, 122, 176
Street musicians, 77–78
Street parades of traveling troupes, 79–80
Stromberg, John, 143
Style, Musical, 95–98, 100
Subjects of songs, 91–95, 102, 112–13, 123–25, 127, 132–33, 140–41, 144–59, 181, 185, 199–200
"Such a Gitting Upstairs," 112
Sullivan, Joseph J., 26, 132
Sullivan, Marion Dix, 29, 101
Summer resorts, 70–71
"Sunshine of Paradise Alley, The," 145, 176
"Susan Jane," 134
Sutton, Harry O., 157
"Sweet By and By," 62, 105, 107
"Sweet Echo Dell," 127
"Sweet Genevieve," 96, 103
"Sweet Marie," 49
"Sweet Mary Ann," 112, 114
"Sweet Matilda," 90
"Sweet Rosie O'Grady," 29, 66
Syncopation, 87, 115–16, 143, 165, 177, 184, 186–87, 191, 193–95, 197

Tabrar, Joseph, 159
Taggart, George, 156
"Take Me Out to the Ball Game," 50, 158, 203
Tanguay, Eva, 60, 62–63
"Ta-ra-ra-bom-der-e," 65, 86, 89, 151
Tastes, 4–6, 7–8, 12, 14–19, 28, 32, 34, 39–41, 75, 92, 131, 138, 164
Taylor, Tell, 145, 167
"Teasing," 203
Techniques of songwriting, 29–31
Templeton, Fay, 57, 62, 64, 66
Tempo, 108–109, 114–16, 130, 168, 177–79, 183–84, 190, 193–94
Text and text structure, 92, 134, 166–67, 174
"That Is Love," 10

Theater capacities, 73
Theater managers, 10
Theatre Comique (Seattle), 69
"There's a Light in the Window," 124
Thomas, George H., 52
Thornton, James, 66, 141, 158
"Throw Him Down, McCloskey," 58
"Thy Beaming Eyes," 173
Time signatures. *See* Meter, musical
Tinkering, 77
Tin Pan Alley, 9, 14, 15, 27, 46–47, 84, 96, 138, 159, 198–206
Titles and title-tags, 95, 107, 114, 130, 166, 177, 188, 194
Tonality. *See* Keys
Trevathan, Charles, E., 151, 182, 184
Trip to Chinatown, A, 58
Tucker, Henry, 96
Tucker, Sophie, 51, 58, 60, 61, 65, 66–67, 72, 74
Tucker, Tommy, 124
Twain, Mark, 2–3, 31–32, 84–85, 121, 144
"Twelve Months Ago To-night," 125
23rd Street Theatre (New York), 10
Two-person acts, 80
Two-step, 183

Udall, Lyn, 158
"Under the Anheuser Bush," 150, 185
"Under the Bamboo Tree," 25, 65, 80, 181, 187–88
University of Michigan, 24
Urban audience, 9, 13, 120, 138, 164

Values, changes in, 8
Values in popular song, 4, 15, 17
Vamp, 134, 169, 178, 196
Variety, 2, 8, 26, 34, 45, 47, 69, 70, 72–74
Variety, 51
Variety and vaudeville circuits, 25, 44, 72, 75
Vaudeville, 10–11, 15, 74–76, 80, 172
Verse of a song, 91, 94–97, 163–64, 167, 169
Vesta, Nettie, 51
Victoria, Vesta, 50, 74
Vienna Gardens (San Francisco), 69
Vocal range, 109–10, 117, 171, 174, 189–90, 194–97

Von Suppé, Franz, 176
Von Tilzer, Albert, 203–204
Von Tilzer, Harry, 25, 31, 32, 39, 43, 61, 86, 139, 141, 145, 147, 150, 152, 154, 158, 167, 188–89, 193, 195, 197, 204
Vulgarity, 84, 89, 185, 203

Wages for performances, 60–61, 68
Wagner, Richard, 7, 132
"Wait 'Till the Sun Shines, Nellie," 31, 71, 147
"Waiting," 174
Walker, George, 25, 69
Waltz song, 40, 122, 175, 175–81
Ward, Charles B., 49, 176
Warfield, David, 57
Warman, Cy, 49
Warren, Charles Denier, 40
Washington Post March, 183
"We Parted by the River," 27, 106–107, 110
Webb, C. W., 133
Weber and Fields, 57, 74
West, Arthur, 50
Westendorf, Thomas, 14, 43, 102, 105
"What Is Home Without a Mother," 101
"When My Baby Smiles at Me," 204
"When the 'Evening Star' Went Down," 126
"When the Sun Has Set," 44
"When You Want 'Em, You Can't Get 'Em," 204
"When You Were Sweet Sixteen," 141
"Where Did You Get That Hat?," 26, 86, 132
"Where Is My Wandering Boy Tonight?," 52
"Whispering Hope," 103, 122, 175
"Whistling Coon," 184
White, C. F., 129
"White Wings," 10, 42
Whiting, George, 156
Whiting, L. E., 24
Whitman, Walt, 121
Whitson, Beth Slater, 44, 177
Whittier, Charles Leroy, 79
"Why Did They Dig Ma's Grave So Deep?," 24, 105–106
Wickes, E. M., 13, 22, 97

Widow Jones, The, 151
"Widow Nolan's Goat," 132
Wiesenthal, Thomas, 202
Wigwam, The (San Francisco), 69
"Will You Love Me in December as
    You Do in May?," 24, 25, 141–42
Williams, Bert, 25, 32, 35, 57, 64, 68–
    69, 184
Williams, Gus, 74
Williams, Harry H., 141, 159, 167,
    196
Wilson, Jack, 185
Wine bars, 66
Wingate, Philip, 159, 178
Winner, Joseph E., 132
Winner, Septimus, 101, 103, 122, 175–
    76
"Winter," 193, 195
Winter Garden (New York), 66
Winters, Banks, 42
"With All Her Faults I Love Her Still,"
    33, 129–30
Witmark, Isidore, 13, 30, 33, 39, 42,
    45–46
Witmark, Julie, 50
M. Witmark and Sons (publisher), 25,
    40, 41–43, 50
Witt, Max S., 156

Women, 10, 13, 14–15, 28–29, 56, 127–
    28, 130, 150–53, 155–57
Wood, C. F., 124
Woodbury, Isaac, 101
"Woodman! Spare That Tree," 132
Woodward, Willis (publisher), 38, 42
Woodworth, Samuel, 132
Work, Henry Clay, 48, 88, 108, 111,
    125–27, 132–33
Working class, 12
World's Columbian Exposition, 45, 87,
    143

"Yankee Doodle Boy, The," 197
"You Naughty, Naughty Men," 129,
    152
"Your Eyes Have Told Me So," 203
"You're a Grand Old Flag," 197
"You've Been a Good Old Wagon, But
    You've Done Broke Down," 143,
    186, 204
"You're the Flower of My Heart, Sweet
    Adeline," 165
Young, Rida Johnson, 104, 159

Zelter, Carl Friedrich, 122
Ziegfeld Follies, 64
"Zip Coon," 117